THE BORDERLANDS OF RACE

THE BORDERLANDS OF RACE

Mexican Segregation in a South Texas Town

JENNIFER R. NÁJERA

UNIVERSITY OF TEXAS PRESS *Austin*

First edition, 2015
First paperback printing, 2016

Requests for permission to reproduce material from this work should be sent to:
Permissions
University of Texas Press
P.O. Box 7819
Austin, TX 78713-7819
http://utpress.utexas.edu/index.php/rp-form

♾ The paper used in this book meets the minimum requirements of ANSI/NISO Z39.48-1992 (R1997) (Permanence of Paper).

LIBRARY OF CONGRESS CATALOGING-IN-PUBLICATION DATA
Nájera, Jennifer R., 1975–
The borderlands of race : Mexican segregation in a South Texas town / Jennifer R. Nájera. — First edition.
pages cm
Includes bibliographical references and index.
ISBN 978-0-292-76755-3 (cloth : alkaline paper)
1. Mexican Americans—Segregation—Texas—La Feria—History—20th century. 2. Mexican Americans—Civil rights—Texas—La Feria—History—20th century. 3. Mexican Americans—Texas—La Feria—Biography. 4. Race discrimination—Texas—La Feria—History—20th century. 5. Social movements—Texas—La Feria—History—20th century. 6. La Feria (Tex.)—Race relations—History—20th century. 7. Texas, South—Race relations—History—20th century. 8. Oral history—Texas—La Feria. I. Title.
F394.L125N25 2015
305.8968′720764495—dc23 2014023108

ISBN 978-1-4773-1129-5, paperback
doi:10.7560/767553

TO THE MEXICAN-ORIGIN PEOPLE OF LA FERIA

CONTENTS

ACKNOWLEDGMENTS

MEXICAN SEGREGATION was not something that I learned about in my kindergarten through twelfth-grade classrooms; I learned about this history at home, from stories that my mom and her sisters recounted to me, my siblings, and my cousins as we were growing up. As a young adult, I realized how fortunate I was to have been reared in a family of storytellers because it provided me a history, indeed, a historical ethnography that I might not have otherwise known existed. I'm grateful for the first road trip that I took with my mom to her hometown of La Feria, Texas, where I was able to map these stories of the past onto a place and begin an intellectual journey that has been both personally affective and academically rewarding.

This book would not have been possible without at least two generations of generous Mexican-origin people from La Feria, who graciously shared their memories, their recollections, their photographs, and their interpretations of the past with me over the last decade. I have been amazed at people's astute recollections of events that occurred sometimes seventy years prior. Interviewing them and listening to hours of their stories was one of the best and most eye-opening parts of my educational journey thus far. I am so grateful to them all.

In addition to my interviewees in La Feria, I would like to thank those people in the community who became my friends and supporters throughout my research process. Gloria Casas; JoAnn Mireles; the Loya family, especially Gloria, Anna Lisa, and Leti; the Chapa family; and Janie Betancourt made me feel like I had a home in La Feria during the year that I lived there and for many years afterward. Amparo Verduzco championed my project and enabled me to meet many people of her generation over the years. Carlos Cantú and Reyes Rodriguez likewise helped to facilitate my research and offered thoughtful answers to my questions about the history of the town's racial dynamics. Cristina Ballí and Celeste de Luna have been my valley confidantes and *comadres* during my many research trips to La Feria.

I am also grateful for the mentorship and academic support that I received during my graduate training in Texas and as a professor in California. Martha Menchaca taught me that anthropology could be a powerful vehicle for excavating and examining the past. José Limón and Richard Flores helped me to more deeply understand the poetics of everyday life. John Moran Gonzales, Angela Valenzuela, Emilio Zamora, and Teresa Palomo Acosta all provided advice and mentorship at critical moments along the way. Dylan Rodriguez and Alfredo Mirandé both provided me with encouragement and institutional support as I was completing the second leg of my La Feria research, and Karen Mary Dávalos has helped me to more gracefully traverse the bridge between anthropology and Chicano/a Studies.

Several people offered feedback and support during the production of this book. Victoria Bomberry, Olga Herrera, Veronica Martinez-Matsuda, Robert Perez, Isabela Quintana, and Cristina Salinas all offered thoughtful suggestions for revision and the development of my ideas during my writing process. I am grateful to UC–Riverside graduate and undergraduate students Lisette Lasater and Jenelle Nila, who helped me to organize my research materials and to prepare them for final submission. Your work with me helped more than you know.

The majority of the research for this book was made possible by a grant from the Social Science Research Council Program on International Migration and research grants from the University of California Academic Senate. The UCLA Institute for American Cultures provided an essential postdoctoral writing fellowship through the Chicano/a Studies Research Center.

The University of Texas diaspora of borderlands students has provided me with the intellectual community and support that have enabled me to complete this manuscript. Gilberto Rosas and Brenda Sendejo have been dear colleagues, friends, and supporters during my time in graduate school and beyond. Olga Herrera, Veronica Martinez-Matsuda, Laura K. Padilla, Isabela Quintana, Virginia Raymond, and Cristina Salinas have inspired and challenged me, offered myriad forms of help, and been the first people I have turned to during both challenging and joyful moments along this journey. Words cannot express how much your friendship has meant to me over the past fifteen years.

I am grateful to my parents, Joe and Rose Najera, who both inculcated me with a strong sense of family and the importance of knowing our historical roots. My sister and brother, Sandra Moran and Paul Najera, have graciously listened and offered advice and sympathy. To my husband, partner, and best friend, Joseph Sepúlveda, who has constantly been by my side with encouragement and love, thank you. Finally, to Eliana and Adalia, this *historia* is yours, too.

THE BORDERLANDS OF RACE

INTRODUCTION: MEXICAN INFLECTIONS OF ETHNOGRAPHY AND HISTORY

IN 1957, Arthur J. Rubel began his fieldwork in a small, racially segregated town in the Lower Rio Grande Valley of South Texas that he called "New Lots." His goal was to conduct ethnographic research about "Mexiquito," the segregated Mexican area of town. Rubel spent the first ten days of his time in the field walking along every street in the city and entering every store. Each time he entered a place of business, he introduced himself and described his research agenda to the proprietors, clerks, and customers of the store. Reflecting on these early stages of fieldwork in the preface to his book *Across the Tracks: Mexican-Americans in a Texas City*, Rubel recalls that many Mexican Americans "expressed concern that their people were not fairly presented in the pages of the current elementary and high-school texts and asked that [he] undertake to 'set the record straight' as to the part played by *la raza* in the development of Texas" (1971, xxiv). Rubel responded by emphasizing the historical aspects of his research to assuage the concerns of these Mexican-origin community members. Ultimately, however, he decided to publish a standard ethnography, which, though including a chapter of broad history, was largely a synchronic account of the Mexican community in New Lots.

Over four decades later, in the summer of 2002, I began my fieldwork in La Feria, a small, previously racially segregated town in the Lower Rio Grande Valley of South Texas. Like Rubel, I approached the field as a trained anthropologist. As such, my goal was to conduct ethnographic research about the social relationships between Mexican Americans and Mexican immigrants in the postsegregation period. Unlike Rubel, I had a personal connection to my field site. Though I had never lived there myself, it was the town to which my family had migrated from Mexico in the mid-1940s, and it was the place where my mother was born and raised. When I arrived in La Feria, I spent my first several weeks in town establishing contacts to which I was referred by colleagues and family. I also began to engage in community life by attending school board meetings, frequenting local restaurants, and attending Mass on Sundays at the one Catholic church in town. When I met and introduced myself to people, I made an effort to describe my research project about immigrants and Mexican Americans. Whereas in general people usually cursorily acknowledged my interest in immigration, most Mexican American people wanted to talk to me about the history of segregation in the community, often asking if my mother had ever mentioned it. As a Mexican American woman who came of age in La Feria in the 1950s and 1960s, my mother had vivid memories of the segregation she experienced, and she had indeed inculcated me with those stories. For my mother's contemporaries who had remained in La Feria, the specter of segregation still haunted the present. Though the phenomenon of Mexican segregation was not my primary research interest, it was apparent to me that people wanted to talk about this history. Rather than pay superficial attention to their historical concerns, as Rubel had done a generation before me, I decided to examine the history of Mexican segregation in La Feria more deeply from an ethnographic perspective.

This book is the culmination of that research. It is a historical ethnography about the culture of segregation in La Feria, Texas, from 1915 through the late 1980s. I argue that there were three stages of segregation: its establishment in the first part of the twentieth century; its accommodated form in the 1940s; and its gradual unraveling after the civil rights and Chicano movements. I examine how social movements and subsequent changes to federal and state policy shaped people's experiences of segregation throughout these different time periods. I also highlight how the ambiguous racial positionalities of Mexican people allowed some of them to be exceptions to Anglo rules of racial dominance during the era of segregation. This work concerns itself with the contradictions, inconsistencies, and indeed the messiness of Mexican segregation. I do not read these contradictions as indicative of the permeability of racial borders during the period of segregation; rather, I argue that the structure of segregation prevailed well beyond landmark national legal mandates of desegregation precisely because of such processes of selective and limited incorporation. I will demonstrate that because of the durability of segregationist structures, Mexican racial integration was necessarily pushed forward by grassroots actions in conjunction with state and federal policies. As such, this ethnographic examination of the history of Mexican segregation illuminates larger issues about race, nation, and belonging in the U.S.–Mexico borderlands.

Despite the absence of a federal or Texas state mandate, people of Mexican origin frequently faced de facto racial segregation, most acutely during the first part of the twentieth century. Though they experienced segregation in a manner similar to blacks and other people of color in the United States, the structure of Mexican segregation differed from the strict racial divides of the Jim Crow South. My research reveals that there were several Mexican-origin people who were exceptions to the racial rule of white dominance in South Texas. While such Mexican exceptionality became more common after World War II, there were some notable exceptions to the rule of racial segregation as early as the 1920s and 1930s. Exceptional Mexican people were usually of higher socioeconomic status, had the ability to speak English, possessed a kind of Anglo[1] cultural fluency, and were often light skinned. Very rarely, however, were these exceptional Mexican people allowed full access to Anglo society. Though granted limited opportunities within the realms of education, business, and—to a lesser degree—politics, their incorporation into the Anglo power structure was always constricted, especially in spheres that involved direct contact with the racialized Mexican body. Instances of absolute racial separation as well as the exceptions were distinguishing characteristics of Mexican segregation in South Texas. These amounted to highly complex structures of racial inequality.

The contradictions in the structure of Mexican segregation actually made processes of desegregation all the more difficult. Indeed, despite major court cases that abolished the legal practice of segregation across the country beginning in the 1940s, La Feria's original "Mexican School," Sam Houston Elementary School, remained segregated until 1972. Segregation persisted in the local Catholic church until even later. Because Mexican segregation in La Feria was based on custom rather than law,[2] it could not necessarily be mandated out of practice. Certainly, desegregation was buttressed by antisegregation court cases, federal mandates, incentives, and threats of noncompliance. This book pays close attention to how the Mexican community was able to push toward a racially integrated community through everyday actions supported by the emerging policies of nondiscrimination. It examines how integration occurred in practice, detailing how Mexicans and Anglos struggled with the process of integration and the ways in which they confronted, negotiated, and renegotiated power relations in different public spheres. While in some cases the process of integration was of an overtly contested and political nature, other instances revealed that integration occurred through subtle changes in everyday practice. When looking at the agents of change in the various chapters of this book, it is clear that Mexican-origin individuals and groups used their multiple positionalities—race, ethnicity, class, and gender—to promote racial integration on a local level.

HISTORICAL ETHNOGRAPHY AS CRITICAL ETHNOGRAPHY

First, the concept of the "traditional culture," as presently used by social scientists, must totally be dropped. Instead, the concept of the historical culture must be adopted.

OCTAVIO IGNACIO ROMANO-V, "THE ANTHROPOLOGY AND THE SOCIOLOGY OF THE MEXICAN AMERICANS: THE DISTORTION OF MEXICAN AMERICAN HISTORY" (1968)

The anthropologist Octavio Romano wrote the words in the preceding epigraph in direct response to the kind of research and writing that Arthur J. Rubel, his onetime colleague, conducted in New Lots. As graduate students, Romano and Rubel shared the same mentor: the then newly minted Berkeley Ph.D. William Madsen. As students, the two conducted fieldwork as Madsen's research assistants in the Lower Rio Grande Valley of South Texas. While Madsen and Rubel penned ethnographies based on their research over the following decade, Romano, buttressed by the Chicano/a movement, penned a scathing critique of anthropologists and sociologists such as Madsen and Rubel in his essay "The Anthropology and Sociology of the Mexican Americans: The Distortion of Mexican American History." In this critical piece, Romano maintains that social scientists who conducted research in U.S. communities comprising people of Mexican origin from the early twentieth century through the 1960s perpetuated and promoted colonial and racist representations of Mexican Americans. At the heart of Romano's critique is the refusal of then contemporary anthropologists and social scientists to engage in a historical analysis of culture. He argues that such texts represented Mexican Americans as passive victims of their own, supposedly deficient, culture, which restricted their economic, political, and social advancement.[3] This analysis, Romano asserts, ignores a history of resistance, particularly in terms of labor organizing, the prevalence of which he documents from the late nineteenth century through the twentieth (Romano-V 1968, 48). Ultimately, Romano argues that the principal factor behind Mexican Americans' poverty and disfranchisement was not their "culture" but rather a dominant Anglo society against which Mexicans had ardently struggled throughout their history as part of the United States.

This book likewise offers a historical analysis of culture, and it does so by weaving together the threads of ethnography left behind by scholars such as Rubel and Romano, as well as contemporary scholars in Chicano/a Studies and anthropology who have called for greater accountability and critical analysis in the ethnographies that we produce. I understand accountability in two primary ways. First, accountability can honor the desires of our communities for research and writing that is meaningful and accessible to them. I went to La Feria with a research plan but was compelled to change that plan to respond to the stories that people wanted to tell me. It is my hope that this book respectfully treats people's concerns about the history of Mexican and Mexican American segregation in the town. Second, I understand accountability as creating a viable space in academia for community knowledge. In her essay "Chicana/o Studies and Anthropology: The Dialogue That Never Was," Karen Mary Dávalos writes, "Chicana/o scholarship is not simply additive but transformative. [It does] not recover the history, literature, sociology, folklore, law, and art of Mexican Americans simply to enhance library collections. The work of Chicana/o scholars calls for change" (1998, 32). This work about Mexican segregation in La Feria, Texas, is not meant to be an addendum to mainstream ethnographies and/or histories; rather, it is meant to transform and deepen the way that we understand the history and culture of Mexican segregation in the United States. In its analysis and methodology, this book heeds Romano's call for historical analysis of culture in a way that decolonizes, or as Dávalos says, "redistribute[s] power both inside and outside the academy" (1998, 32).

In order to offer a critical, historical analysis of the culture of Mexican segregation in this book, I have relied on methods of historical anthropology. The field of historical anthropology emerged in the early twentieth century and has undergone many incarnations; debates about when and how anthropologists should use historical methodologies continue today. In the introduction to his edited volume *From the Margins: Historical Anthropology and Its Futures*, the anthropologist Brian Keith Axel asserts that it is important to understand the project of historical anthropology not as a dialogue between the two fields or even as a matter of borrowing methodologies. Rather, he argues that "historical anthropology may productively deploy the tensions and conflicts of the institutionally defined relationship between history and anthropology to generate a new, critical practice of knowledge production" (2002, 12). Axel argues that while multiple methods may be used, the goal of historical anthropology is to provide a distinct way in which anthropologists can produce knowledge. He argues that this type of critical historical ethnography is essential to understanding the "production of people." Such methods push the temporal boundaries of anthropological analysis, which largely remains ahistorical, and challenges history's conceptions of space and time by presenting microlevel rather than broad geographical accounts of the past. The purpose of this book is to more deeply understand Mexican segregation through the dual lenses of anthropology and history in order to critically interrogate the way that this culture of segregation shifted throughout the twentieth century.

Approaching the history of Mexican segregation from an ethnographic standpoint is important because it allows for an examination of how segregation functioned in a particular local context. Such a microlevel analysis allows for a more nuanced understanding of the way that Mexican segregation functioned and allows us, as Trouillot argues, to make "better generalizations" about larger historical-social phenomena. He asserts:

> When it comes to the past . . . we often move from the general to the particular as if our historical master tropes—colonialism, slavery, racism, and the domination they register . . .—could actually help paint concrete situations on the ground. . . . Yet useful as these master tropes may be in sketching the horizon of an era and the outer limits of a social formation, they cannot convey the lived realities of actual populations, past or present. (2002, 190)

While Mexican segregation was initiated by the state in various forms of government—federal, state, and local—it was enacted and experienced as everyday practice. In La Feria, as in other communities throughout the Southwest, Mexican people's experiences of segregation were contingent upon how they engaged with the Anglo community, the extent to which they accepted or resisted practices of segregation, and their social and economic positionalities. I argue that we should not take Mexican segregation for granted as a monolith that functioned in the same way throughout the U.S. Southwest. By prioritizing a microlevel analysis, this ethnography reveals specificities that help us to understand the larger phenomenon of Mexican segregation more clearly.

In addition to an emphasis on microlevel analysis, another key aspect of this text as a historical ethnography is how practices and lived experiences of segregation changed over time. I agree with Comaroff and Comaroff's argument that historical anthropology should be dedicated to "exploring processes that make and transform particular worlds—processes that reciprocally shape subjects and contexts, that allow certain things to be said and done" (1992, 31). In this way, historical anthropology allows for an analysis that can encompass the way that the culture of Mexican segregation in La Feria changed throughout the twentieth century. Segregation of Mexican people manifested itself differently in the early, middle, and latter parts of the twentieth century. I argue that various historical moments—defined by racial projects such as colonization, legislation by the state, and community organization—affected and changed the culture of segregation. This research reiterates Renato Rosaldo's rumination that "change rather than structure becomes society's most enduring state, and time rather than space becomes its most encompassing medium" (1993, 103).

As a historical ethnography that critically examines Mexican segregation, this book also engages in the field of critical race studies by contributing to the ways that we understand histories of racial formation in the United States. In their groundbreaking work *Racial Formation in the United States: From the 1960s to the 1990s*, Omi and Winant (1994) propose that through the course of U.S. history, there have existed particular "racial formations" that have defined the way that we, as a society, understand race and racial hierarchy as a natural order. They argue that through "racial projects," people attempt to reorient our understandings of race and often push to redistribute resources along racial lines. Such racial projects can include state mandates as well as collective action. A key part of their analysis is that racial formation is processual in nature and that we must understand racial categories as being "created, inhabited, transformed, and destroyed" (55) as society moves from one racial formation to the next. In the case of La Feria, I outline three major stages of segregation that correspond to three distinct racial formations. It is clear that over these three periods "being Mexican" held different racial connotations. Perhaps most notably, certain categories of Mexican people were able to claim greater rights throughout the three distinct racial formations I outline in this book. These categorical differences reveal how race functioned in different ways for Mexican people throughout the twentieth century.

I employ methods that include local archival research as well as field research to develop this historical ethnography. I approached the former ethnographically and the latter to inform historical questions. Comaroff and Comaroff assert that "historical ethnography . . . must begin by constructing its own archive" and urge anthropologists to "work both in and outside the official record" (1992, 34). In constructing an archive for this book, I relied heavily on historical sources from La Feria, Texas, such as school board minutes, city commissioner records, yearbooks, local newspapers, and property records. Within this local context, the archives formed a narrative about the town that posited Anglos as the dominant social actors of history. There was so little mention of Mexican-origin people in these historical materials, it appeared as if they did not exist. Meanwhile, the burgeoning agricultural industry, which was the backbone of La Feria's economy, was being propelled forward on the backs of Mexicano labor.[4] Mexican people's invisibility in the official town records became significant to my analysis of segregation because it indicated how completely Anglo members had marginalized Mexican people. In creating an archive of local town issues, Anglo settlers actively "imagined" a community devoid of Mexicans. In order to address this bias in the historical record, and in order to understand the way Mexican people experienced segregation in La Feria over time, I conducted oral history interviews with several Mexican longtime residents of the community.[5]

Chicano/a and feminist scholars have often relied on oral history narratives to reconstitute subjugated historical perspectives.[6] Oral history narratives often provide an alternative account of historical events, which can be corroborated using archival sources. Vansina (1985) argues, however, that the value of oral sources is not their "testimony of fact" but rather the ways that they testify to the values of a people. Put another way, Alessandro Portelli states, "Oral sources may not add much to what we know, for instance, of the material cost of a strike to the workers involved; but they tell us a good deal about its psychological costs" (1998, 67). Oral history narratives tell us about the histories that people experience, but they also talk about what people choose to remember, how they remember, and the impact of that memory on their current lives. Oral history narratives are key to this project because as Comaroff and Comaroff insist, within historical ethnography, the "methodological concern is less with events than with meaningful practices" (1992, 37). For this book, I relied on twenty-eight qualitative interviews with lifelong residents of the town. These interviews were geared specifically toward generating Mexican and/or Mexican American perspectives about La Feria's past. During my initial year of fieldwork, from 2002 to 2003, and in the decade afterward, I conducted several other interviews about contemporary issues for Mexican people in the community, and I engaged in countless conversations with townspeople about the history of segregation and its legacy.

As an anthropologist, my goal has been to read the archive that I have constructed about Mexican people in La Feria ethnographically. Guha advises us to "distinguish different types of documents and their relations to the forces of domination they purported to represent" (quoted in Axel 2002).[7] The Anglo perspective represented in the local historical records, as well as the Mexican perspective represented in the oral histories that I have collected, has been culturally and historically constituted. I have paid specific attention to how Mexican people were represented in local archives (if at all) and to the privilege that the writers of the records enjoyed in the early history of the town. On the other hand, the oral histories I use in this book illuminate what Mexican life was like within the context of a racially segregated town. Many people remember the same things, corroborating each other's stories. Much of what people remember corresponds to archival material. In my analysis of oral history narratives in this book, I look for historical content, but also the ways that people interpret their own stories. Remembering the era of Mexican segregation and instances of racial discrimination was difficult. While some of my interviewees spoke openly and, at times, angrily about what they had endured, others scarcely mentioned it, focusing instead on their positive life experiences and how the community had changed for the better. I navigate these narratives carefully, with an abiding desire to respect the perspectives of the people who lived through segregation, but also with an abiding desire to shed light on this difficult aspect of Mexican American history in Texas. The significance of these oral narratives lies not only within the particular history they delineate but also in the way that they reveal the emotional impact of segregation, both then and now.

Finally, my engagement in periods of fieldwork in La Feria over the past ten years has had a major influence in the way that this historical ethnography has taken shape. The opportunity to discuss documentary sources and oral histories with local people has influenced both my narration and my analysis of Mexican segregation in La Feria.[8] As I shared with people what I found by way of local history, Mexican American people often "spoke back" to archival sources, encouraging me both to critically interrogate the official historical record and to think beyond it. Even among the oral histories that I collected, my research collaborators would ask questions about what I had learned from other interviews and offer their own analysis as to why people had interpreted historical moments in particular ways. In terms of the many contradictions within the culture of segregation, Mexican people offered varying explanations as to why racial discrimination occurred in some arenas while in others it did not. Often people differed as to ideas about when practices of segregation finally abated. Engagement with local people about historical sources was thus a key aspect of my methodology and sociohistorical analysis.

The tools of ethnography, history, and critical race studies have been essential for breaking open the representation and the analysis of Mexican segregation in Texas during the twentieth century. Though the patterns revealed in previous studies of segregation are apparent here, as a historical ethnography this book enables a more intimate understanding of the way that Mexican people experienced and responded to segregation in their everyday lives. It demonstrates the messiness of Mexican segregation, which was a direct result of the myriad ways that Mexican people were racialized during the twentieth century. In addition to noting the contradictions and inconsistencies relevant to the treatment of Mexicans, this book also reveals those nonnegotiable spaces where Mexicans were never allowed, thus exposing the true depth of the racist ideologies that undergirded practices of segregation. Finally, this book helps us to understand how practices of segregation endured well past the passage of major civil rights legislation. By examining the impact of the racial ambiguity of Mexican people on their experiences of segregation, this book provides a unique perspective about the history of segregation and racial integration, serving to complicate our understandings of the history of race and racial formation in the United States.

ORGANIZATION OF THE BOOK

The Borderlands of Race is organized into two main sections. Part 1, "The Culture of Mexican Segregation," explores how the culture of segregation was established in La Feria, Texas, and how over the first five decades of the twentieth century, it was sustained through practices of limited incorporation of Mexican people into Anglo-dominant spheres. Chapter 1, "The Borderlands of Race and Rights," introduces relevant discourses about race and the Texas-Mexico border in the early part of the 1900s in order to frame the phenomenon of Mexican segregation in La Feria. This chapter also introduces theories of cultural citizenship as a way to understand how people of Mexican origin created cultural space for themselves within segregated spheres, thereby broadening the scope of belonging in town. Chapter 2, "Establishing a Culture of Segregation," focuses on the period from the town's incorporation in 1915 through the 1930s, when, because of its general development, the town established structures and practices of segregation. This chapter looks at the patterns of racial exclusions that emerged in the town's social, economic, and political spheres. Chapter 3, "Formal and Informal Mexican Education within the Context of Segregation," examines the struggle over education within a segregated community. While Anglo people controlled the education of children at the segregated Mexican elementary school, Mexican community members enacted forms of public pedagogy as a counterpoint to Anglo education and as a response to racist Anglo ideologies. Chapter 4, "An Accommodated Form of Segregation," highlights the historical moment when the structures of segregation shifted to enable some flexibility around previously strictly drawn lines of racial exclusion. Focusing on the period beginning in the late 1940s, this chapter ethnographically examines the contradictory experiences of segregation and the durability of racial thinking that led to the maintenance of a racially stratified community.

Part 2 of the book, "Processes of Racial Integration," examines the uneven process of desegregation in the community. Because of the selective incorporation of Mexican people into Anglo spheres, a sweeping legal reform of race relations was untenable. This section demonstrates how racial integration occurred at the grassroots level of individual and group actions. Chapter 5, "Troubling the Culture of School Segregation: Mexican American Teachers and the Path to Desegregation," examines the experiences of the first Mexican American teachers employed at the "Mexican School" in town and the impact that they had on their students as an opening toward integration. Chapter 6, "Surgiendo de la Base: Community Movement and the Desegregation of the Catholic Church," demonstrates how Catholics of Mexican origin used popular religious practices to create a culturally relevant space for themselves in the local Catholic parish. This chapter demonstrates how Mexican people's cultural and micropolitical actions served as a basis for the desegregation of the church.

This examination of the culture of Mexican segregation builds upon and challenges our understandings of the interplay between race and rights in the United States. In this historical ethnography, we see the way that race was mediated by socioeconomic status, skin color, and culture, which led to varied experiences of segregation among Mexican-origin people. Despite contradictions present within the structures and practices of segregation, both Anglos and Mexicans commonly understood La Feria's racial hierarchy for much of the twentieth century. Buttressed by civil rights legislation of the late 1960s and 1970s, everyday people took actions that ultimately challenged racial/racist ideologies and created meaningful spaces for Mexicans in historically dominant Anglo spheres. *The Borderlands of Race* testifies to the changing culture of Mexican segregation and the myriad ways that people claimed rights and created meaningful space for themselves in a South Texas border community.

PART 1

THE CULTURE OF MEXICAN SEGREGATION

CHAPTER ONE

THE BORDERLANDS OF RACE AND RIGHTS

ON A BRIGHT midsummer morning, I approach a white, wood-framed house on the north side of the railroad tracks, in a neighborhood commonly referred to as *el pueblo mexicano*. I have scheduled an interview with Amalia Barrera, a Mexican American woman in her eighties, who has spent the majority of her life in La Feria. She is delicate in her old age, fair skinned, and she speaks to me in perfect Spanish. We sit together in her living room on two worn sofas next to a window that filters in orange light. A small fan buzzes back and forth between us as she speaks.

Playing the clarinet for the school band in the early 1940s is one of Barrera's most vivid memories. She recalled for me the day, in seventh grade, when she was promoted to First Band. She was nervous, so she arrived early. The band director instructed her to sit in the fourth seat. She outplayed the student in the fourth seat, so he moved her to the third. Despite the difficulty of the pieces, she tells me, "*Me puse toda*." She gave it her all. Ultimately, Barrera outplayed the other student clarinet players to assume the first seat. Her large brown eyes still gleam as she recounts that for the rest of the day students she did not even know approached her to extend their congratulations. She played in the band through junior high and high school in La Feria, and it was one of the most memorable activities of her young life.

Later that afternoon, I drive to the south side of town for an interview with a Mexican American couple. Emilio Valenzuela is about five years younger than Barrera and is likewise a lifelong resident of La Feria. Unlike Barrera, he left school in the fourth grade to begin working in the fields. After serving in the military, he was able to establish a small business on the Mexican side of town. His wife, Elizabeth, was not originally from La Feria but moved there after they married in the late 1940s. The two of them speak to me primarily in English, using a few Spanish phrases and words throughout our interview. We sit comfortably in the living room, their grandchildren's voices, laughter, and pattering footsteps providing the soundtrack to our conversation.

Mrs. Valenzuela intimates to me that she never experienced discrimination until she moved to La Feria. She recounts a story from when her children were still young and attending elementary school in the 1950s. At that point in their lives, the Valenzuelas lived in *el pueblo mexicano* and their children attended Sam Houston Elementary School, the segregated Mexican school. Fourth grade was the year when Mexican children began to be "integrated" into the Anglo schools on the south side of the tracks. It was Mrs. Valenzuela's desire for her children to be in the band, so she approached the band teacher about involving her son. The teacher informed her that it was too late because children began their band classes prior to the fourth grade (in the segregated Anglo school). "It made me very upset," remembers Mrs. Valenzuela, "and I told him so." She remarked to him that it was unfair for the children from Sam Houston who could not join because they matriculated to the school with band classes in fourth grade. She continues, "Later, the superintendent called me and said they would let my son get in the band, but the only instrument he could play were [*sic*] the drums. I said, 'No thanks.'" Mr. Valenzuela then stated frankly, "They didn't want any Mexicans in the band."

I tell Mr. and Mrs. Valenzuela how their story stands in contrast to the one that Barrera had recounted to me that very same morning. Fifteen years before their son was edged out of band in La Feria, Barrera remembered her experience playing the clarinet as one of the more joyful experiences of her time in school. They both nod knowingly. "She was born into . . . high society," Mrs. Valenzuela says. She continues, "Yeah, if you had the money, I mean, it was different."

THE ABOVE ETHNOGRAPHIC ENCOUNTER illustrates the contradictory nature of Mexican segregation in La Feria, Texas, during the first half of the twentieth century. While most Mexican-origin people concur that segregation was pervasive in most areas of public life, there were always exceptions. In this case, the Valenzuelas clearly understood Amalia Barrera's foray into the La Feria band to be the result of her family's class position in town. Indeed, her parents were both well-educated, longtime residents of the Valley, and her father owned a small business on the Mexican side of town during the first few decades of the twentieth century. Furthermore, Barrera was light skinned. All of these factors likely contributed to her experiences of inclusion in the school band in the early 1940s. Emilio Valenzuela, on the other hand, as someone with a darker complexion who had less formal education and entered the workforce as a farm laborer, experienced much more discrimination. Although his time in the armed services helped him and his young family to gain economic stability, they still struggled for equal treatment well into the 1950s in the racialized terrain of La Feria.

From the period immediately following the Mexican-American War through the mid-twentieth century, race and racialization always determined the extent to which Mexican-origin people were able to claim rights in the United States. During each of the three periods of segregation and desegregation in La Feria, Mexicans were considered to be racially *other*, distinct from Anglos in the region; nevertheless, some Mexican people were always granted more privileges than others depending on a host of factors, including socioeconomic status and skin color. Furthermore, depending on the stage of segregation, Mexican people were able to claim different kinds of rights for themselves. Indeed, Anglo and Mexican social relations in South Texas have always been fraught with tension, and segregation was often a contradictory experience for Mexican people. Through different periods, Anglo-Mexican social relations shifted to accommodate the changing economy, national and international projects, and grassroots social movements. This chapter will help to provide a framework for how we might understand the phenomenon of Mexican segregation in its various incarnations in La Feria, Texas.

In many ways, de jure Mexican segregation was at odds with de facto practices of segregation. I argue that though the law granted people of Mexican origin certain rights that other nonwhite races did not have, physical and symbolic violence against Mexican people relegated them to the margins of the nation-state. Though the segregation of Mexican people was not legally permitted because the state defined Mexicans as racially "white," the customary practice of Mexican segregation was often more powerful and enduring than egalitarian legal mandates. This was especially true in light of immigration restrictions that cast Mexican-origin people as "foreign" and ineligible for rights, regardless of their actual citizenship status (Ngai 2004). Indeed, racially charged nationalist discourses in the early twentieth century determined internal racial boundaries within the United States. Furthermore, the national, increasingly policed, border just a few miles south of the town of La Feria mirrored geographic boundaries in the city. Practices of segregation enforced these racialized boundaries and set the stage for the ways that Mexican people experienced citizenship and belonging in their town. A crucial yet often overlooked aspect of Mexican segregation is the phenomenon of "exceptionality." Through the two early periods of segregation, there were always Mexican people who were able to cross racial boundaries, in limited ways, at particular junctures in their lives. In this chapter, I will begin to examine how the permeability of the line of segregation led to practices of segregation well beyond national mandates for desegregation.

It is important to understand the active role that Mexican-origin people assumed in shaping the culture of segregation during the first part of the twentieth century and their role in pushing forward the process of desegregation during the latter part. I argue that they often did so by engaging in acts of cultural citizenship. Flores and Benmayor define cultural citizenship as a "range of social practices, which, taken together, claim and establish a distinct social space for Latinos in this country" (Flores and Benmayor 1997, 1). Because Anglos marginalized Mexicans in La Feria, the latter group engaged in social and cultural practices within their segregated communities to create a viable space for themselves within the town. In this way, Mexican-origin people were able to give deeper meaning to their position as citizens of the town (and the nation), effectively broadening the scope of belonging in the community. They practiced cultural citizenship differently during the various stages of segregation, and this had varying impacts in terms of rights and resources. They reflected what William Flores and Rina Benmayor refer to as "emergent Latino consciousness and social and political development" (1997, 1). Cultural citizenship as a lens by which to understand Mexican people's actions within the context of segregation helps to give nuance to micropolitical actions, highlights overt instances of resistance, and unearths the moments in between.

I situate my discussion about the contours of Mexican segregation in La Feria within a larger regional setting and history. The following section provides a brief history of the Lower Rio Grande Valley, emphasizing the way that race functioned in the region, particularly during the agricultural development of Texas in the twentieth century.

SHIFTING RACIAL FORMATIONS IN SOUTH TEXAS HISTORY

The area encompassing present-day La Feria was part of the Nuevo Santander Spanish colony in the middle of the eighteenth century. The first inhabitants of this region, located on Mexico's northern frontier, were indigenous peoples. Scholars have asserted that Maya, Otomi, Nahua, Karankawa, and Coahuiltecan Indians occupied Nuevo Santander at different points in time before the extensive Spanish colonization led by José de Escandón in the mid-1700s (Alonzo 1998; Chavana 2002; Menchaca 2001; McNail 1975). At the same time that Spanish colonists displaced indigenous people in the region, they were securing for themselves a respite from the racial caste system of New Spain. In the colonial Mexican interior, white Spaniards and criollos enjoyed a fuller spectrum of rights and privileges under the Spanish Crown than did mestizos, Afro-mestizos, and indigenous Mexicans. The Spanish Crown relaxed the *casta* system as an incentive for its subjects to colonize its northern frontier. Nevertheless, its persistence within the interior of colonial Mexico inspired a strong source of resentment against Spain. In fact, discontent with the *casta* system was a major impetus for the Mexican War for Independence from 1810 to 1821 (Menchaca 2001).[1]

Even as Spanish and Mexican colonies were taking root, white settlers from the United States petitioned for permission to colonize Texas. The process began with the Spanish government and ended with the Mexican government granting to these settlers limited colonization rights. This second wave of colonization, like the first, brought with it racial tensions between whites, mixed-race Mexicans, and indigenous people. The historian Arnoldo de Leon has argued that attitudes toward Mexicans during this time were generally negative, and Anglo settlers to the region largely viewed Mexican inhabitants as racially inferior (De Leon 1983). In places like New Mexico, indigenous and mixed-race people often tried to perform those racial identities and mannerisms that would allow them greater legal and social rights (Gómez 2007). This double colonization of Mexico's northern frontier resulted in Texas's declaration of independence from Mexico just fifteen years after Mexico had gained its independence from Spain. The anthropologist Richard Flores (2002) has cautioned us not to view Texas Independence as a kind of war between the races, urging us instead to understand the specific Texas-local politics that spurred the move for independence. The Mexican-American War, however, did assume racial overtones, to the extent that at least one scholar casts as excessively violent and egregious (Acuña 1988). The racial cast of both of these wars had serious impacts on the lives of those Mexicans who chose to remain in Texas after it became part of the United States.

In the decades following the Mexican-American War in the middle of the nineteenth century, postwar society in Texas was held together by a tenuous peace structure between Anglos and the Tejano elite, often Spanish land-grant families (Montejano 1987). This peace structure was buttressed by the ranching economy that remained in place after the war. Anglos and Mexican elites lived in a delicate economic and social balance wherein they conducted business together and intermarried, many times for the purpose of merging property (Acosta 2003; Montejano 1987).[2] Nonelite Mexicans, that is to say, the majority of Mexicans who remained in the newly acquired U.S. territories, did not experience postwar "peace" at all. More accurately, from the middle of the nineteenth century through the beginning of the twentieth, there was a great deal of violence perpetrated against Mexicans, both overtly and psycho-

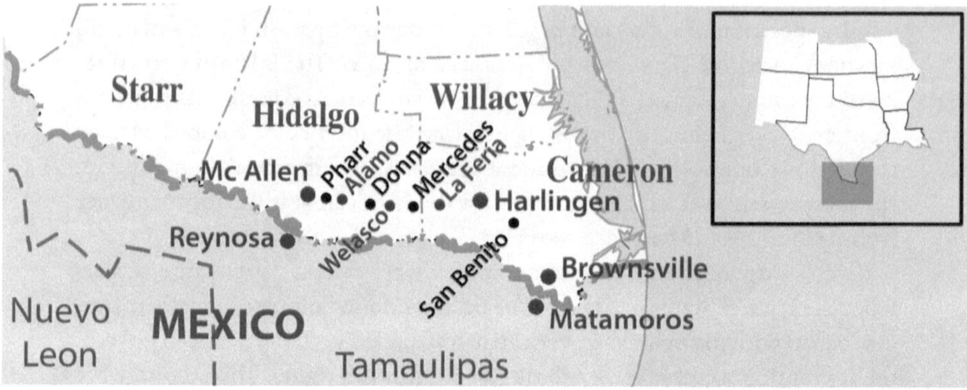

MAP 1.1. Rio Grande Valley. Map by Karthick Ramakrishnan

logically. Nevertheless, Anglos who settled in South Texas during the early postwar period did differentiate between the elite class of Mexicans and the laboring class of Mexicans. Class status, in other words, determined the way Mexicans were racialized during this time, and Mexicans who could align themselves economically with Anglos were able to claim more rights. Soon this period of "peace" yielded to a new era, ushered in by the introduction of the railroads to South Texas.

The railroad arrived in the Rio Grande Valley (the "Magic Valley," as it was advertised to land speculators) in 1904 (see map 1.1). Financed by prominent businessmen in the region, the railroad connected Brownsville with the Corpus Christi terminal of the Missouri Pacific Railroad (Montejano 1987, 107). After this regional railway was connected to the San Antonio line in 1909, it began to experience much more traffic, thus initiating significant social and economic changes to the Valley. Notably, the railroad facilitated the shift from ranching to farming as a primary regional industry. Once the ranchers were firmly connected to outside markets, they began to break up their own land holdings into smaller parcels and sell them to northern colonists (107). Montejano asserts that "with the railroad came farmers, and behind them came land developers, irrigation engineers, and northern produce brokers" (107). These new settlers were not ranchers and thus not necessarily interested in maintaining an economy based on ranching. Land speculators saw farming as a more lucrative economic activity because they could buy large amounts of land and sell it in smaller tracts to farmers for profit. Furthermore, this new, regionally diverse population of Anglos did not distinguish between Mexican elites and working-class Mexicanos. In fact, part of the advertising campaign for land speculators showed not only plentiful land but also plentiful Mexican laborers. Ultimately, the nascent farming industry coupled with the new, larger population of Anglos gave rise to racial- and class-stratified and segregated towns, which severely constricted the rights of Mexican people in the region.

In La Feria, Anglo settlers in the early 1900s recognized the importance of the railroad to the further development of their town. Although the first freight train made a stop in La Feria in 1910, the nearest station was in Bixby, one mile west. According to one local historian, the only railroad stop made in La Feria was to pick up mail, which was gathered in a bag and hung on a post; there was no stop made for passengers or freight (McNail 1975, 9). After some failed attempts to obtain their own railroad station, some local Anglo residents decided to take matters into their own hands. Operating heavy jacks to raise the Bixby station off its foundation and rolling it on a makeshift platform down the tracks to La Feria, early Anglo La Ferians effectively stole Bixby station in 1912 (McNail 1975, 9). The railroad stop in La Feria connected the town with the greater U.S. economy, shifting the local industry from ranching to farming. The city fit squarely into the larger economic trend in South Texas, which Montejano describes as an "agricultural revolution." Bearing in mind that the census during that time redefined what constituted a farm, Montejano argues that the aggregate data indicate a stark shift in the local economy toward farming. He states that the number of farms increased dramatically, while the average farm size decreased. He asserts that this shift indicates the conversion of ranches into farmland as well as the reclamation of unused land in the region for farming. Specifically in Cameron County, in 1910 there were 709 farms with an average size of 770.1 acres. Ten years later there were 1,507 farms averaging 198.6 acres, and by 1930 the 2,936 farms of the region averaged 45.6 acres (Montejano 1987, 109). One local historian recounts that in La Feria, "prospective buyers, being brought in by various land companies . . . , became alarmed about the land situation and wired ahead about specific property, fearing it might all be sold before they arrived" (McNail 1975, 9). The dramatic increase in the number of farms in the region confirms the rapid acquisition of land in La Feria.

The population growth that La Feria experienced during this period further illustrates its prime position as a rail-stop town in the midst of the region's rapidly expanding economy. In 1915, La Feria city records indicate that the town had a population of two hundred, one bank, two churches, and a weekly newspaper called the *La Feria Leader*. By 1925, city estimates place the population between 236 and 825 (Government Service Agency 1999). Eight years later, at the time La Feria was incorporated, it boasted a population of 1,594 residents and ninety businesses (Government Service Agency 1999).

Over the span of sixteen years, the town's population increased eightfold. It is important to consider who the new immigrants to South Texas of this period were and the effect they had not only on the local economies but also on the culture of the cities they began to inhabit. Montejano argues that the Anglos who were new migrants to the region did not have the same understanding of the social system that the previous Anglo inhabitants had; they did not make a distinction between the laboring and aristocratic classes of Mexicans (115). Because the land-owning Mexican elite had been losing their political and economic clout since the mid-1800s, and because Anglo farmers recruited and employed large numbers of Mexicans as farm laborers, new Anglo residents began to conflate the two previously distinct classes. The effects of this racial and class conflation was felt most strongly by the old Mexican elite. Jovita González, a native scholar of the region, interviewed one resident who shared the following:

> We, Texas-Mexicans of the border, although we hold on to our traditions, are proud of our race, are loyal to the United States, in spite of the treatment we receive by some of the new Americans. Before their arrival, there were no racial or social distinctions between us. Their children married ours, ours married theirs, and both were glad and proud of the fact. But since the coming of the "white trash" from the north and middle west we felt the change. They made us feel for the first time that we were Mexicans and that they considered themselves our superiors. (González 2006, 112)

Interestingly, this longtime Valley resident distinguishes between classes of whites the way long-standing Anglos distinguished between classes of Mexicans. He refers to the postwar "peace structure," noting the so-called ethnic harmony that existed before the influx of new Anglos to the region. Unmentioned in this passage is the violence that nonelite Mexicans endured during that time, an issue to which I will return later. With the introduction of the railroad, elite Mexicans began to lose their social, economic, and political standing. Indeed, the significance of class among the Mexican-origin community in Texas lessened while the significance of race increased. Furthermore, the sheer numbers of new Anglos to the region changed the racial dynamics of the social structure in South Texas. Montejano argues that the railroad brought enough Anglos from other parts of the country that white Texans no longer had to admit Mexicans into their social circles. Intermarriages, which had been common during the early period of Anglo settlement in Texas, began to decline. Anglos were now able to form their own, racially exclusive societies (1987, 92). Hence the delicate political and economic balance of the peace structure began to erode, especially in those cities and counties where farming had taken root as the backbone of the local economy.

South Texas political, economic, and social society was now open to a completely different kind of social organization: segregation. Montejano argues that segregation was the formation of a new society, with new class groups and new class relations (163). Simply stated, farmers were Anglo and their laborers were Mexican. He argues that in those places that retained their character as ranching towns, Mexicans experienced less segregation than in farming towns. To Montejano, the shift in the mode of production was what largely propelled segregation.

New farm labor societies proceeded based on what Montejano calls "simple racial exclusions" (1987, 163). By emphasizing the shift in the economy from ranching to farming, the subsequent racialized division of labor, and the decline of the Mexican elite in South Texas, Montejano provides an important basis by which to understand Anglo-Mexican segregation in the region. Nevertheless, the shift in the mode of production alone did not sustain the new social structure of segregation. The legal system, negative racial attitudes about Mexicans, and, especially in South Texas, the rise of a militarized border resulted in the formation of a complex system of segregation in the first decades of the twentieth century.

LEGAL PRECEDENTS AND LOCAL PRACTICES: ESTABLISHING A BASIS FOR SEGREGATION

Legally, Mexican-origin people were uniquely well positioned compared to other people of color living within the boundaries of the United States at the end of the nineteenth and beginning of the twentieth centuries. The Treaty of Guadalupe Hidalgo (1848) was a key legal precedent, granting Mexicans in the conquered territories of the U.S. Southwest citizenship, and subsequent court decisions declared Mexicans legally "white" (Gomez 2008; Menchaca 2001). Nevertheless, Mexican-origin people regularly experienced violent subjugation that severely constricted their citizenship rights during the postwar period. By the beginning of the twentieth century, xenophobic immigration discourses as well as immigration-enforcement efforts along the border rendered most people of Mexican origin an ineligible citizenry in the United States (Ngai 2004). The chasm between de jure and de facto rights reflects Mexican-origin people's fragile claims to whiteness, which was essential to being a fully enfranchised citizen throughout much of the nineteenth and twentieth centuries.

The treaty's grant of citizenship to those Mexican people who chose to remain in the newly acquired U.S. territories was significant because, during this time—and for decades thereafter—the right to naturalization was solely granted to free white persons (Ngai 2004). Granting Mexican people citizenship en masse indicated that in the eyes of the federal government, Mexicans were viewed as "white enough" to be citizens (Gómez 2007). Legal scholar Laura Gómez argues, however, that the citizenship provision of the treaty was "at best, legally vague and, at worst, a deliberate attempt to mislead the Mexican negotiators" (2007, 43). She points to the fact that just twenty years prior, in 1828, the U.S. Supreme Court rendered a decision that made a legal distinction between federal and state citizenship. Gómez emphasizes that the Treaty of Guadalupe Hidalgo granted Mexicans federal citizenship, which was significant in terms of civil rights but would not necessarily enable Mexicans to exercise the political rights that would come with state citizenship. The latter came into sharp relief as states determined their own practices of segregation, many of which would be contingent upon white and nonwhite racial identities.

Questions around Mexican citizenship rights and Mexicans' racial position as "white" in the United Sates were manifested in the U.S. court system soon after the end of the Mexican-American War. Indeed, the legal construction of whiteness was actively waged in the U.S. court system from the 1870s through the first several decades of the twentieth century. Legal scholar Haney Lopez highlights the fact that fifty-two racial prerequisite cases were tried during this time, illustrating how the courts grappled with decisions around who was white enough to become a U.S. citizen (2006). Because only "white" people could be naturalized, the prerequisite cases showed plaintiffs of varying national origins making claims to whiteness in order to be naturalized as U.S. citizens. While race scholars (such as anthropologist Franz Boas) were occasionally called as expert witnesses, the courts took it upon themselves to answer the "categorical question of how to determine racial identity" (Haney Lopez 2006, 3). The logic behind their decisions was frequently based on either scientific evidence or what they deemed "common knowledge," which during different eras proved to be at odds with each other (Haney Lopez 2006; Ngai 2004).

It was in one of these prerequisite cases that the courts established a precedent that Mexicans were, for legal purposes, white. In the case *Rodriguez v. Bexar County* (1897), Ricardo Rodriguez, a Mexican-origin man who had resided in San Antonio for ten years, applied for naturalization. Initially denied by the Bexar County court because of his race, Rodriguez took his case to the Circuit Court of San Antonio. In this case, the naturalization board argued against Rodriguez's petition for citizenship on the basis that he was racially indigenous, citing several legal precedents that established it to be against the law for indigenous people to be naturalized. In an interesting move, Rodriguez's legal representative, T. M. Paschal, did not attempt to prove that Rodriguez was racially white. Rather, Paschal argued that because the Treaty of Guadalupe Hidalgo had extended citizenship to Mexican people in the ceded territories, Mexican immigrants were legally entitled to citizenship, regardless of their racial status. To deny Rodriguez his application to be naturalized would thus be a violation of international law. The district court agreed, deciding in favor of Rodriguez (Martinez 1997; Menchaca 1993; Ngai 2004.) The court's decision based on the Treaty of Guadalupe Hidalgo effectively set the precedent that Mexicans were legally white, even if not racially recognized as such by segregationists.

Ian Haney López argues that "in constructing race, legal rules operate through violence" (2006, 85). In the case of Mexican Americans, however, their legal rights as white citizens were actually undermined by practices of violence—both physical and symbolic. Immediately after the Mexican-American War and through the first part of the twentieth century, the Texas Rangers served as a kind of frontier police force in Texas. Borderlands historians have testified that rather than apply the law objectively, the Rangers effectively promoted the interests of Anglo Texas to acquire land and power. To accomplish this, the Rangers engaged in the violent suppression of Mexicans, especially through practices of lynching (De Leon 1983; Johnson 2003; Paredes 1958). In their research about Mexican lynchings in the U.S. Southwest, Carrigan and Webb (2003) find that between 1848 and 1928, mobs lynched at least 597 Mexicans, with 282 of these murders occurring in Texas.[3] Though their research focuses on lynch mobs and not specifically the Texas Rangers, this study is indicative of the kind of frontier justice that subjugated Mexicans in the new U.S. territory. While international law granted Mexicans citizenship, the prevalence of anti-Mexican violence relegated them to second-class-citizen status.

Whereas overt violence shaped the citizenship experiences of Mexicans during the second half of the nineteenth century, the dawn of the twentieth century brought with it new forms of legality that shaped the lives of Mexican people, especially in the border region. During the 1900s and 1910s, the political boundary between the United States and Mexico was not regularly enforced, and Mexican nationals were able to cross with relative ease to perform day labor or longer, seasonal labor. The establishment of the Border Patrol in 1924, however, ushered in a new era of policing to the border region of South Texas. Like the Texas Rangers, the Border Patrol was a national force formed to police the border. Historian Mae Ngai argues that although the

Border Patrol was charged with enforcing civil laws, their activities "assumed the character of criminal pursuit and apprehension" (2006, 69) as they vigorously pursued "illegal aliens." To this end, Border Patrol officers would practice racial profiling, interrogating Mexican laborers on roads and in towns as well as conducting sweeps to apprehend suspected "illegals." Within the context of my research in La Feria, regional popular lore and at least one oral history interview recalls that during an immigration raid of farmworkers, even U.S. citizens of Mexican origin would flee the Border Patrol agents for fear of deportation. In their capacity as border-enforcement officers, the Border Patrol helped to create an environment rife with deepening racial hostilities between Mexicans and Anglos. Though the Border Patrol did not engage in the same types of violent activities as the Texas Rangers, the fear that they instilled in the Mexican population of South Texas mirrored that of the previous generation. In fact, as late as the 1950s, Mexican-origin people in La Feria referred to Border Patrol agents as "*rinches*," a Spanish word used pejoratively to refer to the Texas Rangers.

At the end of the 1920s, though Mexican people in the United States were legally well positioned, their racial aspect rendered their rights tenuous. They were eligible for citizenship, they were legally considered white, and they had not been targeted with an immigration quota as part of the Immigration Act of 1924, also known as the Johnson-Reed Act. Ngai argues, however, that the presence of the Border Patrol and the emergence of a category of "illegality" prohibited U.S. Mexicans from enjoying their full rights as citizens. She states that "as numerical restriction assumed primacy in immigration policy, its enforcement aspects—inspection procedures, deportation, the Border Patrol, criminal prosecution, and irregular categories of immigration—created many thousands of illegal immigrants" (Ngai 2004, 71). In other words, that Mexicans were exempt from immigration restrictions did not mean that immigration policy, particularly its modes of enforcement, did not have a marked impact on Mexican people's lives on the U.S. side of the border. Furthermore, U.S. politicians and lobbyists actively debated the "Mexican problem"—the steady immigration of Mexican people who crossed the border to work in the burgeoning agricultural industry of South Texas and elsewhere in the southwestern United States. Those who argued for the restriction of Mexican immigration cited statistics demonstrating that Mexican people were likely to become a public charge. These statistics were buttressed by allegations that Mexicans were mentally inferior and unhealthy (Ngai 2004, 53). On the other side of the debate, farm lobbyists supported a more open and flexible border to serve their interests of importing cheap labor. Within this immigration discourse were, at worst, immigration restrictionists, who believed that Mexicans and other nonwhite races would contaminate the American way of life and, at best, lobbyists who were looking to exploit Mexican labor.

Determining and guarding the external boundaries of the United States were closely related to concerns about Mexicans' potential cultural impact on the nation. Though the federal court upheld the provision of the Treaty of Guadalupe Hidalgo that legally rendered Mexicans eligible for citizenship, there were obviously many who believed Mexican people were an ineligible citizenry. Montejano argues that the "Mexican problem" that occupied so many scholars and academics was not so much about assimilation as it was "a question of locating another inferior race in American society" (1987, 181). He continues, "There was general agreement, in Texas and elsewhere, that Mexicans were not a legitimate citizenry of the United States. They were outside the civic order, and references to American national integrity and Texas history were often ill-disguised claims of Anglo Supremacy" (181). Indeed it seemed that from Texas to Washington, D.C., politicians viewed Mexicans as racially and culturally inferior, and they feared the impact that Mexican people would have on the fabric of American life. Though the law officially granted Mexican-origin people more potential rights than other nonwhite groups in the United States during this time, law enforcement and discourses around immigration revealed thinly veiled ideas about the racial inferiority of Mexicans and their status as an ineligible citizenry. If legally Mexicans could not be barred from American civic life the way that other nonwhite groups had been through immigration quotas and outright denials of civil rights, the unwritten policy was to systematically subjugate Mexicans so that they were socially, economically, and politically marginalized, regardless of their citizenship status. This created a de facto racial border within the boundaries of the United States. One of the main ways that such racial borders were constructed and maintained was through practices of racial segregation.

The Supreme Court case *Plessy v. Ferguson* (1896) was perhaps the most powerful legal ruling supporting practices of racial segregation in the United States, legalizing all forms of social segregation (Menchaca 1993). In the *Plessy* ruling, the court granted the states the right to determine who was considered white and nonwhite for the purposes of segregation. Because of the ambiguous racial status of Mexican people, the states often grappled with whether to classify them as white or as Indian. There were several local and state court cases in the Southwest to determine the legality of Mexican segregation, most of which based their rulings on the racial status of Mexican people (Menchaca 1993; Valencia 2008). The outcomes of these types of court cases, many of which centered on education, were varied, often depending on the local context and the amount of community activism propelling the case forward. However, even if state and local courts ruled against the legality of racial segregation, Anglo-run school districts and other government entities successfully enacted de facto policies of segregation throughout the U.S. Southwest. Latino Studies scholar Suzanne Oboler emphasizes the fact that after the *Plessy v. Ferguson* decision in 1896, segregation became a reality for nonwhite people in the United States by law and "by custom" (1995, 31). She asserts that "newly and often violently created customary practices frequently came to define [Latinos'] lack of citizenship rights and to shape their experiences more clearly than the 'law of the land'" (38). Though Mexican-origin people could claim legal whiteness, customary practices of segregation defined their subordinate positions in society much as more formal measures did for those minorities that were segregated by law. I suggest that the emergence of Mexican segregation in the first decades of the twentieth century was a powerful mechanism by which to police the social, political, and economic boundaries between Mexicans and Anglos in the United States.

Mexican segregation supported the racialized capitalist development that was occurring in the Southwest at the beginning of the twentieth century. First, Mexican segregation established racial divisions between Anglos and Mexicans. Especially because of Mexicans' mixed-race status, practices of segregation literally separated them from whites and, by extension, claims to the rights of whiteness (Haney López 2006, 84). Oboler argues that segregation helped to establish the "internal boundaries of the 'national community' such that the public self-image of the American nation could be invoked primarily in white-only terms" (1995, 31). The internal boundaries set by practices of racial segregation circumscribed lines of inclusion and exclusion in the nation-state and brought to bear the relationship between race and citizenship. Again, even though many people of Mexican origin were citizens and/or eligible for citizenship, practices and structures of segregation precluded them from claiming citizenship rights, indicating to them that they did not truly belong within the boundaries of the nation-state. Ngai argues that particularly within the context of farm-labor economies like La Feria's, segregation "stripped Mexicans of the claim of belonging," creating and maintaining a "foreign" workforce that had limited access to rights, thereby ensuring Anglo economic and political dominance (2006, 133). It is important to highlight that in cities such as Los Angeles and El Paso, strong and stable Mexican communities developed at the turn of the twentieth century, and within those contexts, Mexicans had more access to both resources and rights.[4]

The struggle to define who belonged to the nation-state was perhaps most actively waged and felt in the local communities along the U.S.-Mexico border. Railroad tracks created physical borders between Mexican and Anglo communities in various towns and cities throughout the Southwest, and the border town of La Feria was no different. The railroad bisected it into two racially divided neighborhoods. While this physical border was not policed the way that the national border was, it was a division that had national overtones. Mexicans referred to the north side of town as *el pueblo mexicano* ("the Mexican town") and the south side of town as *el pueblo americano*" ("the American town"). They did not refer to the south side as "Anglo" or by any other racial term connoting white people; they referred to it as "American." The Anglo population similarly utilized the language of nation when referring to the north side of town, which they called "Mexicata" or "Mexiquito," the latter literally meaning "little Mexico." This discourse of nation highlighted the segregationist politics of the town. Anglos did not view Mexican-origin people—even those who had inhabited the area for generations—as "American." In the same manner that Ngai describes, in this agricultural community, Mexicans were ascribed foreign identities and thus not entitled to the same kinds of rights as their Anglo American counterparts. When Mexican people were permitted into Anglo spheres, each such occasion was an exception determined by either an Anglo individual or an Anglo-dominated power structure. In short, during this period, there was little distinction between national and racial borders in La Feria. Everyone in the community at least implicitly understood that racial borders were related to a national discourse of belonging.

After an intense era of vigilante border violence at the hands of the Texas Rangers, the modern era brought with it increased border enforcement that largely cast Mexicans as a "foreign" workforce regardless of their citizenship status. Furthermore, practices of segregation, initially targeted toward African Americans and Native Americans, became the de facto law of the land for towns and cities with significant numbers of Mexican people. Segregation delineated the limits of Mexican "whiteness," often reinforcing ideas about Mexicans as an ineligible citizenry, and rendered tenuous their claims of belonging to the United States.

CROSSING RACIAL BORDERS, MAINTAINING ANGLO DOMINANCE

De facto segregation was the reality for Mexican-origin people across South Texas during the early twentieth century. Nevertheless, there were always a few individuals who were exceptions to the rule of racial segregation in the region. The amount of wealth that a family or individual possessed often determined whether a person was able to cross racial boundaries. In addition to class status, exceptions to the rule of racial segregation were based on factors such as education, gender, and Anglo cultural fluency. Even so, within the context of de facto segregation, neither class nor any other factor guaranteed acceptance into Anglo spheres of influence; Mexican people often struggled to be included. Such inclusion was always tenuous; most Mexican people who gained access to Anglo society also experienced limitations within it.

In his book *White but Not Equal*, the historian Ignacio García acknowledges that various factors affected the way that Mexican-origin people experienced segregation in their communities during the middle of the twentieth century. He states: "De facto segregation . . . [was] effective because de facto exclusion . . . made class, color, gender, education, and political ties qualifiers for acceptance. This meant that only those with money, education, and political connections could participate, and even then only if they insisted. These qualifiers [laid] the burden of inclusion on the Mexican Americans themselves" (2009, 6). In other words, though race was the primary means of segregating Mexicans, de facto segregation in Texas was more than a system of simple racial exclusions. Garcia argues that segregation was maintained through a complex system of qualifiers that allowed some Mexicans to "pass" into certain realms of Anglo society. Indeed, class, complexion, education, and social connections affected the ways that Mexicans experienced segregation. Nevertheless, even an alignment of all of these factors did not guarantee acceptance into Anglo spheres. Mexican people often had to fight for rights of inclusion, and even when they "won," such instances of acceptance were the exceptions to the general rule of racial dominance. Furthermore, as I demonstrate in following chapters, even exceptional Mexican people experienced racial stigma.

Though rare, instances of Mexican exceptionality occurred in farm communities like La Feria as early as the 1920s and 1930s, the period when Mexican segregation was intensifying throughout South Texas. During this time, those Mexicans who were exceptions to the rule of racial segregation were usually people whose families were longtime residents of the region. Many belonged to the original Spanish land-grant families who had managed to maintain a modicum of wealth and influence, primarily through the land that they had retained. In La Feria, these people frequently established themselves as business owners on the Mexican side of town and would often serve as liaisons between the Mexican and Anglo communities, especially within the realm of labor. For example, a well-positioned Mexican American might be the contact person through whom Anglos would contract Mexican laborers. However, because so many land-grant families in Texas had been disenfranchised,[5] these exceptional figures were uncommon in La Feria during the first few decades of the twentieth century.

The phenomenon of Mexicans crossing racial boundaries in La Feria began to occur more frequently in the 1940s and 1950s. Several Chicano historians have noted this period as a turning point for the Mexican American community (García 2009; Gutierrez 1995; Sanchez 1995). Mexican Americans participated in large numbers in World War II, which led to a greater investment in and increased claims to their citizenship rights upon their return to the States from their military service. Furthermore, the economic stimulus of the war and the bracero program (1942 through 1964), which brought increased traffic to Mexican American businesses, gave many Mexican Americans an economic boost, which led to more upward mobility. Racial ambiguity, increased economic mobility, and widening opportunities for education (mostly high school, but also some college) were all factors that gave Mexican people greater access to Anglo spheres. Nevertheless, those Mexican people who crossed racial boundaries were not fully incorporated into Anglo society. García describes the flexibility of the social structure of segregation. He states: "Mexican American class fluidity made it difficult to establish laws that covered all Mexican Americans, so most of the practices and rules that did discriminate were focused on the lower working class. The fluidity also allowed a few Mexican American elites . . . to move in and out of some social circles as long as they did not overreach" (2009, 14). García's argument is important because it indicates the importance of socioeconomic status as a major influence on the way that Mexican people experienced segregation. García's reference to Mexican "elites" referenced their economic standing in the community, but it most likely also referred to aspects of cultural capital, such as English-Spanish bilingualism, manner of dress, and level of formal education. The case of La Feria illustrates that neither class status nor cultural capital allows Mexican-origin people to fully transcend the perception of their race. Even those Mexican people who were permitted into Anglo spheres of influence in La Feria experienced segregation in ways that limited their incorporation into the town as full citizens, especially at the level of the racialized Mexican body. In other words, despite the fluidity that class status granted Mexican people, race was always a factor that differentiated even middle class Mexican people from their Anglo counterparts, and race limited the ways in which they were able to participate in society.

While the phenomenon of Mexican exceptionality is intriguing within a historical context of racial segregation and discrimination, it is more important to analyze how this exceptionality led to the persistence of segregation beyond landmark civil rights legislation. As García's work on Mexican jury discrimination indicates, a town's ability to point to exceptions to the racial rule of Anglo dominance made discrimination lawsuits difficult to win.

He states that "de facto discrimination had always allowed a certain amount of fluidity among the races in Texas and because of that fluidity there were Mexican Americans who could prove to be the exception in every case" (2009, 40). This was perhaps the most frustrating aspect of Mexican segregation for advocates of desegregation. Because Mexican segregation occurred as custom rather than by law and because there were always exceptional Mexicans who were able to break racial boundaries, discrimination was difficult to prove and desegregation was difficult to legislate. The latter part of this book will discuss the persistence of racial segregation by custom, which made it necessary for integration to occur not only by law but also as local practice.

CLAIMING AND CREATING RIGHTS

The racial logic that characterized South Texas throughout much of the twentieth century marginalized Mexican-origin people economically, politically, and socially. Regardless of their citizenship status, Mexicans were treated as second-class members of society. While the ethnographic chapters in this book will discuss how racialization led Mexicans to experience and navigate the structure of segregation in different ways, this section highlights how people of Mexican origin forged community and strategically used Mexican culture and values to create a space of belonging for themselves in the town. Sometimes they sought to belong by performing cultural identities that were acceptable to Anglos. Other times, people reinforced the bonds within the Mexican community and held strong to Mexican cultural identities. While the latter might be understood as "resistance," people's everyday actions also acutely speak to their desires to belong, to create community, and to claim basic human rights, such as respect and dignity. The concept of cultural citizenship provides a useful frame of reference for understanding how Mexicans forged community to claim rights of membership in La Feria.

Often used as a way to make sense of the discrepancies between de jure and de facto rights, cultural citizenship can be understood as what Rina Benmayor calls a "borderlands paradigm" (Benmayor 2002, 99). Though Mexicans were considered legally white and were eligible for citizenship, immigration enforcement and practices of segregation rendered them marginal to the nation-state. Indeed the anthropologist Renato Rosaldo encourages us to understand the difference between the legal renderings of citizens as "equal before the law" and "the substantive level of exclusionary and marginalizing practices" (1997, 27). If we understand that Mexican-origin people during this period occupied a borderlands space in terms of rights, cultural citizenship allows us "to see the notion of rights as it is defined not by the legal code but by the cultural foundations and practices of people themselves" (Benmayor, Torruelas, and Jarabe quoted in Coll 2010, 5). The historical ethnography presented in the following chapters illustrates how Mexican people's actions, ranging from the everyday to the ritualistic, can be understood as both claiming and creating rights. These claims to rights must first be understood as community building.

The social analysts Stuart Hall and David Held posit that "citizenship has entailed a discussion and a struggle over the meaning and scope of membership of the community in which one lives" (quoted in Rosaldo 1997, 30). Who are considered full members of a society? How do subordinated groups struggle to broaden the scope of belonging? Flores (2003) argues that forging community, creating space, and claiming rights are all essential elements of cultural citizenship. Within a segregated city like La Feria, Mexicans were relegated to the part of the town north of the railroad tracks. While it lacked the infrastructure of the Anglo side of town, the Mexican community found ways to render itself culturally relevant by creating an ethos of reciprocity and mutualism through everyday actions as well as through staged cultural celebrations. Scholars have categorized such activities as economic survival strategies, political maneuvering, and cultural resistance. Within the local context of La Feria, these actions might have been acts of contestation, but they were also acts of affirmation and cultural production, part of what the anthropologist Carlos Vélez-Ibáñez calls the "cultural basis of political action" (1996, 93). In claiming the segregated neighborhood as their own place and, as we will see in later chapters, in creating transnational U.S.-Mexican relationships and sensibilities, Mexican-origin people in La Feria created a space of belonging for themselves within the borders of the United States.

Through the lens of cultural citizenship, Mexican community building and the creation of culturally relevant space in La Feria illustrate the people's claims to such rights as respect and dignity, which become particularly important in the context of a racially subordinated community. Furthermore, scholars in anthropology represent cultural citizenship as "processual rather than simply a static bundle of rights and entitlements" (Coll 2010, 7–8). In the context of La Feria, Mexican people's claims for rights shift through the different periods of segregation. Whereas during the first period of segregation the emphasis is on creating an ethos of mutualism and reinforcing Mexican heritage, during the latter stage, Mexican people use their culture and values to actually desegregate Anglo-dominant spheres. The anthropologist Kathleen Coll reminds us that cultural citizenship recognizes that "all members of a society seek to claim their rights without being either marginalized or forced to assimilate to hegemonic norms" (2010, 141). I build upon her argument by asserting that claiming cultural space can have varying impacts on a community during different periods of time. Regardless of the depth of the impact of claiming space and rights, cultural citizenship is about community empowerment.

The law undoubtedly shaped the way that segregation was manifested in the first half of the twentieth century. Civil rights movements and subsequent legislation were also instrumental to the desegregation of communities all over the country. This ethnographic examination of Mexican people's lives and their claims of cultural citizenship provides a way for us to understand more deeply how Mexicans experienced and responded to segregation in their everyday lives and how they pushed desegregation forward at the local level. Though Mexican residents of La Feria rarely espoused oppositional politics, throughout the twentieth century we can see a clear trajectory of Mexican people claiming and expanding their rights as members of the community.

RACIAL SEGREGATION, a social structure that emerged in the early twentieth century with the arrival of the railroad in South Texas, was a defining characteristic of Mexican social and political life. In this chapter, I have argued that although on paper the law seemed to ensure that Mexican-origin people could claim citizenship and the rights of "whiteness," violence and discrimination characterized their experiences immediately after the Mexican-American War. As the economy of the region shifted toward agribusiness, racial segregation emerged as the major structure of social and political organization. Because Mexicans could not be legally segregated owing to their racial status as white, segregation occurred most strongly as local customs, which were pervasive throughout the Southwest. However, these regular customs of segregation were fraught with contradictions precisely because Mexican people's racial aspects ranged from white to indigenous. Factors such as class status, education, gender, and Anglo cultural fluency further complicated the structure of segregation in South Texas. I have argued that Mexican people's borderlands experience of race was reflective of the proximity of that U.S.-Mexico border, just a few miles south of La Feria. As this national border was increasingly policed after the establishment of the Border Patrol in 1924, towns in the border region of the Lower Rio Grande Valley became vigilant about maintaining racial boundaries within their city limits as well. Nevertheless, Mexican people found ways to claim rights for themselves through their everyday actions, creating culturally relevant spaces for themselves even in the strictest era of racial segregation.

CHAPTER TWO

ESTABLISHING A CULTURE OF SEGREGATION

IT WAS EARLY ENOUGH in the morning that the air was still dewy and cool, though the white summer sun was already beginning to shine brightly through the homes on a crowded block of *el pueblo mexicano*. I had returned for the third time to this small white house intent upon talking to Santiago Martinez, whose schedule always seemed to conflict with my own. That morning, I found the ninety-year-old lifelong resident of La Feria sitting, shirtless, on the porch enjoying the cool morning while eating a plate of *migas*. When he saw me, he stood graciously and said, "*Pásale*," telling me that his wife was inside. I tried to explain to Mr. Martinez that I was there to see him, but he continued to usher me inside the house toward his wife. When she told him that I was there to see him, he muttered that he already had enough nurses and did not need another. Mrs. Martinez explained that I was not a nurse but had come to talk to him about the history of La Feria.

Once he realized why I had come, he made himself comfortable on the couch, and I sat across from him. Still shirtless and gesticulating broadly, he stated loudly, "*¡Qué bueno que me preguntas éso!*"

Santiago Martinez migrated from northern Mexico to La Feria with his family in 1923, when he was five years old. He recounts that he knew the first residents of the town and that during his youth his family lived in extreme poverty. He recalls, "*No conocíamos el dinero, oiga, no lo conocíamos. Un dólar era como mil dólares.*" ["We never saw money, I tell you. One dollar for us was like a thousand dollars."] Never having attended school, Martinez taught himself how to read and write and spent his entire life working in the fields. After marrying Margarita, who was from another part of South Texas, they, like many Mexican-origin people of their generation, migrated to California to work in the fields each summer. During our interview, the Martinezes shared with me the black-and-white pictures that chronicled their trips to California.

They recounted for me all the dance halls that played Tejano music up and down the Valley, where they would go to dance. Mr. Martinez's memory, despite his age, was still sharp, and he and his wife filled my morning with vivid storytelling.

When I asked him about segregation or discrimination against Mexicans, both Mr. and Mrs. Martinez shook their heads thoughtfully and said no. Mr. Martinez recalled, *"Pues yo anduve trabajando en muchas partes, y casi éramos puros mexicanos; en la tomatera puros mexicanos, y alguna americana de mayordomo, o americano de mayordomo; acá en la bodega también puros mexicanos, la mayordoma era mexicana, el mayordomo también. No, no . . . Yo nunca sentí discriminación ni nada."* ["I've worked in a lot of places, and it was almost all Mexicans; in the tomato cannery, it was all Mexicans with an Anglo supervisor; here in the packing shed it was also all Mexican, the supervisor was Mexican. No, no . . . I never felt any kind of discrimination."]

After our interview, I wondered why the Martinezes' perspective on segregation was so different from what I had heard previously. I realized that they had never experienced overt discrimination precisely because they had lived in such a segregated Mexican world. Because Mr. Martinez had not attended La Feria schools and because the couple did not regularly attend church, they did not experience the same kind of racial tensions that other Mexican-origin people in town had experienced. During their time working in the fields, the cannery, and the packing sheds, their coworkers were all Mexican, as were the majority of their supervisors. In their leisure time, they attended Mexican dances, which played Spanish-language Tejano music, catering toward a Mexican crowd. While they were regularly in community with Mexican-origin people throughout the Valley and in the migrant stream, they were so segregated from Anglo people that they did not feel a strong sense of racism or discrimination. The Martinezes' story provides a way for us to understand the rigid racial boundaries that characterized Mexican segregation during the first few decades of the twentieth century. As farm communities along the Rio Grande Valley emerged during this time, their development was often marked with the purposeful spatial separation of Anglos who would run the town and Mexicans who would labor in its fields.

THE CITY OF La Feria emerged as a prototypical farm town in South Texas at the turn of the twentieth century. Anglo settlers from the Midwest purchased the tract of land that would encompass the city, and unlike South Texas towns that developed in the 1800s with ranch economies, La Feria, with its farm-based economy, developed a rigid social order of segregation from its inception in 1915 through the 1930s. In this chapter I will illustrate how the development of segregation in the first decades of the twentieth century reflected local and national concerns about the "Mexican problem." Broadly speaking, the Mexican problem was that Anglo-run farms, which had quickly become the backbone of a new economy, were dependent upon Mexican labor to sustain them; however, Anglo settlers did not want Mexican people to have a social or cultural impact on their communities. In other words, Anglos needed Mexicans to be present for the labor that they could provide but did not want their presence in society as a whole. Anglo settlers strategically developed farm towns along the border in ways that amplified their economic strengths in farming while keeping their local Mexican populations socially, economically, and politically subordinate through practices of segregation. While segregation during this time was nearly absolute, there was at least one Mexican family that was able to cross the local racial divide. This phenomenon would not become common until the 1940s.

This chapter illustrates what I designate as the first stage of racial segregation for Mexican people in La Feria. In the period from the incorporation of the town through the 1930s, the structure of segregation was such that each community—Anglo and Mexican—was almost completely separate. The place where the two populations had the most contact was in the realm of labor, most of which was fieldwork. Other major points of contact were in the school system and in the local Catholic church. High levels of school attrition and spatial designations within the sanctuary of the church, however, buttressed the notion that Mexicans and Anglos should remain segregated in social spaces. Indeed, the legal scholar Ian Haney López has argued that such practices of spatial separation helped to fix racial boundaries (2006, 84). Popular understandings about the racial superiority of Anglos, the shift in the local economy from ranching to farming, and the influx of new Anglo settlers from parts of the country where the logic of black-white segregation was well established all provided the ideological justification for segregation.

Furthermore, in this chapter I demonstrate the interplay between race and rights for Mexican-origin people during this early epoch of segregation. After the Mexican-American War, while all Mexicans suffered varying levels of disenfranchisement and violations of their rights as new U.S. citizens, the elite class of Mexicans was able to attain more rights than the "peon" class. At the turn of the twentieth century, however, Mexican racial segregation emerged as the de facto social structure. In La Feria, segregation corresponded to limited rights and opportunities for Mexican people. Socially, economically, and politically, they were largely subordinate to Anglo people. There were, however, some descendants of land-grant families whose wealth (and often, racial aspect) allowed them some nominal acceptance within the Anglo-dominant city. One such well-known Mexican family lived in a house on the south side of the tracks, and a few others owned businesses on that side of town. City records reflect the willingness of Anglos to engage with the head of this exceptional Mexican household, which illustrates that his racial ambiguity and, perhaps more important at this juncture, his class status allowed him to claim rights that poor, racialized Mexicans could not. Nevertheless, exceptional Mexican people were by no means incorporated into Anglo society; rather, their main affinities were with the local Mexican community.

LOCAL FOUNDATIONS OF SEGREGATION

Spurred by the rapid development of the railroad, Anglo settlement and development around La Feria began in 1907. In 1909, S. J. "Duke" Schnorenberg and other local developers purchased a six-thousand-acre tract of land that encompassed La Feria. That same year, Schnorenberg formed the La Feria Townsite Company, and the La Feria Post Office was established. Schnorenberg built the La Feria Hotel in 1910 on Old Highway 83. Also in 1910, another prominent Anglo settler, and an Illinois native, Bailey H. Dunlap, established the Cameron County Bank of La Feria. These modern developments connected La Feria more easily to neighboring town sites and industries, which Anglo settlers were rapidly populating. Despite the long-standing Spanish and Mexican settlement of the region, when the citizens of La Feria filed the request to officially incorporate the city in 1915, of the fifteen signatories, not one had a Spanish surname (McNail 1975).

La Feria's City Commission records reflect the rapid establishment of the city's infrastructure during the first fifteen years after its request for incorporation. This construction boom involved contracting vendors and laborers to pave streets; install power lines, including streetlights; and build the framework for distributing natural gas, water, and wastewater. Unrecorded in these records is the simultaneous development of the "Mexican Town."[1] While the city was developing its infrastructure from 1915 through 1930, it also established a separate part of town where Mexican people were to reside. That the establishment of residential segregation in La Feria was never debated or explicitly recorded by city officials leads us to understand that Mexican residential separation was not intended to emerge as de jure segregation. In his study of segregation and suburbanization in the South, the historian Matthew Lassiter (2006) challenges the distinction between "de jure" and "de facto" segregation altogether, calling it an "artificial dichotomy" when considering that racialized suburbanization was financed by the state. In La Feria, where eco-

FIGURE 2.1. View of La Feria, Texas. Runyon (Robert) Photograph Collection, RUN03014, the Dolph Briscoe Center for American History, the University of Texas at Austin

nomic resources and political power lay squarely in the hands of Anglo residents, de jure and de facto segregation were similarly conflated. Though there were no racially explicit housing covenants, the Mexican town, which was spatially separate from Anglo neighborhoods and businesses, was constructed using money from the state.

The same railroad that facilitated a shift in the local economy from ranching toward farming increased the arm of American influence and industry. It delivered carloads of new Anglos to the region and served to literally divide La Feria and other Valley towns into two stratified communities—Anglos on one side of the tracks, Mexicans on the other (Foley 1988; Madsen 1973; Richardson 1999; Rubel 1966). The physical characteristics of Anglo and Mexican neighborhoods in South Texas reflected the dramatic social hierarchy between the two groups. David Montejano notes that "American neighborhoods of handsome wood frame houses, paved streets, and enclosed sewers stood in sharp contrast with Mexican towns of corrugated tin shacks, dirt roads and outdoor privies" (1987, 168). The "American" and "Mexican" towns in La Feria exhibited similar kinds of physical discrepancies. The spatial characteristics of segregation in La Feria can be seen in a map that reflects the areas of the city that were part of its original town site (see map 2.1). In the Mexican neighborhood, north of the railroad tracks, housing lots are significantly smaller than those south of the tracks, where Anglos lived. Houses in the Mexican neighborhood were constructed such that there would be five feet on either side of the structure—from house to property line—so that two homes next to each other would be ten feet apart, the minimal amount of distance to be in compliance with fire-safety codes.[2] These so-called shotgun houses were wood framed, and many did not have indoor plumbing. Antonia Garza, who grew up in La Feria's Mexican neighborhood in the 1930s and 1940s, recalls the Mexican community fondly despite the lack of infrastructure. She states, "I remember we had a big circle, and a lot of people lived in the area where we lived. We had the potty thing, you know, the outhouse, in the center, and we all used to use that." In contrast, Anglo residents of the south side of town enjoyed much more space, and there was generally better infrastructure in their neighborhoods, including sidewalks, gutters, street dividers, landscaping, and public parks. The only areas on the south side of town that were designed to occupy a small space comparable to the Mexican residential area on the north side of town were located in the business and commercial district south of the railroad tracks along Main Street. Furthermore, all of La Feria's original public buildings, where city business was conducted (e.g., city hall, the school district office), were located south of the railroad tracks, on the Anglo side of town, indicating this part of town to be the official center of local government and commerce. The sole government-operated facility located in the Mexican part of the city at its inception was, perhaps not surprisingly, the city jail.

The burgeoning farming industry was the engine of La Feria's fledgling economy, as was true for most of the towns in the Lower Rio Grande Valley. Records from the local newspaper illustrate how this new industry resulted in the rapid growth of the town. While in 1915 the town recorded a population of merely 200 people, the 1930 census counted 1,594 residents in La Feria. This population boom resulted in the development of new residential areas south of the railroad tracks, the progress of the city's bank, and the establishment of new businesses. Newspaper accounts that detailed the modern foundations of the town were paralleled in number only by those that highlighted the local agricultural industry. The management of citrus and cotton crops, the mechanics of cotton ginning, and concerns about water management and pests that might affect crops were all of interest to new local residents. Sev-

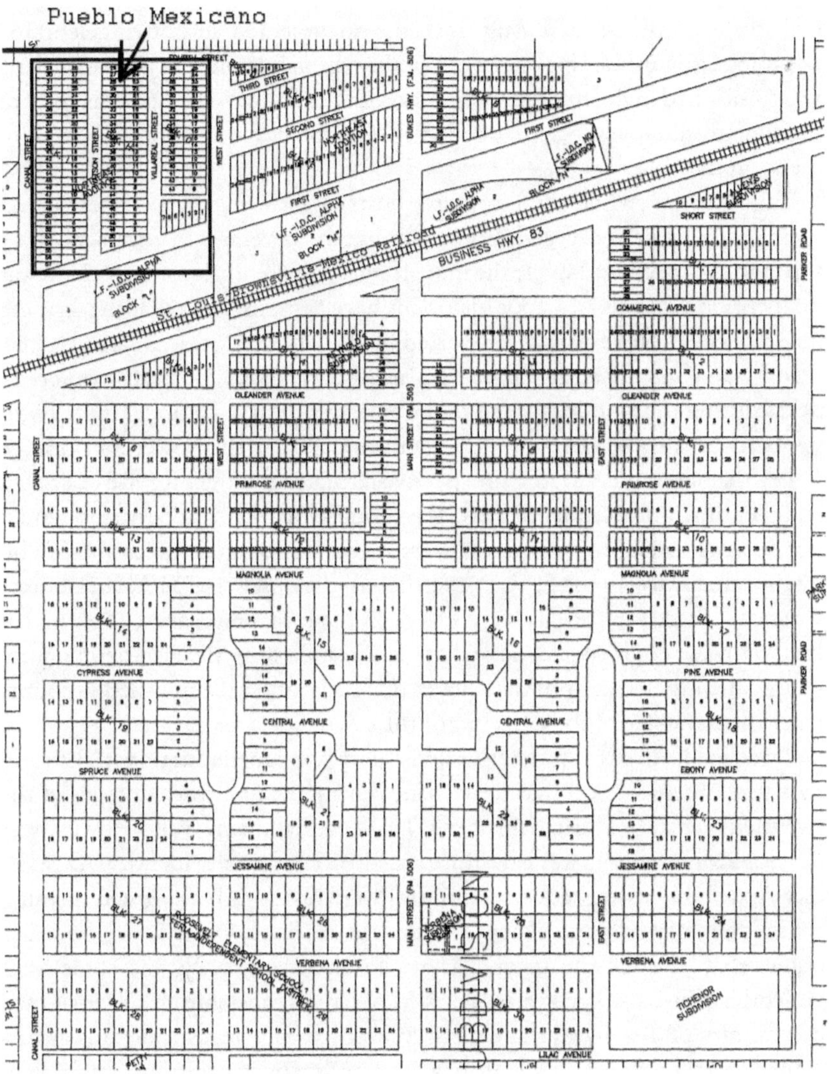

MAP 2.1. City of La Feria, Texas, cropped to show town site in 1915. Courtesy of City of La Feria

eral stories in the press during this time documented and often celebrated booming agricultural shipments out of the region by train and truck. La Feria was positioned in the middle of the local agricultural revolution; a prominent headline from November 1929 reported that the city was third in fruit shipments in the Valley.

Interestingly, while the farming industry—farmers, their concerns, and their crops—received a significant amount of coverage in the local news through the 1920s, and while the industry was apparently booming, there was no mention of laborers. Labor historians have demonstrated that the farming industry of South Texas was supported by the labor of Mexican farmworkers (Montejano 1987; Zamora 1993). In his history about Mexican workers in Texas during the first decades of the twentieth century, Zamora (1993) highlights advertising by farm-development companies in the Lower Rio Grande Valley that attempted to lure prospective farmers with the promise of "cheap and plentiful" Mexican labor (32). The promise of abundant farmland would not be as appealing to speculators were there not also guarantees about who might actually toil in the fields. Nevertheless, the number of Mexican laborers was not recorded in the city's records or in the local newspaper. Their invisibility in these contexts indicates that, as a population, Mexican people were marginal to the social political life of La Feria; indeed published accounts place them outside of the citizenry of the town.

I would like to suggest that this invisibility was a manifestation of the rigid structure of segregation that took shape during the first three decades of the twentieth century. During this time, La Feria, like many Valley towns, was developing not only an infrastructure but also a community identity. As Benedict Anderson has argued, communities were historically imagined through the medium of newspapers (1991). In the case of Texas, John Morán González argues that through the 1930s, "Anglo Texans customarily, and sometimes violently, refused to recognize Texas-Mexican membership in the imagined community of Texas and the United States, treating Texas Mexicans as foreigners, even those who came from a family of many generations' standing in the state" (2009, 12). Invisibility in local newspaper accounts and city records indicates not that Mexican people were absent in La Feria but rather that they existed outside of the imagined community. Anglos in La Feria did not incorporate Mexican people into the image of the community that they were building for themselves. In fact, a land development company from Pharr, Texas, just twenty-five miles west of La Feria, appealed to prospective speculators by printing the following: "The great advantage of Mexican labor is its dependability. The men are expert farmers, competent, willing and contented. *They hold their place without attempting to mingle socially with the Americans*, and are segregated in their own districts and have their own schools and churches" (quoted in Zamora 1993, 32; emphasis added). The development of new farm communities along the Lower Rio Grande Valley was thus based on an abundant supply of Mexican labor along with guarantees of Mexican segregation. The ideal community for prospective buyers was the Anglo-dominant farm community with a separate, socially and politically invisible Mexican laboring population. For Anglos arriving in the region, such a community would be governed by a structure of segregation.

Mexican segregation in La Feria through the 1930s was fairly stringent, scarcely allowing Mexican people to cross into Anglo spheres. Residential segregation set the context for the myriad ways in which Mexican people were segregated in La Feria. Celia Garcia, who was a child living in La Feria's Mexican neighborhood in the 1930s, recalled that even the cemeteries were segregated during the early years of the town's history, the years of her childhood.

> Eran duros esos tiempos. Nunca se me ha olvidado todo lo que hacían [los americanos]. Había un cemeterio donde eran puros americanos. Uno [un mexicano] tenía que ir al Rancho Solis o a la Capilla [para enterar a los muertos]. De que había discriminación!
>
> [Those were difficult times. I never have forgotten what the Anglos did. There was a cemetery that was all Anglo. If you were Mexican, you had to go to the Solis Ranch or La Capilla to be buried. In all things there was discrimination!]

La Feria Cemetery, now a historical landmark, was established in 1920. A local history (McNail 1975) confirms Garcia's memory by listing the names of the first families buried there. Despite Mexican-origin people having occupied the region surrounding La Feria since the middle of the eighteenth century, none of the first families buried in the La Feria cemetery had Spanish surnames. In 1929, members of the Solis family—a family that had inhabited the region since the 1700s—filed an official petition that confirmed the apportionment of some of their family's land as a cemetery. According to the Texas Historical Commission, Solis Cemetery began interring bodies in the late nineteenth century and is recorded as a cemetery that holds "graves of Hispanic origin" (fig. 2.2). Though the justifications for this second cemetery are not in the historical record, we might surmise that the long-established Solis family donated their land so that their fellow Mexican community members might have a local place to bury their dead, since they were not permitted to do so in La Feria Cemetery. Though, as Garcia recalls, "in all things there was discrimi-

FIGURE 2.2. Mexican Cemetery. Runyon (Robert) Photograph Collection, RUN03024, the Dolph Briscoe Center for American History, the University of Texas at Austin

nation," perhaps nowhere was Mexican segregation more marked than in the local Catholic church and in the La Feria school system.

RACIAL DIVISIONS IN THE LOCAL CATHOLIC CHURCH

The first Catholic church in La Feria benefited from the faith practices of one of the town's early land speculators, as well as from the French missionaries whose ministry was prevalent in South Texas. As I mentioned earlier, the first part of the twentieth century marked a period of intense Anglo settlement in the Rio Grande Valley in general and La Feria in particular. In 1907, S. J. Schnorenberg and other developers from Minnesota bought the six-thousand-acre strip of land that encompassed the present-day site of La Feria. Schnorenberg, who was Catholic, donated land for the construction of a Catholic church, St. Francis Xavier (McNail 1975; St. Francis Xavier Catholic Church 1930–1980). The Oblate Fathers, the order that had been sent to evangelize South Texas in the middle of the eighteenth century, served the wooden mission that was constructed on the site and dedicated in 1912. The Oblate Fathers served La Feria until 1930, when La Feria attained its status as a parish and was then ministered by diocesan clergy (St. Francis Xavier Catholic

Church 1930–1980).[3] La Feria's Catholic church received its first pastor, H. J. Schmidter, in 1930.[4]

In Texas during the first half of the twentieth century, Catholic ministry to Mexicans expanded, but in the process it often reinforced separate Anglo and Mexican spheres. In 1930 the Missionary Catechists of Divine Providence, an order exclusively of Mexican American women, compelled the Church to expand its ministries (Treviño n.d.). The Catholic Church Extension Society and the American Board of Catholic Missions financed much of this expansion, providing money for "Mexican work" during the first half of the twentieth century (Treviño n.d.). Despite this outreach to the Mexican population in Texas, Catholic Mexican ministry in the state was characterized by institutional segregation (Martinez 2005; Treviño 2006). Some of this segregation was reflected in the missions that were established in rural areas to serve Mexicans. For example, shortly after St. Francis Xavier gained status as a parish, it began a mission church in Santa Rosa with the support of the Catholic Church Extension Society (*St. Francis Xavier Catholic Church* 1930–1980). Eight miles north of La Feria, Santa Rosa has historically boasted a higher Mexican-origin population than La Feria. Santa Rosa thus became a de facto "Mexican Church."[5]

Despite the existence of the Santa Rosa Mexican church, for Mexican Catholics in La Feria, St. Francis Xavier was their local church. Though not segregated by mandate of the diocese, the culture of the local parish reflected the ethos of segregation by not allowing people to practice popular Mexican religious customs and by relegating them to a separate side of the sanctuary. Certainly Anglos and Mexicans had different ideas about what it meant to be Catholic in the community during this time. Mexican Catholicism has historically been marked by popular religious practices (*religión popular*), which extend beyond the liturgical elements of the Mass. These popular religious practices reflected both the quotidian ways that Mexican people worshipped and could also be associated with a culturally specific holiday, such as El Día de los Muertos (Day of the Dead). Though popular faith practices were common to Mexican people during this time, they were foreign to Anglo Catholics. This cultural clash coupled with the logic of racial segregation led to the marginalization of Mexican people within the parish.

The suppression of Mexican popular religious practices began early in the local church's existence. Maria Zamarripa was a daughter of one of the original Spanish colonial families who had settled near the area that would become La Feria. She vividly recalled how the Anglo Catholics inhibited her family's faith practices when she attended church as a young girl with her family in the early 1940s.

Veníamos a la iglesia, a pie, descalzas, con muy pocos recursos. . . . Me acuerdo que a la iglesia mi mamá nos traíba chiquitas porque mi hermano, se llama Joe Sánchez, fue a la invasión. . . . No no más la familia de nosotros. Otras familias también. A la iglesia entraban de rodillas. Entramos de rodillas. Al uso de antes.

Entonces nos criticaban y nos iban y nos levantaban [los americanos]. . . .

Y decían que no quieren que nos hinquen. . . .

Mucha gente iba de rodillas hasta el altar a pagar su manda porque sus hijos estaban en la guerra de la invasión. . . .

Entonces los hicieron que se levantaran. Como dando de entender que era ridículo. Que ésto no se hacía así. Entonces ya. Poco a poco ya la gente no se usaba eso.

We would go to church on foot, barefoot, with very few resources. . . . I remember that my mother would take us when we were little because my brother, his name is Joe Sánchez, went to war. . . . It wasn't just our family. It was other families as well. They would enter the church on their knees. We would enter on our knees. The way it used to be done.

Then [the Anglos] would criticize us and they would go and pick us up. . . .

And they would say that they didn't want us kneeling. . . .

A lot of people would go on their knees to the altar to pay their obligation because their sons were in the war. . . .

Then [the Anglos] would make them get up. With the idea that what they were doing was ridiculous. That that was not their way. Then it ended. Little by little, people stopped doing it.

The preceding narrative testifies as to how local Anglos established a religious hegemony at St. Francis Xavier. Zamarripa asserts that her family, as well as others, expressed their religious devotion by traveling on foot to La Feria for Sunday Mass. Expressions of religious piety were especially important to Mexican people during that period because many of their sons were fighting in World War II. In order to pay their religious obligation, the Mexican custom was to enter the church and proceed to the altar on their knees. While common to Mexican-origin people, Zamarripa states that this custom seemed "ridiculous" to Anglo members of the congregation. The historian Robert Orsi argues, "The American Catholic Church could not [locate immigrants in the U.S.] . . . its cultural distaste for the immigrants amounted to an existential rejection of their value system" (1985, 189). Within the context of the La Feria Catholic church, this rejection of immigrant values resulted in the physical policing of such practices. Zamarripa remembers that Anglo parishioners would literally lift up Mexican people from their knees, forcibly establishing the boundaries of what they deemed was acceptable behavior in the church.

Indeed, the popular religious practices of immigrants in the U.S. Catholic Church were a source of contention in parishes in different parts of the United States. In his study about the *festa* of the Madonna of Mount Carmel in New York City, Orsi (1985) details how the American Catholic clergy attempted to stymie Italian immigrants' devotions to the Madonna, especially in the late nineteenth and early twentieth centuries. The public nature of the *festa* and its simultaneous expressions of revelry and penitence moved beyond sanctioned liturgical practices of U.S. Catholicism. Orsi argues that the American church downtown viewed this Italian devotional practice as "pagan and primitive" (1985, 221). Despite the objections of American Church officials and their attempts to ban the *festa*, the growing Italian immigrant community, with the support of certain Italian and Italian American clergy, was able to sustain and develop this popular religious practice. Within the context of segregated South Texas, with its racially segmented labor market and history of racial violence, however, such Mexican popular practices began to wane.

Apart from the suppression of Mexican popular religious practices, Anglo parishioners enforced spatial boundaries at St. Francis Xavier that mimicked practices of segregation in La Feria. The town's old Catholic church, which has since been converted into a small chapel, was constructed according to pre–Vatican II standards so that there were two long columns of pews facing the altar. Anglos sat in the left section of pews and Mexicans were expected to sit in the right section. In my interviews with Mexican residents, several people recounted to me that Anglo ushers would make them feel "very uncomfortable" if they were to sit in the wrong section of pews.[6] Outside of Mass, St. Francis Xavier Church ministered to its Mexican community by providing a form of religious education in Spanish. Norma Sánchez, a lifelong Mexican American parishioner at St. Francis, recalls attending a form of catechism at the church in the early 1950s. Though there were no formal catechism classes then, as there are today, she remembers that one of the town's prominent Mexican American women, Bertha Gavito,[7] would meet with Mexican-origin Catholic children to teach them prayers in Spanish.

It was apparent from the early decades of the town's existence that the Anglo community extended their economic and political power into the local parish. Maria Zamarripa's husband, Pablo Zamarripa, who was similarly a descendent of one of the Spanish settlers to the region in the eighteenth century, recounted, "*Como ellos, los americanos, habían hecho la iglesia, ellos creían como dueños*." ("Because the Anglos had built the church, they felt like they owned it.") For Mexican Catholics, this meant that the church would not provide a reprieve from the marginalization and segregation they experienced in other realms of the town.

SEGREGATION IN LA FERIA SCHOOLS

It was the spring of 1925 when the *La Feria News* recorded that a group of concerned citizens approached the school board about the problem of overcrowding in La Feria schools (fig. 2.3). Their proposed solution was to build a separate school for Mexicans and to locate it on the north side of the railroad tracks. Though this citizen action seemed to be the impetus for Mexican school segregation, it was actually the result of the seeds of racial segregation that had already been planted in the school system. School board records prior to 1925 reveal the employment of a teacher for the Mexican students, which indicates that even within the integrated school, Mexican students were already being separated, though we do not know to what extent. Furthermore, over one year prior to that story in the newspaper, in February 1924, the school board appointed a committee to investigate a site on the north side of the railroad tracks for a Mexican school building. Citizen action notwithstanding, within the first ten years of the town's request for incorporation, the push for Mexican school segregation in La Feria had already gained momentum. By the fall of 1926, the Mexican School, as it was then called, was open and had enrolled students.

It is important to understand the culture of Mexican school segregation in La Feria within the context of the Americanization programs that were prevalent in Mexican schools throughout the Southwest, as well as the policies and practices specific to Mexican education in Texas in the 1920s and 1930s. In many ways, the culture of segregation within La Feria's Mexican school reflected another aspect of how Anglo people attempted to address the "Mexican problem." The historian Guadalupe San Miguel (1987) argues that popular discourses among Anglos during that time revealed their concern with how to educate a growing Mexican population whose primary language was not English and whose culture was distinct from that of Anglo Texans. San Miguel and other scholars (Blanton 2004; González 1990) suggest that the Mexican problem was not about how to educate Mexican children in general but rather how to educate them to become "Americanized" while at the same time maintaining their subordinate social and economic status in the community. Anglo educators and policy makers in Texas and across the Southwest focused on language and culture as a way to address this challenge.

Texas educators repeatedly asserted that fluency in the English language was key to citizenship and belonging in the state. In 1923, the state superintendent of public instruction, Annie Webb Blanton, stated, "If you desire to be one with us, stay, and we welcome you; but if you wish to preserve, in our state, the language and the customs of another land, you have no right to do

FIGURE 2.3. School Building, La Feria, Texas. Runyon (Robert) Photograph Collection, RUN03019, the Dolph Briscoe Center for American History, the University of Texas at Austin

this" (quoted in San Miguel 1987, 32). Blanton's position had been bolstered five years earlier by a state legislative package that included a bill making English the exclusive language of public instruction. The dictates of this bill applied to teachers, principals, superintendents, board members, and all other public school personnel, and also declared it a criminal offense to teach in any language other than English (San Miguel 1987, 33). Americanization programs made English-language learning the cornerstone of their curricula and the key to citizenship. In his book *Chicano Education in the Era of Segregation*, Gilbert González states, "Presumably, the English-speaking child became an equal and full member of society, whereas the child who failed to learn English retained 'the culture, ideals, customs, thought and attitudes of another race and another people'" (1990, 42). In other words, educators viewed English-language fluency to be inextricably linked to being a true American. Language, though important in the context of education, was not the only aspect of culture that Texas educators sought to address in the education of Mexican children. Superintendent Blanton viewed language and culture rooted in Mexican traditions as a problem, particularly among Mexican-origin people who lived along the border. She wrote in 1923, "In certain counties along our border are many men and women, born and reared in the Lone Star State, who speak a foreign tongue and cherish the habits and ways of another country" (quoted in San Miguel 1987, 33). The habits and ways to which she refers included language but also knowledge and celebrations of Mexican history and culture as well as the maintenance of social relations between Mexicans on both sides of the border.

The irony, of course, was that though Blanton and undoubtedly many educators throughout Texas held the desire for Mexican students to culturally assimilate, they were not nearly as invested in the students' actual social and economic incorporation into Anglo society. Especially in communities where farm economies dominated, it was in the best interest of the Anglo power structure to educate Mexican children only to the extent that they would be good workers. While educators held mixed views about how well to educate Mexican children, the position of farmers from the region was quite clear. One South Texas grower expressed a representative sentiment when he stated, "Educating the Mexicans is educating them away from the job, away from the dirt. He learns English and wants to be a boss. He doesn't want to grub" (quoted in Montejano 1987, 193). South Texas farmers believed that overeducating Mexicans would run contrary to their economic interests. The problem facing educators was thus for them to be able to educate Mexicans enough to shed their Mexican culture and to become more Americanized, but not so much that they would become a viable part of the citizenry.

Americanization programs during this time undoubtedly meant to bolster a national and even state identity. Indeed, John Moran González (2009) and Richard Flores (2002) have effectively argued that the 1930s marked a defining moment in the formation of a modern Texas identity, when the Anglo power structure began to reimagine and rewrite Texas history to omit or diminish the contributions of Mexican people to the development of the state in favor of a more Anglo-oriented purview. One cannot ignore, however, the connection between nation- and state-building projects like school Americanization programs and race. The development of a modern, Anglocentric Texas identity required, among other things, a lower tolerance for linguistic and cultural diversity. Thinly veiled under the discourse of Americanization was an Anglo bias against Mexicans, whom they believed to be of an inferior race (De Leon 1983). Americanization programs and practices of segregation belied the connections Anglos were forging between nation and state building and white supremacy.

Ironically, the same Americanization programs that were supposed to help

Mexican students to acculturate to Anglo society were often used as a justification for segregation. As noted, educators believed that in order to become proficient in English, Mexican students had to be separated for a certain number of years during primary school. Mexican schools throughout the Southwest, however, were often substandard facilities that were not equal to the corresponding Anglo schools in town (González 1990; San Miguel 1987). The separate and unequal practices of education for Mexican students reinforced the belief that Mexican students were racially inferior to their Anglo counterparts.

Mexican and black children were systemically segregated in La Feria. The Mexican School in La Feria, which opened in 1926, was for Mexican children enrolled in first through third grades. Although the Anglo citizenry who had initially demanded a Mexican school stated that it was to ease the problem of overcrowding, the justification for the maintenance of the school quickly shifted to helping develop English-language skills (Armour 1932). After the third grade, the district allowed Mexican students to attend school on the Anglo side of the tracks to complete elementary school, junior high, and high school. Within these schools, however, Mexican people recall that they were placed on separate curricular tracks from their Anglo counterparts. In other words, although after the third grade Mexicans and Anglos attended "integrated" schools, they were separated within the schools based on their race. Perhaps not surprisingly, the number of Mexican students enrolled dwindled in each progressive grade (Armour 1932).

There were a few black families—ranging from 1.5 percent to 3 percent of the total population—who lived in the city limits of La Feria in the first part of the twentieth century. Of these families there were always approximately two dozen children enrolled in a "Negro School." This school was initially rented per contract with the Negro Baptist Church and employed one teacher, a young African American woman named Evia Campbell.[8] Miss Campbell instructed grades one through six, after which time black students were expected to enter into the workforce or travel out of the Valley to attend high school. Further educational opportunities for black students in La Feria would not open up until the late 1940s and early 1950s.

Like many farming communities that developed in the Lower Rio Grande Valley after the arrival of the railroad during the first few decades of the twentieth century, La Feria was a city marked by racial segregation. Early Anglo residents crafted a city with racially stratified social, political, and economic realms. Anglos, who lived on the south side of the railroad tracks, held political positions of power and social influence. This social and political stratification was buttressed by the burgeoning farm industry, where they dominated the means of production, hiring a predominantly Mexican labor force. Overall, Mexican people were disenfranchised within the city's official system of power. They were relegated to segregated and inferior places to live, work, worship, and be educated. Within this very strict structure of segregation, few Mexican people were able to cross racial boundaries. One person who did so was Virginio M. Villareal.[9]

CROSSING RACIAL BOUNDARIES

The Villareal family established themselves in the region of the Lower Rio Grande Valley by the 1700s, having received *porciones* (land grants) from the Spanish Crown. Many such families established towns and ranchos in the region long before the arrival of Anglo settlers (Alonzo 1998; Chavana 2002). Though we do not know the specific trajectory of the branch of the Villareal family to which Virginio belonged, we know that like many long-standing Tejano families, the land where they had settled was governed by Spain, Mexico, Texas, and, finally, the United States during a relatively short span in the nineteenth century. It was the last shift in government that marked the most dramatic change for Tejano families, as they had to navigate a new racialized economic structure that placed Mexicans at the bottom of local economic, political, and social systems. In addition to having to contend with the shift from ranching to farming, they had to navigate the new racial boundaries that accompanied it.

Virginio Villareal was born in Santa Maria, Texas, southwest of La Feria, in 1872, just twenty-four years after the end of the Mexican-American War. He married Eulogia Solis,[10] the daughter of another well-established Tejano family, in 1897. During the early years of their marriage, Virginio Villareal and Eulogia lived in a house next door to his parents near Mercedes, Texas, where he helped to farm his father's land. Beginning in 1913, he began to buy and sell land in and around the La Feria grant, even selling land to one of La Feria's most prominent Anglo citizens, Bailey Dunlap. It is important to keep in mind that with the shift in the economy from ranching to farming, even land-grant Mexican families found themselves at an economic disadvantage. Though such families were land wealthy, they did not have the same kind of liquid capital that Anglo settlers had (Montejano 1987). Villareal, however, managed to create a living for himself through land brokerage.

Around 1914, just before La Feria was incorporated by the state, Villareal and his wife erected a house in the town, on the south side of the railroad tracks. They would be the only Mexican family to establish a residence on the Anglo side of town until the 1940s. During the same time, V. M. Villareal applied for a tax license to operate a beer saloon in the Mexican neighborhood, north of the railroad tracks. As a land broker and a small-business owner who owned a home on the south side of the railroad tracks, Villareal made connections with city officials. His pattern of residence and his business on the Mexican side of town enabled him to make contacts in the Mexican community that allowed him to also broker Mexican labor for city projects. The city of La Feria regularly paid Villareal for services rendered, such as cleaning and cutting weeds, hauling sand and gravel, laying city water pipes, and draining areas of the city that flooded.[11]

Interestingly, at the time of the census in 1920, Villareal, his wife, and their adopted daughter, Beatris,[12] were again living in the neighboring town of Mercedes.[13] Though it is unclear why the family might have temporarily moved from their home in La Feria, we know that border violence stemming from the Plan de San Diego had run rampant in previous years. The Plan de San Diego, written in 1915, was a call to arms for Mexicans and other oppressed racial minorities (blacks and Native Americans) to take back the lands that were lost in the Mexican-American War. While the plan did not reflect the political ideology of all Mexican-origin peoples in the region, it incited violence throughout South Texas, including in the Lower Rio Grande Valley in the form of attacks against Anglo adult men as well as the destruction of property. These raids were met with even more indiscriminate and intense violence from the Texas Rangers and groups of vigilante Anglos, and, ultimately, the U.S. government ended the uprising (Johnson 2003).[14] Indeed by June of 1916, the La Feria Board of Commissioners issued a town curfew of 9:30 p.m. owing to "the unsettled condition of affairs now existing in this section of the state." The Villareal family, with their three-year-old daughter, might have felt more secure in Mercedes, where they could live near family in a Mexican neighborhood. Several other Mexican families in the region actually took refuge in Mexico (Johnson 2003).

Even with this brief time away from his family's La Feria home, Virginio Villareal continued to conduct business in La Feria. From the late teens through the mid-1920s, Villareal sustained his work as a labor contractor with the city. From the middle of the 1920s, however, he began to focus more on real estate transactions in and around La Feria.[15] Census records indicate that by 1930 he and his family lived in La Feria and that he owned a real estate business, conducting transactions with both Anglo and Mexican people in town. His daughter, Beatris, graduated from La Feria High School and performed the secretarial work for her father's business. Villareal was active in his real estate business almost until the time of his death in 1940.[16]

Long after his death, Villareal continued to live in the memories of

Mexican-origin people who had lived through this early period of La Feria's history. Celia Garcia remembers that "Don Virginio" sold property in and around La Feria, and that his wife, "Doña Locha," was a Solis. She recalls that Villareal always wore a suit and that he lived across the tracks in the Anglo neighborhood. She recounts the following story that she heard as a child in La Feria in the late 1920s and early 1930s:

> Había un hombre mexicano que no quiso a los mexicanos. Se llamaba Alfredo. He owned a cleaners in La Feria, where the glass store now is.
>
> One day Don Alfredo was cutting Don Virginio's hair y que Alfredo le dijo, "Si yo sabía donde tuviera la sangre mexicana, me la quitara." Y que Virginio le volteó y le dice, "Hijo de la Chingada. Si te la quitaras, te quedaría pura cuacha.

> There was a Mexican man who didn't like other Mexicans. His name was Alfredo. He owned a cleaners in La Feria, where the glass store now is.
>
> One day Don Alfredo was cutting Don Virginio's hair and Alfredo said to him, "If I knew where I had Mexican blood, I would take it out." And Virginio turned and said to him, "Son of a whore. If you were to take it out, you'd be left with nothing but shit!"

As a young girl during the time period when Villareal was an adult in La Feria, we know that Garcia could not have been a witness to the conversation that occurred between Villareal and his friend. Regardless, the story became a kind of folklore about the two men, and it is significant for what it reveals about Mexican attitudes about race and race relations during this time. Villareal's friend, a fellow Mexican business owner, tried to denounce his Mexicanness, going so far as to say that he wanted to remove whatever Mexican blood ran through his veins. Villareal, in turn, offered his friend a violent verbal reprimand, stating that the friend's bloodlines that were not Mexican were worthless. In this way, Villareal at once valorized their Mexicanness—race and, most likely, culture—and derided any non-Mexican, presumably "white," blood his friend might have had. In this story, Villareal emerges almost as a folk hero. He is someone who lives on the Anglo side of town, is fully bilingual, is impeccably dressed, and is economically well positioned in an era of intense discrimination and segregation. He is someone who shows himself to be in all ways equal to (if not better than) any Anglo in town. What makes Villareal's response heroic is that he nevertheless maintains himself as a champion for Mexicanness, proud of his heritage and cultural background.

The antihero in Celia Garcia's story is more of a tragic figure than a villain for Mexican-origin people in La Feria. The increasing prevalence of segregation and discrimination toward Mexicans led Villareal's friend to wish that he were not Mexican. Garcia recalls that this man and his family lived in the *pueblo mexicano*, near the Mexican School, and that his children would never speak Spanish. In fact, the 1930 census recorded that within this family, each of the children had English-language versions of Spanish first names, whereas the children of all the neighboring families had Spanish first and last names. Garcia's memory of the children aligns with the aforementioned story. We might surmise that this man encouraged his children to speak English, perhaps believing that the more Americanized they were, the less discrimination they would experience. Garcia, however, remembers this man and his family as having turned their backs on their community while at the same time viewing Villareal, who lived in the Anglo community, as a more loyal Mexicano.

Virginio Villareal was a singular exception to the rule of racial segregation during the early years of La Feria's history. Economically, he integrated himself into the Anglo community while maintaining social ties to the Mexican community. We do not know how Villareal managed to navigate the rigid racial boundaries between Anglos and Mexicans. The one thing that we know facilitated his economic incorporation into Anglo La Feria was his ability to buy and sell land. As the descendant of a land-grant family, he was able to convert some of his land holdings into liquid capital and make a business of real estate. I would like to suggest that it was not purely money that enabled his entry into Anglo spheres, as there were other descendants of land-grant families living in and around La Feria during that time who were not accorded similar acceptance. Villareal and his family were notably white, according to the 1930 census. While this census designation was granted to those American-born Mexican people whose parents were also born in the United States, Villareal's mother was born in Alabama. Among Mexican people of mixed race, Villareal might very well have been on the "whiter" side of the Mexican racial spectrum. This racial aspect certainly would have helped Anglos to accept him as a neighbor and businessperson in the community. In addition to race, the legal scholar Laura Gómez suggests that cultural performance was key in colonial contexts in which race corresponded to rights. She states that "racial identity had a strong performance aspect—where people performed knowingly and variably performed race in different social contexts" (2007, 52). From Garcia's recollection, we understand that Villareal was often well dressed, wearing suits to conduct business in town. Furthermore, records reflect that he was a fluent English speaker, as well as being proficient in reading and writing English. With this cultural capital, Villareal had the skills to perform race in Anglo society as well as among Mexicans. I would suggest that during this period of intense racial segregation, only a "white" Mexican with economic and cultural capital could be granted access to Anglo spheres in La Feria.

FROM 1915 THROUGH THE 1930S, Anglo residents in La Feria forged a racially stratified community in its social, political, and economic realms. Anglos, who lived on the south side of the railroad tracks, held political positions of power and social influence. Furthermore, the local farm industry was run by Anglo growers and supported by Mexican labor. Mexicans, on the other hand, lived in a separate neighborhood on the north side of the railroad tracks, which Anglo residents referred to as "Mexiquito" or "Mexicata," reinforcing not only racial but also national borders between them and their Mexican cohabitants of the town. Within the context of the city power structure, Mexicans were largely disenfranchised, as could be seen in their locations of contact—the farms, the local school system, and the local Catholic church. Nevertheless, Mexican people in La Feria were able to create their own culturally cohesive community. As we will see in the next chapter, despite a strong ideology of segregation and systematic disenfranchisement in the school system, Mexican residents of *el pueblo mexicano* maintained a deep sense of their Mexican identity and forged communal bonds to provide each other economic and social support.

CHAPTER THREE

FORMAL AND INFORMAL MEXICAN EDUCATION WITHIN THE CONTEXT OF SEGREGATION

> *Si en la escuela americana a que concurren nuestros niños se les enseña la Biografía de Washington y no la de Hidalgo y en vez de hechas gloriosas de Juárez se la refieren las hazañas de Lincoln, por más que estas sean nobles y justas, no conocerá ese niño las glorias de su Patria, no la amará y hasta verá con indiferencia a los coterráneos de sus padres.* NICASIO IDAR[1]

In the epigraph to this chapter, Nicasio Idar, editor and publisher of the Spanish-language newspaper *La Crónica*, laments the kind of schooling that Mexican-origin children received in Texas at the beginning of the twentieth century. He articulates what many Mexican parents must have been feeling as their children were subjected to a barrage of Americanization programs with an emphasis on English-language instruction in segregated, under-resourced schools throughout South Texas. While some scholars have discussed the ways in which Mexican people fought for equity in the school system through lawsuits and protests, few, if any, have looked substantively at the ways in which Mexican-origin people responded to negative schooling in the form of public pedagogy. In this chapter, I argue that community events and activities served as countereducational projects to the anti-Mexican schooling Mexican children received in the segregated elementary school in La Feria. Examining the tensions between Anglo ideology and pedagogy within the context of formal schooling and Mexican understandings of education, as well as their community's countereducational projects, is vital to understanding the culture of segregation in the 1920s and 1930s.

This chapter will examine the formal and informal education of Mexicans in the community of La Feria during the first three decades of the twentieth century. I argue that community-based informal education was a crucial component in the economic and cultural survival of the Mexican community from the first stage of stringent segregation through the 1930s. As in much of the Southwest, local practices of education, while purportedly trying to teach Mexican children to be English speaking and knowledgeable about Anglo American history and culture, resulted in the majority of children dropping out before high school (many before completing junior high) and then entering positions of menial labor. I argue that despite and perhaps because of such formal schooling, local Mexican people engaged in an educational project of their own. Partly as resistance and partly as an economic and cultural survival mechanism, Mexican people reinforced a Mexicanist cultural identity among both children and adults in their community through the establishment of mutual-aid societies, participation in Mexican historical and cultural celebrations, and the formation of *escuelitas* that taught children to read and write Spanish.

Formal and informal practices of education are crucial to understanding the culture of Mexican segregation in La Feria prior to 1940. In the previous chapter, I focused on the ways in which Anglo residents of La Feria built a racially segregated community. Bolstered by the booming farming industry, which facilitated a racially stratified economic system, segregation was prevalent in all aspects of life for Anglos and Mexicans, from the institutional to the informal. This chapter will delve more deeply into the ideology and culture of Mexican segregation through a close examination of the local Mexican school and teachers' attitudes toward Mexican students who proceeded through the so-called integrated educational pipeline. Moreover, this chapter will demonstrate how Mexican-origin people in La Feria, like many Mexican people throughout South Texas, became extremely adept at forging their own self-sufficient communities within the context of segregation. The establishment and reinforcement of a Mexicanist cultural identity was central to Mexican community building. The positive reinforcement of Mexican history and culture created a sense of belonging both to the U.S. Mexican community and to an imagined Mexican community abroad.

During the 1920s and 1930s, Anglos in La Feria generally viewed Mexican-origin people as outside of the town's citizenry and regularly denied them equal rights. This chapter will more deeply explore the relationship between race and rights, particularly as they are manifested in the educational system. In the La Feria school district during the 1930s, Mexican children were exposed to an English-only curriculum that focused on teaching children about Anglo American history and culture. Though very much aligned with similar assimilationist projects across the U.S. Southwest, this educational approach was at times confusing and upsetting to children whose language and culture were Mexican. The irony of such an education was that while Mexican children were being schooled about the glories of U.S. citizenship, their families and their community were routinely relegated to second-class-citizen status. I argue that events in the Mexican community in La Feria that celebrated Mexican history and culture as well as mutual-aid society activities and the establishment of alternative schools, known in the region as *escuelitas*, provided opportunities for Mexican people to engage in practices of cultural citizenship. Though their legal rights were regularly violated, these acts of cultural affirmation helped Mexicans in La Feria to create a legitimate space for themselves in the community. Marginalized by local Anglos because of their race, Mexican and Mexican American residents used their segregated neighborhood as a place that valued and celebrated Mexican culture. These acts of cultural resistance, though not necessarily politically oppositional, enabled *mexicanos* to claim human rights in their community, such as the right to respect and dignity (Flores 2003).

Before discussing the education and countereducation of Mexican children and Mexican-origin people in La Feria, I will begin with an examination of the general trends of Mexican education in the U.S. Southwest during the first part of the twentieth century.

THE EARLY EDUCATION OF MEXICAN CHILDREN

Scholars have argued that the school system has served as the major institution by which to shape young people into "citizens" of the United States. In their article "Conflict and Consensus in American Public Education," David Tyack and Elizabeth Hansot state that historically "the common school was an official agency for defining and creating citizenship in ethnocultural terms" (1981, 3). A major guiding philosophy among educators has been that public schools should transmit core "American" morals and values to young citizens (1981, 7). While the period following the civil rights movements of the 1960s and 1970s has regularly challenged how society and its schools define Americanism, during the early twentieth century it was commonplace for educators to teach about American history and social values in a way that transmitted Anglo social and cultural dominance. Compulsory schooling laws that emerged during the first two decades of the twentieth century ensured that culturally and racially diverse children would be exposed to this type of American education (Orozco 2009). Local records indicate that in 1921, La Feria's school district passed an ordinance to comply with compulsory schooling laws such that any child who was seven years old at the beginning of the school year would be expected to enroll.

By the 1930s, both state and private agencies subjected Mexican American children to many types of Americanization projects. González (1990) persuasively argues that, from the 1930s through the 1950s, many of these Americanization efforts were born of the belief that Mexican-origin people were less socially evolved than their Anglo counterparts. The goal of many of these Americanization programs inside and outside the schools was to promote so-called civilization (González 1990; Ruiz 1998). Programs included English, nutrition, child rearing, hygiene, homemaking, and sewing, as well as other vocational subjects (González 1990, 46). Such programs were often aimed specifically at Mexican girls, who were seen as future American homemakers and the social carriers of culture (González 1990; Ruiz 1998). Also central to the project of Americanization was the acquisition of English-language skills. San Miguel (1987) states that Americanization programs were based on a curriculum that would "imbue the non-English child with the habits, customs, and ideals for which America stood and particularly to teach her or him the English language" (1987, 58). González asserts that several educators throughout the Southwest equated language with culture and felt that Mexican children's learning would be retarded until their use of Spanish had been completely eradicated (1990, 41). Indeed, though the initial justification for establishing a separate Mexican school was to ameliorate the problem of overcrowding, Basil Armour, the principal of La Feria's Mexican School during the 1920s and 1930s, insisted that such a segregated school was necessary for pedagogical purposes, namely English-language instruction.

Certainly, Americanization programs and segregated Mexican schools informed and reinforced each other in theory and practice. The Texas case *Del Rio ISD v. Salvatierra* perhaps set the precedent for using pedagogy as a justification for Mexican school segregation. In 1930, Jesús Salvatierra, along with some other Mexican parents, filed a lawsuit against the school district, alleging that Mexicans were being denied the privileges of "other white races." In May of 1930, Judge Joseph Jones decided in favor of Salvatierra, granting an injunction (Valencia 2008).[2] González (1990) argues that the Salvatierra case "enunciated the doctrine that Mexicans could not be legally segregated . . . on the basis of race . . . that the only basis for separate schooling for Mexicans was educational (language, culture, etc.)" (1990, 28). Indeed when the Salvatierra case was taken to the San Antonio Court of Appeals, testimony by the superintendent maintained that the rationale for the segregation of Mexican students was predominantly for pedagogical purposes because of Mexican students' deficient English-language abilities (*Del Rio ISD v. Salvatierra, et al.*, 1930). The San Antonio Court of Appeals voided the earlier court's injunction in October 1930, granting power to the school district to segregate Mexican students (Valencia 2008). In the Salvatierra case and in schools around the Southwest, justifications for Mexican-school segregation included race, but more often they relied on arguments about Mexican students' language ability, hygiene, alleged intelligence deficiencies, and supposedly inherent racial inferiority (Gonzalez 1990; Menchaca 1993; San Miguel 1987). The pedagogical imperative of teaching English as a key component of Americanization programs reinforced the need for segregation throughout Texas and the rest of the U.S. Southwest.

At best, the Americanization projects of this era had as a goal the assimilation of Mexican children into society as citizens with particular American values and ideals. However, San Miguel argues that "assimilationist curricular practices were in contrast to the exclusionary ones promoted by local school administrators" (1987, 58). In practice, the promotion of American ideals was undercut by the quality of education that Mexican American children received throughout the Southwest. Various authors have described Mexican schools as substandard, often in overcrowded and dilapidated buildings with poor or no recreational facilities. Furthermore, these schools often had inadequate teaching materials, many times utilizing old textbooks unwanted by local Anglo schools (González 1990; Houston 2000; San Miguel 1987). With regard to instructors, González asserts that many teachers in Mexican schools were generally paid less than those who worked in Anglo schools and that moving from a Mexican school to an "American" school was often viewed as a promotion for teachers (1990, 22).

The Mexican School in La Feria was likely similar to other such schools across the Southwest, though the historical records do not speak to its condition or resources in the early twentieth century. We do know, however, that teachers in the Mexican School earned wages comparable to those of teachers in schools on the south side of the tracks. School board records indicate policies to pay teachers based on the number of years they had attended college, and in general, education levels for teachers across the La Feria school system were similar. At the Mexican School, teacher and principal salaries corresponded to their levels of education. Even so, it is important to note that the principal and all the teachers at this school throughout the 1930s were Anglo. Evia Campbell, the African American woman who assumed teaching responsibilities for the segregated black school during this period, was paid an average of 40 percent less than the other teachers in the district. Other employees of the Mexican School, including bus drivers with Spanish surnames and black janitors, consistently earned less money than their counterparts on the south side of the tracks who worked for Anglo schools. In other words, though teachers in La Feria's Mexican School were paid wages comparable to those of teachers at the Anglo school, a racialized dual-wage system still applied to nonwhite employees of the school. This disparity had implications for the future of the Mexican students in La Feria's school system.

Another problem that Mexican children encountered in their education during the early part of the twentieth century was a lack of enforcement of the compulsory schooling law (Acosta 2003; González 1990; San Miguel 1987). Oftentimes Mexican-origin children would miss school in order to work to help support their families. Within agricultural regions, these absences occurred more frequently during that particular area's crop seasons. During the summer, many Mexican families, especially in the Rio Grande Valley, worked as migrants on farms in Arizona, New Mexico, and California in order to supplement the meager incomes they earned in Texas. Summer migrations often began before the school year officially ended and lasted well into the fall (Goldfarb 1981; Wells 1978). These work patterns, coupled with the lack of enforcement of the compulsory schooling laws, led many Mexican children to miss large periods of school instruction and, ultimately, to be left back. It was not infrequent, even throughout the early 1960s, to see teenage students in Mexican elementary schools (González 1990).

Circumstances such as these were clear obstacles in the education of Mexican-origin students throughout the Southwest. Indeed, several researchers have shown that prior to the 1970s, Mexican students were far more likely to drop out of school than were their Anglo counterparts (Armour 1932; González 1990; San Miguel 1987). Those Mexican-origin students who did complete their education through high school contended with issues such as tracking and placement in vocational education programs. González (1990) asserts that in the first half of the twentieth century, there were disproportionately high numbers of Mexican children enrolled in vocational training. He states that "in theory and practice [vocational training was for] . . . students of inferior mental ability" (77). His implication is that the placement of such high numbers of Mexican students in vocational training reveals that teachers and administrators viewed these students as intellectually inferior. González argues that, ideally, vocational training should have been a stepping-stone toward middle-class status for those students who had not been adequately prepared for college. As González suggests, the problem as noted in La Feria was that Mexican-origin students were placed in vocational training because teachers and administrators did not deem them suitable to pursue higher education. Indeed, as we will see later in this chapter, vocational training was seen as the educational culmination for Mexican students who made it through the educational pipeline.

In sum, prior to the 1960s and 1970s, the educational experiences of children of Mexican origin in the southwestern United States seemed to promote "cross-purposes" (San Miguel 1987). On the one hand was the objective of inculcating Mexican children with "American" ideals, morals, values, and culture, including the rapid acquisition of the English language. This type of education was a means by which to shape young Mexican students into American citizens. On the other hand, this American education was promoted within segregated Mexican schools, which were typically inferior facilities with poor educational resources. Furthermore, low expectations of Mexican students, lack of enforcement of the compulsory schooling laws, tracking, and vocational training contributed to high dropout rates of Mexican students and a continual funneling of these students into the working class. In other words, although Mexican children were educated to be American citizens, at a very early age they were relegated to second-class-citizen status. They were ingrained with ideas about the U.S. imagined community, but they were not granted the same access to it as their Anglo counterparts.

EDUCATION AT SAM HOUSTON ELEMENTARY SCHOOL

It seems that segregation in the first few grades is best for the Mexican child in order to enable him to become adjusted and to aid him in overcoming his language handicap. This segregation ought to be based upon pedagogical reasons only.
BASIL ARMOUR, PRINCIPAL OF LA FERIA'S MEXICAN SCHOOL

Ahí fui yo, al Sam Houston School primary. Era Mexiquita, le decían y de los tracks para allá, le decían Mexiquita. . . . Porque los mexicanos vivían para allá, para aquel lado across the tracks, y la escuela esa era la Mexican school for Mexicans. Más antes era muy discriminatoria a la gente, los americanos.[3] AMALIA SILVA

Anglo residents of La Feria established the Mexican School, later renamed Sam Houston Elementary School,[4] in the fall of 1926. Located in the Mexican neighborhood on the north side of the railroad tracks, Sam Houston was intended to serve Mexican students from first through third grade. Basil Armour was the Anglo principal of the Mexican School from spring 1928 through the end of the 1930s. He earned a master's degree in sociology from Texas A&M in 1932, writing a master's thesis entitled "Mexican Social Problems of the RGV," based on research he conducted in La Feria's Mexican School. A few months later, he published an article for the *Texas Observer*, a statewide educational journal, entitled "Problems in the Education of the Mexican Child," in which he argued, as excerpted above, that segregation should be used solely for pedagogical purposes, ostensibly until Mexican children gained a command of the English language. On the other hand, Amalia Silva, a lifelong resident of La Feria who attended kindergarten through twelfth grade in the 1930s and 1940s, recalls spending the first few years of her primary schooling at Sam Houston Elementary School, La Feria's segregated Mexican school. Though she lived on the outskirts of town on her father's small farm, she remembers that that Anglos referred to the Mexican neighborhood as "Mexiquita" (Little Mexico) and that they had established a separate school for Mexicans in that neighborhood. Silva understands it was Anglo discrimination that led to the establishment of a separate Mexican school despite Armour's insistence that segregation was solely a means to attain English-language fluency. Tensions between Anglo pedagogies at Sam Houston Elementary School and Mexican public pedagogies are key to understanding the culture of segregation in the 1920s and 1930s.

As the principal of Sam Houston Elementary School, Basil Armour published pieces that indicate a generally positive attitude about Mexican children and their propensity to learn. He attributes Mexican students' lower test scores to language problems and is quick to cite examples of Mexican valedictorians and salutatorians in neighboring districts. Armour focused on the performing arts as a way to engage Mexican students at Sam Houston Elementary. He argued that among Mexican students, even low-performing, working-class children exhibited exceptional abilities in the arts. Armour was not alone in these beliefs about Mexican children's penchant for the arts. González states that Anglos often viewed Mexican culture as "gay" and "lighthearted," devoted to "color, music, and dancing" (1990, 40) and that educators often paternalistically viewed Mexicans as especially talented in arts and crafts. In his study on Texas schools, San Miguel (1987) reveals similar findings, stating that "despite the variety of scholarly studies challenging these stereotypes, teachers . . . continued to believe that Mexican children had special expressive abilities and talents" (45). Based on these beliefs, he states, teachers often advocated for more classes to enhance these supposedly "natural" artistic abilities. Indeed school board records indicate that in La Feria's Mexican School, Principal Armour incorporated the arts into the curriculum for his Mexican students. School board records also reflect that he purchased a piano for the Mexican School, using his own funds as well as a partial loan from the school board. Armour helped to organize what he considered to be successful performances both at the Mexican School and in conjunction with the Anglo schools, including an operetta at the Mexican School, a Presidents' Day celebration, and a May fete. In discussing these programs at the Mexican School, Armour observes, "Mexican children enjoy taking part in school programs. The fathers and mothers seem to enjoy seeing their children in school programs, although they are often unable to understand a word that is said" (1932, 30). Armour's observations reflect his belief that both children and parents enjoy the school performances at Sam Houston Elementary School in spite of cultural differences.

Interestingly, we might see a different kind of performance being played out in the English-only classrooms of Sam Houston. Elena Ramirez, who was born in La Feria to immigrant parents in the late 1920s, recounted the following anecdote to me about learning English at the Mexican School:

> Para pedir para ir al baño decían, "May I bescuze?" Nosotros creíamos que decíamos, "May I bescuze," era los excusados. Ya de grande decíamos: "¿por qué diríamos 'bescuze'?" Es que nos enseñaban que dijéramos, "May I be excused?" y nosotros como no sabíamos mucho inglés, pues nosotros creíamos que así se llama el excusado, 'bescuze.' Entonces pedíamos, "May I go to the bescuze?" . . . [laughs] Así aprendimos el inglés nosotros. Porque los papás de nosotros eran mexicanos, no sabían nada de inglés y vamos con unas maestras americanas, ¿te puedes imaginar? It was hard.

> To ask to go to the bathroom, they said, "May I bescuze?" We thought that saying, "May I be excused" was the bathroom. As we got older we would say, "Why did we say 'bescuze'?" It's that they taught us to say, "May I be excused?" and because we didn't know very much English, well, we thought that was how to say 'bathroom,' 'bescuze.' So we would ask, "May I go to the bescuze?" [laughs] That's how we learned English. Because our parents were Mexican and didn't speak any English and then we would go with Anglo [English-speaking] teachers. Can you imagine? It was hard.

Though Armour focuses on the effectiveness of the schoolwide performances in his *Texas Observer* article and in his master's thesis, perhaps more interesting and telling are the microperformances in which Mexican children engaged in their day-to-day lives at school. As Ramirez narrates the anecdote of learning how to "be excused" to use the bathroom, she is still struck by its absurdity. She remembers all of her Mexican peers sharing the experience of calling the bathroom, "bescuze" because they did not understand that their teachers were attempting to teach them to be polite. The children believed they were just learning a basic way to ask to use the school facilities. She laughs at the memory, perhaps recalling her childhood innocence, but then asserts how difficult it was for her and for her peers to mediate their home lives with their lives at school. While Armour maintains that the children at Sam Houston enjoyed the performative aspect of the education they received at Sam Houston, he does not consider Mexican children's everyday microperformances as they attempted to learn English and proper Anglo manners. These quotidian performances reflected the cutural distance that his students had to bridge as they navigated back and forth between Mexican and Anglo worlds on a daily basis.

Mexican parents of children at Sam Houston had their own educational imperatives regardless of their levels of English-language fluency and formal education. Records reveal the existence of a Mexican PTA during the late 1920s. In fact, the Mexican PTA organized a community carnival at the Mexican School in 1927, an event so successful that Armour himself attempted to reproduce it just two years later, in 1929. That year, he organized the event along with teachers and the "American" PTA, advertising it in the local newspaper as "an interesting program, including the coronation of a queen" (*La Feria News*, 11/8/29). As we will see, the Mexican parents were most likely bringing to the school a festival that was similar to one they were already enacting in *el pueblo mexicano*. The Mexican PTA might very well have been trying to incorporate some of their public pedagogical practices into the segregated Mexican school. Principal Armour's plug for the carnival in the newspaper encouraged the "American population as well as the Mexican . . . to attend the affair."

Armour is an interesting figure in the history of Mexican education in La Feria. As a scholar and a principal, he seems to be invested in developing an educational model that would genuinely serve Mexican children. He generously assesses their educational potential, and he promotes the arts because he believes that is a strength upon which a Mexican curriculum can be built. Though it might be based on stereotypical cultural beliefs, Armour goes so far as to purchase a piano for Sam Houston School, partially out of his own funds. Furthermore, that he invited Anglos to attend a school event on the Mexican side of town, even advertising it in the local newspaper, indicates his desire to bring the Mexican and Anglo communities together. It is unclear how well he was able to serve as a cultural or racial bridge during this time. Despite Armour's best efforts and intentions, structural barriers and pervasive negative racial attitudes helped maintain a high rate of school attrition for Mexican children and practices of school segregation until the 1970s.

After Mexican children completed third grade at Sam Houston, they attended schools alongside Anglo children on the south side of town. Even so, several Mexican-origin people recall experiencing segregation even within the supposedly integrated schools. The schools in the district organized the students into two tracks—A and B. These tracks generally corresponded to Anglo and Mexican students, respectively, though there were some exceptional

Mexican students placed in the A track. Menchaca argues that oftentimes skin color was a determining factor in whether or not children of Mexican origin were placed in segregated schools or, in this case, the A or B tracks (1993). While skin color might have been a mitigating factor in La Feria, my interviews with La Feria residents further reveal that Mexican-origin children whose parents were business owners within the Mexican community were permitted to attend white schools and were often tracked into college-prep classes while their working-class counterparts remained in lower-level classes.[5] Here we see the intersection of race and class determining a child's experience of segregation in the public school system. On the other hand, none of my interviewees recall any white children ever being placed in the B track. While over the decades there might have been some exceptions to this trend, the overwhelming majority of people's memories about race-based tracking indicate consistent racial application through the first half of the twentieth century.

Teachers in the La Feria School District diverged from Armour's assessment of Mexican students' academic potential. In his 1939 master's thesis about student failure in La Feria schools, J. B. Smith, the superintendent of the La Feria School District at that time, highlights the differing attitudes that teachers had toward Mexican versus Anglo students and student failure. Whereas teachers mostly attributed Anglo school failure to "lack of effort," they overwhelmingly opined that Mexican school failure was due to "low IQ," listing language difficulties as a distant second reason. Unlike Armour's optimistic article about the abilities of Mexican children, Smith's survey of teachers points to their ideas about the natural abilities of Mexican versus Anglo students. Teachers believed that Anglo students would be less likely to fail if they would only put forth a greater effort in their classes. On the other hand, they believed that regardless of effort, Mexican children failed because of low-level intellectual ability (Smith 1939). One can only speculate how these attitudes about children's intelligence might have been manifested in teachers' pedagogies toward Anglo and Mexican children. These low academic expectations for Mexican children might be seen as a factor contributing to the dramatic levels of Mexican school attrition throughout the La Feria School District.

According to Armour's article in the *Texas Observer* (1932), the enrollment of Mexican children in La Feria schools was concentrated in the lower grades, and there were high levels of school attrition for Mexican children. Armour notes, however, that from 1926 to 1932 the enrollment of Mexican children in the school system rose from 127 to 400, a dramatic increase of 215 percent. School board records indicate uneven growth during that time. Whereas 1930 records indicate that the district had just completed a building addition to the Mexican School, in the fall of 1931 enrollment seemed to stagnate or decrease. This statistic corresponded to the board's decision to discontinue bus service in an effort to save money because of the ongoing economic depression. Bus service was reinstated in the fall of 1932, and two months later the surge in numbers of Mexican children enrolled at the Mexican School necessitated hiring another teacher. Though the Mexican School was ostensibly a neighborhood facility, many Mexican families worked and lived on farms in the areas outside of the city limits. The remoteness of these farms and the number of families that did not own a motor vehicle during this time precluded Mexican children from attending school without reliable bus service. School enrollment for Mexican children thus corresponded not only to the number of school-age children in the district but also to whether or not they had access to school.

These fluctuations related primarily to Mexican children enrolled in elementary school. Levels of attrition for Mexican children through high school were abysmal. Armour observes that 51 percent of Mexican children were enrolled in the first three grades, while only 3.1 percent were enrolled in high school. The enrollment of Anglo children, on the other hand, was more evenly distributed across all of the grades. Broader studies about school attrition during the period of Mexican segregation reveal that this phenomenon was due to a variety of reasons. These included failure to enforce the compulsory-schooling law, the fact that many children belonged to migrant families and missed significant amounts of school at a time, and the fact that older students often dropped out of school to contribute to the labor and income of their families (González 1990). Families' unstable economic situations, poor school infrastructure, and negative teacher attitudes toward Mexican students undoubtedly contributed to poor performance and low levels of attendance in school. Although these structural factors played a role in the levels of attrition among Mexican students in La Feria, I contend that everyday experiences of Mexican students, especially as they progressed through the "integrated" schools, must also be considered as push-out factors.

Oral histories of Mexican students who graduated from La Feria High School in the mid-1940s (elementary school students during the 1930s) reveal that anti-Mexican discrimination in the schools was perhaps one of the more painful factors that contributed to school attrition. For example, Mexican alumni recall that Anglo students did not socialize with them. Though some Mexican students recall having Anglo acquaintances, they did not have Anglo friends. Amalia Silva remembers, "*No teníamos amigos americanos porque nos rechazaban. No nos querían.*" [We didn't have American friends because they rejected us. They didn't like us.] She felt that Anglos rejected social relations with Mexican students within the context of the integrated school. In terms of school incorporation, Mexican alumni recall that they were limited in the activities in which they could participate. While sports teams generally seemed to welcome Mexican student participation, other extracurricular activities were more exclusive. Elena Ramirez recalls that she was the only Mexican girl to be given a part in a school play, but that, even so, it was a minor role. A couple of my interviewees recall being able to participate in the choral club. These inclusions correspond to Anglo beliefs about Mexican students' propensity for the arts. Ramirez recalled that during her time at La Feria High School (early and mid-1940s) there were never any Mexican cheerleaders or baton twirlers, which can be confirmed through a survey of the town's high school yearbooks. This school policy directly reflected racist Anglo attitudes about the inferiority of Mexican bodies, a topic to which I will return in chapter 4. Overall, the social slights and exclusions that Mexican students endured during their high school years were racial microaggressions[6] that characterized the culture of segregation in La Feria schools during this time. These oral histories demonstrate the ethos of segregation and racial superiority that followed Mexican students to the supposedly integrated schools south of the railroad tracks.

Finally, I would like to suggest that educators' ideas about the "Mexican problem" were a contributing factor in the high rate of attrition in Mexican schools. Though approaching the problem in education from different perspectives, even the sympathetic principal of the Mexican School concurs with Superintendent Smith about the solution to low academic achievement. For both men, the remedy for the difficulties Mexican students faced in school—namely, school failure and attrition—was to increase vocational courses for them. Armour cites a list of those that exist in other Valley towns, such as vocational agriculture and manual training for boys and home economics for girls. In other words, despite Armour's insistence that Mexican children had the same academic potential as their Anglo counterparts as well as special artistic talents, ultimately Mexican children were to assume the same laboring positions as their parents—farmworkers, manual laborers, and housekeepers for the dominant Anglo class. The disproportionate placement of Mexican-origin students in vocational training again exposed teacher and administrator attitudes toward these students as intellectually inferior. Vocational courses were indeed the solution to the Mexican problem for Anglos. They would provide Mexican students a basic education, focused primarily on language and acculturation, while at the same time preparing them to occupy the same subordinate economic and social positions as the generation before them.

Within the system of Mexican school segregation at Sam Houston Elementary School and in the upper grades, there were nevertheless some Anglo teachers who were kind and supportive. Elena Ramirez recalls some elementary school teachers who were "*muy lindas*" and "*dedicadas*." Though perhaps ill equipped to effectively handle a classroom of Spanish-dominant children, some teachers were kind and dedicated to their education. In an essay she wrote for a reunion of the class of 1945, Molly Salazar-Lozano recalls two "exceptional teachers" in her primary school years at Sam Houston Elementary School. She states that Mrs. Moran "instill[ed] in us an awareness of what [was] going on in the world around us, and I thank [her] for arousing in me the curiosity and love for reading[,] which is my favorite pastime to this day" (Salazar-Lozano 1995). Finally, Antonia Garza, who completed her K–12 education in La Feria in the 1940s, recalls that a teacher singled her out for exceptional music abilities and proceeded to give her singing lessons free of charge and chauffeur her to performances at ladies' clubs around neighboring Valley towns. Though not calling for educational equity between Anglo and Mexican students, Armour in his capacity as principal of the Mexican School and the aforementioned teachers represent a cross-section of the Anglo community that sought to edify Mexican children. Beyond the formal system, however, Mexican children in La Feria received a meaningful education from the adults in their community. This education, which promoted a Mexicanist ideology and the basis for a strong cultural identity, in many ways served to counteract the one they received in the segregated La Feria public schools.

CREATING AND CELEBRATING A MEXICANIST IDENTITY AS A COUNTEREDUCATIONAL PROJECT

In 1930, a census worker canvassed the streets of La Feria's segregated Mexican neighborhood, collecting information about its various households. While walking along the few unpaved streets that composed *el pueblo mexicano*, he likely noticed brightly painted wood-framed houses crowded together. The close proximity of these homes bred familiarity and a strong sense of community among the families who lived along these few streets. He might have seen children from these families playing together in the streets or perhaps a group of them gathered to attend Spanish lessons at the Mexican hall. This census worker would also have observed a few small Mexican restaurants and grocery stores, a tortilla mill, and a billiard hall as he walked along Villareal Street, the "Main Street" of the neighborhood. Though just a small area in the northwest corner of La Feria, the *pueblo mexicano* was a vibrant center of Mexican community life. During the era of segregation, the points of contact between

Mexicans and Anglos in the agricultural fields and in the school system were, at worst, marked by violence and, at best, fraught with racial tension; the Mexican neighborhood, on the other hand, despite its infrastructural weaknesses, was often a safe haven for Mexican people. It was an insular community where Mexicans celebrated and reinforced a proud Mexicanist identity that stood in stark contrast to negative attitudes about Mexicans that were promulgated in La Feria schools and in the town in general.

The census worker who recorded details about the population of La Feria was charged with a variety of questions about residents' ages, places of birth, and occupations. Among the data that he was to collect was a question about race. Though previous censuses classified Mexican people as "White," in 1930, for the first time, census enumerators were instructed to classify Mexican-origin people who were born in Mexico and those whose parents were born in Mexico as racially "Mexican." Texas-born Mexicans, on the other hand, who had no immediate kinship ties to Mexico continued to be classified as racially "White" (Hendricks and Patterson 2002; Ngai 2004). This new racial classification of Mexican people was most likely a result of increasing concerns in the 1920s about Mexican immigration to the United States. Those policy makers who would have restricted Mexican immigration faced the powerful agricultural industry that consistently lobbied for a more open border so that they could secure cheap labor. Nevertheless, the establishment of the Border Patrol in 1924 indicates that Mexican migration was a growing concern for nativists in the 1920s.[7] The new 1930 racial classification was a way of marking Mexican immigrants as racially distinct. Despite the fact that Texas-born Mexicans were still "White" in the eyes of the U.S. government, newly arrived Anglos to the region did not distinguish between Tejanos and Mexican immigrants, and the vast majority of Mexican-origin people in La Feria lived in the segregated *pueblo mexicano* regardless of nativity.

Though Tejano families traced their lineages to the region from as far back as the eighteenth century, by 1930 La Feria's *pueblo mexicano* was a predominantly working-class immigrant community. While some immigrant individuals and families had arrived as early as 1870, the number of immigrants in town began to increase dramatically in the early 1920s. The growing demand for farm labor and the new railroad system throughout the United States and Mexico facilitated the arrival of more Mexican immigrants in La Feria and throughout the Lower Rio Grande Valley. These new immigrants lived alongside Tejano families. The historian David Gutiérrez (1995) has written about how relationships between newly arrived Mexican immigrants and those Mexican Americans whose families have longtime roots in the United States have been fraught since the signing of the Treaty of Guadalupe Hidalgo. Though likely to come together because of a shared ethnic identity, Gutiérrez argues that tensions often arose between the two groups, especially around issues of labor competition. Furthermore, racial discrimination led many Mexicanos to want to distance themselves from recently arrived Mexican immigrants who were less Americanized and could not claim citizenship rights (Gonzalez 2009; Gutierrez 1995; Orozco 2009). In La Feria, because the Mexican population was overwhelmingly composed of recent immigrants, shared ethnicity seemed to be a bond in the racially segregated community. Tejanos were more likely to be more economically stable, owning rather than renting their homes and working as merchants or skilled laborers (e.g., mechanics, bricklayers, etc.), though some worked in agriculture. The Tejano merchant class depended on the immigrant community to support their businesses, which were often located in *el pueblo mexicano*.

The majority of working adults in the community—immigrants, native-born Mexican Americans, men and women—were employed as farm laborers. Though work "*en el labor*" would be the predominant occupation of Mexican-origin people through the 1970s, some were able to move into different occupations as early as the 1930s. Despite that few Mexican-origin women had declared an occupation on the 1930 census, in the following decade many women went to work for a newly arrived tomato cannery. Luz Perez, a Mexican American woman born to immigrant parents in La Feria, recounted that after her father's initial employment as a farm laborer, he was able to save enough money to set up a small grocery store in *el pueblo mexicano*. Indeed, many of my interviewees remembered this neighborhood grocery store. Antonia Garza recalls the following:

> Most of the [Mexican] families there did their grocery shopping [at that store]. And I remember [they] used to have a little spiral notebook. And whenever you needed something you'd go and they'd write it down. At the end of the month, if you had the money, you paid or gave so much down. And that's how people did it because some people had money, some people didn't. But Mr. Gutierrez [the store owner]—he helped us, helped the people there.

Perez and her sisters worked as clerks at their father's small grocery store, and she confirmed to me that her father instructed them to let people make their food purchases on a good-faith basis. As an immigrant who began work in the fields before setting up his grocery store, Gutierrez was willing to help other members of the community who perhaps needed groceries sooner than their next paycheck was due from a local farmer. Indeed this type of camaraderie and community support was common in the Mexican neighborhood north of the railroad tracks.

Antonia Garza's mother worked as a housekeeper before setting up a small restaurant in the Mexican neighborhood. Garza recalls that the clientele was mixed—both Mexican and Anglo—but primarily Mexican. Similar to Gutierrez, Garza's mother was cognizant of the economic shortfalls Mexican people in the neighborhood experienced. Garza remembers her mother's willingness to help those in need: "[My mother] was a wonderful person. A wonderful person. If anybody came to the restaurant and didn't have any money, she didn't care. She'd give you the food, and don't worry about it. And I remember her telling me that you would need to help other people when they're in need because a lot of people helped her when she was in need." As with Gutierrez, Antonia Garza's mother purposefully taught her daughter about the importance of helping others, instilling in her the Mexican value of mutualism. While Gutierrez's practice of giving people credit at his grocery store to buy food showed his daughters the importance of supporting his working-class clientele, Garza's mother clearly articulated to her daughter that her generosity stemmed from the knowledge that in the Mexican community, people provided mutual assistance to each other. Though the hungry people who entered Garza's mother's restaurant were not necessarily the same ones who would offer her support, she fed them because of her strong sense of a larger community obligation.

The examples of Gutierrez's grocery store and Garza's mother's restaurant illustrate that within the context of racial segregation, the Mexican working poor often pooled their resources to support each other. Pooling resources occurred in informal ways, as mentioned above, and in formal, more structured ways. The historian Emilio Zamora has written extensively about the prevalence of Mexican mutual-aid societies in Texas. Zamora argues that mutualism emerged out of the experiences and needs of the Mexican community during the first few decades of the twentieth century. He states, "[T]he most important force that contributed to mutualism originated in the experiences that Mexicans shared in Texas. These included a condition of poverty that required the sharing of resources and efforts for survival and advancement, and the problem of discrimination and inequality that called for collective actions of defense and protest" (1993, 92). In this sense, mutual-aid societies were open to both Tejanos and Mexican immigrants, as they were largely relegated to the same conditions of poverty and limited social and economic advancement (Orozco 2009; Zamora 1993). Though some Mexican people in La Feria achieved a level of economic stability (e.g., enough to become small-business owners), the majority of the Mexican community lived in poverty. Furthermore, the structure of segregation precluded opportunities for social and economic advancement. Indeed many Mexican people depended on their fellow community members for their economic survival. To this end, Mexican-origin people in La Feria, and in Mexican communities throughout Texas, created and participated in mutual-aid societies. The prominent mutual-aid society in La Feria was Woodmen of the World (WOW), also known as "Los Hacheros."

Zamora states that mutual-aid societies served a few key purposes. Among them were providing financial assistance to their members, especially in the form of covering medical and burial expenses, offering community events "for entertainment and socializing," and sponsoring public forums that addressed issues pertinent to the Mexican community (1993, 93). Amalia Barrera recounted to me that her father was secretary of Los Hacheros in La Feria and that within the group he helped to organize an auxiliary children's group (fig. 3.1). During our interview at her home in *el pueblo mexicano*, she led me into a side room filled with old framed photographs. There she showed me a large framed picture of a few rows of serious-looking Mexican children with the words "*campo juvenil*" imprinted at the bottom of the photograph. She began to sing a song for me that she still remembered from her days in the group, and she recounted how the children would dress up in traditional Mexican styles for national Mexican holidays, such as the 16th of September and Cinco de Mayo (fig. 3.2).

In addition to the children's camp sponsored by the local WOW mutual-aid organization, there were Mexican adults who invested in employing instructors to teach their children how to read and write in Spanish. These types of *escuelitas* were common in Texas during the nineteenth and twentieth centuries (Acosta 2003; Barrera 2006; González 2006; Zamora 1993). These schools ranged from home schools established for preschool instruction to one-room schools that provided primary-level education. Elida Prado, who immigrated as a small child alongside her parents in the mid-1920s, recalls that an older cousin from Mexico and his wife came to live in her family's house when she was a child. As a form of "rent," Prado's mother asked that the cousin's wife, a young woman from Monterrey, teach Prado how to read and write in Spanish. More formally, Luz Perez remembers an *escuelita* in the *pueblo mexicano* where she and other children in the neighborhood would go to learn Spanish. She recalls that a woman of her parents' generation, Petrita Cavazos,[8] brought a teacher they called Doña Nachita[9] from Monterrey to teach these classes. The education scholar Aida Barrera argues that Mexicans established these *escuelitas* as a response to the inferior conditions of segregated Mexican schools throughout Texas. She states, "The *escuelitas* demonstrated the interest that Texas Mexicans had in providing educational opportunities for their children

FIGURE 3.1. Campo Juvenil, Woodmen of the World, La Feria, Texas, 1933. Photo courtesy of Amparo Verduzco

FIGURE 3.2. *Escuelita* in La Feria, Texas, n.d. Photo courtesy of Amparo Verduzco

as well as their attempts at maintaining their mother culture and language" (2006, 37–38). Indeed when considering the teacher attitudes toward Mexican children that I discussed earlier in this chapter, the establishment of *escuelitas* served as an opportunity for the Mexican community to educate their children directly in a way that would preserve and assign value to their children's heritage language.

If the community's *escuelita* was a direct countereducational response to the public school experience in La Feria, local commemorations of Mexico's national holidays were likewise a form of education that illustrated the kind of Mexicanist ideology that many Mexicans in Texas subscribed to during this time. Zamora states that a Mexicanist orientation was "based on grievances against racial discrimination plus the influence of nationalist thought from Mexico often [blurring] differences in the community" (1993, 86). The historian Cynthia Orozco describes a Mexicanist orientation as placing an emphasis on politics in Mexico and loyalty to *la patria* (Mexico), supporting resistance to Americanization, and raising children with a consciousness of their ties to Mexico (2009, 58). Indeed my interviewees vividly recall the Mexican celebrations that took place in the *pueblo mexicano* of their youth. In retrospect, they do not speak about gaining loyalty to "*la patria*"; their recollections instead affirm a strong sense of community in the *pueblo mexicano* of their youth. Though many of my interviewees were young children at the time of these celebrations in the 1930s, it remains an important part of how they remember the history of Mexican people in La Feria.

"*Alguien tenía un cañón*," Celia Garcia, a Mexican American woman in her 80s, recounted to me. "*No sé de donde le sacaban, pero lo sonaban a las cinco de la mañana.*"[10] Luz Perez, five years younger than Garcia, remembers, "*Nos íbamos a los troques alegóricos, los arreglaban con ribbons de todos colores, verde, blanco y colorado, you know. Y nos vestían de china poblana.*"[11] The "*troques alegóricos*," or floats, would be parked on Villareal Street. Elena Ramirez recalls that the floats were actually people's trucks that they would adorn with red, white, and green decorative paper, but that the people would gather around them, sitting or standing for the program. The program included "*discursos*," or speeches. As Garcia told me, "*Había gente que decía de las historias de aquella época.*"[12] In addition to the recitation of Mexican histories, Ramirez recalls that the children, often dressed in traditional Mexican clothing, such as the *china poblana* dresses that Luz Perez referred to, would sing patriotic songs. As scholars have indicated, celebrating 16 de Septiembre and Cinco de Mayo helped Mexican-origin people to create and reinforce a Mexicanist identity and community ideology. I further argue that these events served as a form of community education. La Feria public schools did not teach children about the history of Mexico, nor did they provide any instruction about Mexican culture or language. On the contrary, during this period, schools were focused on eradicating children's use of the Spanish language and schooling them about American traditions. By celebrating the Mexican national holidays and including a strong component of Mexican history and positive national identity, the Mexican community of La Feria engaged in a kind of countereducational project that ran contrary to Anglo-dominated formal education in town. This was a key part of identity formation for Mexicans during the 1920s and 1930s, the most stringent epoch of Mexican segregation.

In addition to the educational component of the Mexican celebrations, there was also the selection of Mexican "*reinas*," or queens, of the festivities. Though my interviewees were too young to have been considered for queens of the celebration, several had older sisters who were chosen as princesses or queens of Cinco de Mayo or 16 de Septiembre. Garcia recounts, "*Elegían muchachas para la reina, y esas muchachas tenían que agarrar votos. Las reinas tenían coronas muy bonitas y capes made out of velvet.*"[13] The beauty queen component was an important aspect of the events in *el pueblo mexicano*, especially because Mexican girls were banned from participating as cheerleaders and baton twirlers at the local high school, two positions that represented beauty and femininity. The selection of Mexican beauty queens from the community was essential to counter the notion that only Anglo girls could embody beauty and ideal womanhood. Through these contests, Mexican people created a world where young Mexican girls held the standard of beauty within their community, and these young beauty queens were feted appropriately with, as Garcia states, beautiful crowns and long velvet capes. At the time of their interviews, two women recounted to me that at the funeral services for a couple of older women, the family displayed pictures from their days as *reinas* in *el pueblo mexicano* in the 1930s. Such tributes indicate the indelible impression that these contests and festivities made on the lives of Mexican people in La Feria (figs. 3.3 and 3.4).

The 16th of September and Cinco de Mayo were not the only times of year when there would be celebrations in *el pueblo mexicano*. Amalia Barrera recounts, "*La navidad fue muy festejada en La Feria.*"[14] Particularly during December, the Mexican community engaged in various traditions that reflected strong Mexican Catholic traditions. As I discussed in chapter 2, Anglo Catholics largely suppressed Mexican popular religious practices in the local parish. Nevertheless, these practices endured in *el pueblo mexicano*. Community members recall that during the 1930s there would be culturally specific celebrations around December 12th, the Day of the Virgin Guadalupe and

FIGURE 3.3 (*left*). Amparo Verduzco in *china poblana* dress. Photo courtesy of Amparo Verduzco

FIGURE 3.4 (*below*). *Fiestas patrias* in La Feria, Texas. Photo courtesy of Amparo Verduzco

Christmas. For the former, there would be *matachines* performances, a dance ritual that represents the triumph of good over evil. For Christmas, the community hosted events such as Las Posadas, a procession that reenacts the journey Mary and Joseph took as they looked for a place to stay in Bethlehem, and *la Pastorela*, a play that represents the shepherds' quest to find the Baby Jesus. My interviewees recall that these popular religious practices were celebrated in the *pueblo mexicano* with people in the community dancing, playing instruments, and singing. Santiago Martinez recalls Chelo Silva, a young Tejana singer who would become one of the best-selling Spanish-language artists in the 1950s,[15] coming to town to sing for one such festivity.

Many of these celebrations and cultural practices ended in the late 1930s due to a massive repatriation that depleted the immigrant population of the *pueblo mexicano*. Though my interviewees do not recall much about the Depression era, their community felt the impact of the Mexican repatriations, a bilateral government response to the economic downturn at the end of the decade. In the urban hub of Los Angeles, repatriation efforts gained force in the early 1930s just after the stock market crash of 1929 (Sanchez 1995). In this case, unlike that of Mexican deportation, the Mexican government and its representatives in the United States often supported repatriations. In other parts of the United States, generally repatriates returned to their home villages in Mexico or relocated to urban centers (Sanchez 1995, 217). The South Texas case was unique, however, in that the Mexican government offered land in unsettled parts of Northern Mexico as an incentive for Mexicans in South Texas to repatriate (Walsh 2008). Under Mexican president Lázaro Cárdenas, the government began to make a concerted effort to cultivate cotton in the irrigation zones of Mexico's northeastern border region (2008, 98). To achieve this goal, it needed skilled agricultural laborers, like the ones who had migrated to the United States. In order to attract repatriates, the government offered twenty acres of land to each returning Mexican "colonist" (2008, 142).

Santiago Martinez remembers that the prospect of returning to Mexico as landowners was appealing to many people in the community. He recalls, "*En el 39 había un . . . programa de paquete grande. Vino y nos alborotó que para el 18 de marzo iban a dar tierras. Bueno entonces, mi papá también se quería ir, y le dije:—'No señor, si aquí está duro pues allá está peor' . . . Fue el 39 cuando se alborotaron la gente. Varias familias se iban a ir, y nosotros no.*"[16] As a young man in his early twenties at the time, Martinez vividly recalls the "*alboroto*," or frenzy, that the repatriation program caused in the community. While many were inspired to take advantage of the opportunity, including his own father, Martinez reasoned that if things were difficult in the United States, they would be even more difficult in Mexico. He was ultimately grateful for having followed his instinct to stay in the United States when the details of the repatriation plan became clear. The land that the Mexican government was giving to repatriates was unsettled brushland; it was the responsibility of the new colonists to cultivate it into sustainable farmland. Martinez comments, "*Iban a dar tierras—mentiras! Las tierras estaban . . . era monte. La gente tuvo que desenraizarlo.*" (They were going to give land—it was a lie! The lands they were giving were brushland. The people had to dig up the brush in order to plant.) Indeed conditions proved difficult for those who participated in the repatriation program. In some cases, the nearest water was nearly five miles away (Walsh 2008, 139). Furthermore, Mexican repatriates had to clear the land before the government would give them the title to it. Many people ultimately had to rely on their remaining connections in South Texas in order to sustain themselves in Mexico (2008, 142).

While the program had mixed results in Mexico, the impact of the program on the Mexican-origin community in La Feria was definitive. Many people recall that one of the principal organizers of the Mexican festivities, Don Julio Sanchez,[17] was among those who participated in the repatriation effort. With his departure and the departure of many Mexican families in the community, the character of the *pueblo mexicano* was altered dramatically. The national and cultural celebrations, which were such an important part of Mexican community life, ended.

Community life in *el pueblo mexicano* was strong and vibrant throughout the 1930s. Though, and perhaps because, this era marked the establishment of a rigid structure of racial segregation, the Mexican community in La Feria, which was largely immigrant and working class, forged communal ties that helped them to survive economically and thrive socially and culturally. Antonia Garza poignantly reflects on this period of her life as a child in La Feria:

> It was just one happy little place that we grew up with because we were in our little world. Nobody bothered us, and we were happy. It's until we crossed over that—when our problems started because we—you could feel that you were not wanted. You could feel that there was something there that they [local Anglos] didn't want. But there was something going on in Mexican town all the time, all the time. . . . I think everybody that lived there has good memories of the way things were.

Antonia Garza, like many of her contemporaries, fondly remembers growing up in the *pueblo mexicano* and frequently refers to that community as a happy family. Inherent to the happy family sentiment she recalls was their being in their own "little world." As a child, she had limited experiences in the local racialized economic system, and, for Garza, residential segregation facilitated an insular community in which she felt safe and happy. Her positive memories of that time are tainted only when she recalls the experience of leaving the safety of her all-Mexican world, crossing the railroad tracks, and feeling unwanted within the context of the Anglo community.

In many ways, Garza's recollection reflects the nature of Mexican segregation during the first few decades of the twentieth century. The strict structure of racial segregation created two worlds—one Anglo and one Mexican—within the town of La Feria. Anglos maintained control of all of the formal institutions in town, including the local school system. Within this school system, Mexican children were placed in segregated schools, where they were subject to an English-only curriculum, and continued on to schools where they routinely were placed in lower-level academic tracks and were encouraged to pursue vocational training. There were some benevolent Anglo administrators and teachers within the school system who focused on providing Mexicans with positive experiences in the arts as well as basic skills that promoted Americanization and bolstered English-language skills. However, these Anglo educators neither sought to eliminate segregation nor attempted to provide truly equal learning opportunities for Mexican children. In this way, the goals of local public education in La Feria, as in much of the Southwest, seemed to be to deracinate Mexican children and to reproduce a racially stratified socioeconomic system. Nevertheless, Tejanos and Mexicanos in La Feria were able to claim rights for themselves within the context of their segregated community, *el pueblo mexicano*.

Antonia Garza has positive memories of her home community, as do many of her cohort, because the adults therein worked diligently to provide a positive community experience for themselves and their children. In her book about the El Paso area company town, Smeltertown, the historian Monica Perales states, "Residents of such communities were hardly relegated to lives of misery and drudgery. On the contrary, they found ways to construct culturally vibrant and personally meaningful worlds in spite of, and perhaps even because of, the heavy hand of their corporate benefactors" (2010, 59). Similarly, this chapter has shown how, even under the yoke of racial segregation, Mexican people in La Feria created a strong and vibrant community life for themselves, engaging in practices of cultural citizenship. Though they were denied many of their civil and human rights in the Anglo-dominant public sphere because of their race, Mexican people in La Feria were able to create a sense of belonging for themselves in their segregated neighborhood by promoting their culture, specifically through enacting values of mutualism and reinforcing a Mexicanist identity. The ethos of mutualism was both informal and formal, through people's willingness to help each other in difficult economic times as well as by the establishment of a mutual-aid society that provided assistance in the form of insurance and sickness and burial services. In addition to providing mutual economic support to each other, members of the Mexican community established *escuelitas* to teach children Spanish and organized celebrations to commemorate Mexican national holidays and popular Catholic traditions. In this way, local Mexican people reinforced the bonds of community while proudly promoting their heritage culture. Through these collective practices, they created a culturally relevant space for themselves within a segregated community, thus engendering a sense of belonging to their small community in La Feria as well as to a larger, imagined Mexican community. Furthermore, these acts of cultural citizenship provided a crucial countereducational project that created a strong Mexicanist ideology and identity for their children.

CHAPTER FOUR

AN ACCOMMODATED FORM OF SEGREGATION

> *The one-syllable answer to the question "Are Latin Americans refused service in public places of business and amusement in Texas?" would have to be "Yes." But in order to be truthful, and speaking for the State as a whole, that reply must be modified by the addition of the phrases "some Latin Americans" are refused service in "some places of business" in "some Texas towns." At the same time it is admitted that in some rural and semi-rural communities, Anglo American operators of cafes, beer parlors, barbershops, and theaters are adamant in refusing service to any and all Latin Americans.* PAULINE KIBBE

Pauline Kibbe, a member of the Good Neighbor Commission, writes in 1946 about Mexicans in Texas, following her "one-syllable" response to whether or not discrimination exists with a sentence riddled with qualifiers. The Good Neighbor Commission had been established by then Texas governor Coke Stevenson to assuage the concerns of the Mexican government that discrimination was rampant in the state (Kibbe 1946; McWilliams 1948). Because of the Mexican government's negative perception of Texas's racial environment, it blacklisted Texas from receiving workers through the bracero program (McWilliams 1948). Within that political context, Kibbe might have been attempting to soften her assessment of racial discrimination and segregation in the mid-1940s by pointing to the many "exceptions" to such discrimination. Indeed, unlike the 1920s and 1930s, when Mexican segregation was fairly stringent, the 1940s marked the beginning of an era when inconsistencies and contradictions would become characteristics of what I call an accommodated form of segregation. This shift in the culture of Mexican segregation allowed a limited number of Mexican people to access Anglo-dominant spheres. Rather than classify the late 1940s as the beginning of integration, I argue that this period marked the emergence of an accommodated form of segregation because even though exceptional Mexicans emerged and were seemingly able to cross racial boundaries, Anglos continued to dominate all of the major political institutions and public social spaces. While this kind of racial exceptionality might seem to demonstrate the permeability of the line of segregation, in this chapter I will suggest that this apparent fluidity actually demonstrates the durability of segregation as it operated through a process of selective and limited incorporation/inclusion. Anglo people continued to determine the parameters of inclusion and exclusion for Mexican people, and attitudes about Anglo racial superiority were especially crystallized in their treatment of the racialized Mexican body.

During and after World War II, national political developments led to greater opportunities for Mexican people to claim rights normally afforded to Anglos. The aforementioned Good Neighbor Policy placed diplomatic pressure on Texas to present itself as a hospitable environment to the Mexican government so that it would remove the state from its blacklist and include it in the bracero program (McWilliams 1948). When it was finally enacted in Texas in 1947, the bracero program spurred the Texas economy. While bracero labor supported the agricultural industry, bracero purchasing power had a positive economic impact on Mexican-run local businesses (Menchaca 1995). Finally, the establishment of the GI Forum led to an increased number of legal challenges to the discrimination that Mexican-origin people faced, especially in South Texas (Ramos 1998). Not only were Mexican American veterans, especially those who had served in World War II, increasingly invested in claiming their civil rights, they were also more likely to be economically stable in the postwar era. The convergence of increased economic stability for a cross section of the Mexican-origin community, political pressure to lessen discrimination, and civil rights activism opened a small path for Mexican-origin people to claim more rights.

In La Feria, the impact of the Good Neighbor Policy and the GI Forum was limited, reflected by the fact that practices of segregation remained relatively unchanged. Schools, barbershops, cemeteries, and churches remained segregated, and Anglos continued to hold almost all positions of power and influence in the city. However, this chapter will demonstrate that people of Mexican origin, particularly Mexican Americans, did experience increased economic stability in the postwar period. Some Mexican Americans returned from the war with money saved; others had learned trades that had more earning potential than farm labor. Furthermore, the bracero program had a marked impact on the economy of the *pueblo mexicano*; Mexican-owned businesses thrived once local farmers began to contract braceros. Those Mexican-origin veterans, merchants, and their families who emerged more economically stable by the end of the 1940s began to constitute a small class of "exceptional" Mexicans who could cross certain racial boundaries.

Beginning in the late 1940s we can see the interplay between race and rights for people of Mexican origin in La Feria become more complicated and, at times, contradictory. During this time, the majority of the Mexican-origin community worked in the agricultural industry as laborers for local farms, packing sheds, and a cannery.[1] They continued to experience segregation in public spheres. Furthermore, they remained largely disenfranchised, with few civil rights that they could claim in the city's economic and political spheres. Nevertheless, there was a tenuous process of racial integration at work for those Mexican-origin people who were becoming more economically stable. With increased economic capital, a select number of Mexican people gained greater access to the realms of business and education, where Anglos dominated. I argue that in addition to class status, racialization determined the extent to which Mexican-origin people were able to cross previously stringent racial boundaries. Mexicans who were light skinned and also those Mexicans whose formal education enabled them a level of Anglo-Mexican biculturalism were more likely to be able to claim rights. Interestingly, greater access also led to an acute awareness of where the limits of rights for Mexican people in the city were drawn. Even though people of Mexican origin experienced increased economic and social opportunities, Anglos continued to view them as racially inferior, never allowing them the full spectrum of rights that white citizens enjoyed. This accommodated form of segregation, allowing select Mexicans increased but not unlimited rights while the majority of the Mexican population remained disenfranchised, would persist in various spheres until the early 1990s.

POSTWAR SOCIAL CHANGES

Just as the South Texas repatriations of 1939 shifted the character of the Mexican-origin community in La Feria, so did World War II and the postwar era mark important cultural and demographic shifts to the city, the Lower Rio Grande Valley, and the state of Texas as a whole. Whereas in the 1930s, Mexican segregation was characterized by stringent racial boundaries, in the 1940s the structure and the culture of segregation began to change. People of Mexican origin, especially Mexican Americans, were increasingly able to cross racial borders into Anglo neighborhoods, classrooms, and businesses. In this section, I will discuss how the bracero program and Mexican American veterans' activism contributed to what I call an accommodated form of segregation.

The bracero program was instrumental in changing the culture of segregation in South Texas. The program began in 1942 as an emergency wartime measure to address the labor shortage that employers faced with so many American GIs serving abroad. The U.S. and Mexican governments brokered a binational agreement that enabled thousands of Mexican nationals to legally enter the United States to work.[2] By the end of the 1930s, the agriculture industry was the economic backbone of the Lower Rio Grande Valley, and it was dependent upon Mexican immigrant labor. For years prior to the establishment of the bracero program, Texas farmers had lobbied for the establishment of such a guest worker program to provide them an easy supply of low-wage laborers (Ngai 2004).[3] Unfortunately for farmers, however, the Mexican government decided to blacklist Texas from the bracero program in 1943, citing rampant discrimination against Mexicans in the state (McWilliams 1948). That same year, Texas governor Coke Stevenson made a goodwill trip to Mexico to try to persuade the Mexican government to lift the ban. Upon his return to Texas, Stevenson appointed a Good Neighbor Commission. Pauline Kibbe, a member of the commission, wrote about its goals as follows: "The purpose of the Commission is three-fold: (1) to study the problems in Texas and arrive at a definite understanding of their scope and urgency; (2) to formulate, in co-operation with other State agencies, plans for the permanent solution of the problems encountered; (3) to put those plans into effect, with the assistance of other state agencies, local civic, cultural, religious and patriotic organizations, and interested individuals" (1946, 120). While the commission worked to identify problems that Mexicans encountered in Texas and look for solutions, Governor Stevenson issued a proclamation urging Texans to adhere to a Good Neighbor Policy, condemning any discrimination against "fellow citizens of Latin American extraction" (McWilliams 1948, 270). Nevertheless, the Texas ban from the bracero program was not lifted until 1947, when the U.S. and Mexican governments renegotiated the extension of the program. In this and in subsequent renegotiations, the Mexican government lifted its ban on certain U.S. states from the program not because discrimination had decreased, but because it had steadily been losing its power to negotiate in the first years of the program. U.S. growers were increasingly using undocumented labor as leverage to change the program to their liking and were pushing for a unilateral rather than a bilateral agreement. Rather than risk losing all of its negotiating power, Mexico made concessions with the program that ultimately benefitted the U.S. growers over Mexican workers (Kim 2004; Ngai 2004).

The arrival of bracero workers in South Texas had a marked economic impact on the region. While braceros ushered in an era of profits for local farmers, domestic farmworkers saw their wages drop and were largely unable to organize for better wages and working conditions.[4] Not all Mexican Americans and permanent residents fared poorly during the bracero era. An increased number of people in towns meant more business for both Anglo and Mexican merchants (Menchaca 1995). In the La Feria context, where segregation prevailed, braceros were more likely to frequent businesses on the Mexican side of town. Juanita Rodriguez, a native of the region and a teenager living in *el pueblo mexicano* during this time, recalls that there was "*más movimiento*," or "more movement," with the arrival of the braceros. They performed farm labor, including picking and harvesting crops as well as work in packing sheds. Rodriguez remembers that in town, especially along the railroad tracks, there were many packing sheds for fruits and vegetables that were staffed by braceros. Aside from the farm-related industries, braceros frequented local Mexican businesses. Rodriguez saw this clearly through experiences she had in her grandmother's restaurant in *el pueblo mexicano*. She remembers, "*Mi abuelita tenía restaurante y ahí comían muchos de los señores que venían de allá, de los braceros*."[5] Luz Perez, whose father owned a grocery store in the *pueblo mexicano*, recalls that the bracero epoch brought strong business to her father's store (fig. 4.1). She states, "We worked hard [at my father's store] *también. Era mucho porque era ya el tiempo de los braceros by then, y teníamos mucho, mucho [trabajo]. No cerrábamos la tienda hasta la 1:00 de la mañana*."[6] Emilio Valenzuela recalls Villareal Street as a bustling center during the bracero era. "It used to be . . . four beer joints, pool hall, tortillería, and Jerry's Dry Good Store. . . . That was a busy street. . . . Saturdays, oh, it was full of braceros." Local businesses on both sides of the railroad tracks flourished with the arrival of braceros. Coupled with wartime industry, the business that braceros brought gave a boost to the small Mexican American middle class in La Feria. Though a stronger Mexican American middle class meant the potential upward socioeconomic mobility of Mexican people, the problem of racial discrimination remained.

Discrimination against Mexicans, especially within the context of segregation, remained strong in South Texas. In 1946, while working for the Good Neighbor Commission, Kibbe noted the disparities in Mexican neighborhoods in Texas. She wrote, "As a rule, the 'Mexican colony' is devoid of paved streets, sewer lines, frequently even electric power, gas mains, and garbage dis-

FIGURE 4.1. Mexican business-owning families in La Feria. Photo courtesy of Amparo Verduzco

posal service. One can spot such a 'colony' or section in almost every case; it is 'on the wrong side of the tracks'" (124). Most Mexican people—both immigrant and Mexican American—continued to earn low wages as farmworkers with little prospect for mobility (Zamora 2008). As for the economic gains that Mexican Americans were making in the postwar era, these were tempered by discrimination. Despite Mexicans' having made significant occupational gains, particularly during World War II, they experienced lower rates of mobility than Anglos (Zamora 2008). Finally, one cannot ignore the everyday indignities that Mexicans in Texas faced as they were refused service at restaurants, barbershops, and other facilities throughout the state. This type of discrimination was particularly distressing to Mexican American veterans, many of whom had risked their lives to the service of a nation that continued to treat them as second-class citizens.

By the mid-1940s, Mexican American GIs were returning to their home communities in South Texas from their service in World War II. For many Mexican Americans, the decision to join the war effort was most likely a conflicted one. In his monograph about the Mexican American studies pioneer

Américo Paredes, Ramón Saldívar writes that Paredes was ambivalent about joining the service when discrimination against Mexicans in Texas continued to be so prevalent. Saldívar writes, "Like many men and women of color of his generation engaged in the public discourse of the era, Paredes measured the possibility that service in the U.S. Armed Forces might ultimately bolster the validity of the claim to a Mexican American stake in national identity and American citizenship" (2006, 50). Unfortunately, Mexican Americans did not find much changed when they returned from having served in the war. After having invested so much in their country, however, many veterans were emboldened to join Mexican American civil rights organizations to claim their rights as citizens. In the postwar period, Mexican American veterans established the GI Forum and reinvigorated the League of United Latin American Citizens (LULAC), two organizations that were instrumental in fighting for increased rights for the Mexican American community.[7]

In the late 1940s, both the GI Forum and LULAC emerged as organizations distinct from the mutual-aid societies that had been so prevalent in the 1920s and 1930s. Historian Cynthia Orozco argues that prior to the 1940s, Mexican Americans "had to construct their identity in relation to Mexican immigrants who largely identified Mexico as their nation and maintained allegiance to Mexico, resisted Americanization, and promoted Spanish monolingualism" (2009, 41). After the war, however, Mexican, or "Latin American,"[8] organizations began to make claims to their identity as Mexican Americans, a hybrid identity, Orozco argues, that was not possible before the war. Zamora uses the example of a World War II veteran and active LULAC member, José de la Luz Saenz, as someone who "appropriated the wartime language of democracy and justice to recast the Mexican cause for equal rights in hemispheric terms" (2008, 17). Zamora argues that Mexican Americans like Saenz "broaden[ed] their claims for equal rights at home by becoming citizens abroad" (17). Claims to American citizenship and identities became the basis on which LULAC focused its antidiscrimination campaigns.

From its inception in 1929, LULAC primarily issued legal challenges to the kind of discrimination that Mexicans faced. In the mid- to late 1940s, however, with the Good Neighbor Policy at play and the Mexican government expressing concerns about discrimination its workers might face in Texas, LULAC was rejuvenated. It began to work in conjunction with the Mexican consulate to address issues of discrimination and adopted the "egalitarian" language of the Good Neighbor Policy (Zamora 2008, 209). LULAC enjoyed success, filing complaints and initiating protests around segregation in public facilities, jury discrimination, job discrimination, and education (Garcia 1989). Although the Good Neighbor Policy, to which LULAC looked to bolster its cause in the

1940s, was a "significant gesture," it was "not particularly effective" (McWilliams 1948, 270). Though individual cases were won, these amounted to exceptions rather than fundamental changes to the structure of segregation. For example, LULAC lawyer Gus Garcia represented a laborer named Pete Hernandez, who had been convicted of murdering another Mexican American man. Garcia's appeal was based on the fact that Hernandez had been judged by an all-white jury rather than by a jury of his peers. Garcia took this case of jury discrimination to the Supreme Court, and in 1954, the court ruled in his favor (Garcia 1989; García 2009). Despite this high-profile win that would have ostensibly opened the jury pool to Mexican Americans, over twenty years later, in 1970, the U.S. Commission on Civil Rights issued a report that found "serious and widespread under representation of Mexican Americans on grand and petit juries in state courts in many areas of the Southwest" (cited in García 2009, 198). This case illustrates that while important, LULAC's antidiscrimination efforts had a limited impact on the larger Mexican community in the Southwest through the 1940s and 1950s.

The commerce generated by the bracero program and activism of Mexican American civil rights organizations like the GI Forum and LULAC opened a path of increased rights for Mexican-origin people within the structure of segregation. The bracero program spurred the local economy to the benefit of Mexican-owned businesses. This economic activity was significant in that it fostered economic stability for Mexican-origin merchants. Furthermore, because Texas had initially been blacklisted from the program, the governor enacted a Good Neighbor Policy to try to assuage the Mexican government's concerns about discrimination against Mexicans in the state. Mexican American civil rights organizations like LULAC built upon this diplomatic moment to contest discrimination in the courts, and the GI Forum likewise lobbied for the full civil rights of Mexican American veterans. While the latter organization enjoyed a degree of success in the courts, de facto segregation remained a reality for the majority of Mexican-origin people in Texas, especially those in the racialized farm labor sector. These contradictory processes of increasing rights while maintaining a subjugated racialized workforce led to an accommodated form of segregation, one in which people of Mexican origin—at all socioeconomic levels—experienced inconsistencies and contradictions in the rights they could claim.

AN ACCOMMODATED FORM OF SEGREGATION

From 1940 to 1950, La Feria's population grew from 1,644 to 2,952 residents, nearly an 80 percent increase. During this time, segregation in the city shifted such that some of its major structures became more accommodating of Mexicans. Neighborhoods, businesses, and the local schools began to show more flexibility in permitting Mexicans into Anglo spheres, but only to a certain extent. As this section of the chapter will illustrate, though Anglos allowed some Mexican people to cross racial boundaries and enjoy increased civil rights, they did not see these exceptional Mexican people as their racial equals. The persistence of racist attitudes about Mexican inferiority, especially at the level of the body, rigorously maintained certain racial borders.

Neither the economic advances of a cross section of Mexican-origin people nor the work of Mexican American civil rights organizations fundamentally changed the structure of residential segregation in La Feria, though the culture of each part of town began to change. After the repatriation movement in South Texas at the end of the 1930s, the *pueblo mexicano* remained a Mexican space, but the ethnic identity shifted in the town from one that was binational and Mexicanist to one that was Mexican American oriented.[9] A number of Latin American organizations emerged, many of which organized Mexican dances as fund-raisers. One organization, the Artemis Club, was established to "aid in the provision of recreational facilities for Latin Americans" as well as to "attempt to raise funds for a Latin American community hall through the sponsorship of dances, Mexicans suppers and bazaars" (*La Feria News*, January 15, 1948). Other so-called Latin American organizations in La Feria and across the Valley also hosted activities such as *querméses* (festivals) and dances to raise money for the Red Cross (*La Feria News*, March 18, 1948). In this context, Latin American organizations seemed to function in much the same way as mutual-aid societies had in the 1930s in terms of raising money to support the Mexican community. However, they did not promote the same kind of Mexicanist identity as the *mutualistas*; Mexican patriotic festivals were absent from Latin American events. These organizations were focused on supporting Mexican-origin people locally in La Feria and the Valley. The use of the ethnic label "Latin American" also represents a break from the mutual-aid Mexicanist identities. Mexican-origin community leaders in town began to use the language that LULAC had adopted in 1929 as a way to emphasize their social and political investment in the United States.

Interestingly, very few of my interviewees recall the Latin American organizations or their causes as much as they do the events that these organizations sponsored, particularly the dances. Margarita Martinez moved to La Feria from another part of South Texas when she married in 1942. She recalls that during this time, "*cerraban la calle con mecate y . . . ahí hacían baile, y ahí bailaba la gente. Era muy bonito antes.*"[10] She continues, "*Había sociedades de . . . los colones, y quién sabe qué más, y muchas que era la sociedad fulana de tal, y las sociedades . . . en la calle les hacían los bailes*."[11] Martinez and her husband, who, like many of their contemporaries, made their living as farmworkers, were not interested or invested in the "societies" that organized the dances as much as they were in the dances themselves. The anthropologist José Limón argues that for working-class Mexicans in South Texas, dancing offered a "measure of artful control" over the forces of race, class, and gender that subjugated Mexicans in this region for decades (1994, 165). Mexican dances in La Feria occurred in *el pueblo mexicano*, where they would rope off the streets, but also in the local American Legion Hall as well as halls and "*salones*" throughout the Valley. Tejano music and dance were an integral part of Mexican community life in the 1940s and beyond.[12]

In addition to the enjoyment that such events provided, Mexican-origin people sponsored and attended dances and other Mexican community events because practices of segregation precluded them from attending Anglo social events. Elena Ramirez, a graduate of La Feria's class of 1946, shared with me the announcement for a graduation party for her and the five other Mexican graduates that year. The party was to be held at the American Legion Hall, which, at the time, was located on the north side of the railraod tracks, and was to feature the music of Pete Peña's Orquesta. She told me that the Mexican students had raised the necessary money for the dance, and, in turn, could offer a certain number of tickets to family and friends. This graduation party was separate from whatever graduation festivities the Anglo students were holding, not by law, but by everyday logics and enactments of persistent racial segregation. In this era of segregation, Mexican people adjusted to claim rights and make space for themselves in the town. While Mexican-origin organizers began to invest in the rhetoric of America, perhaps investing themselves as citizens, many working-class Mexican people were invested in cultural citizenship, creating and participating in activities that affirmed their cultural practices and preferences.

The *pueblo americano* similarly retained its same demographic through the 1940s and 1950s, as a predominantly Anglo middle- to upper-class section of town. During this epoch, however, there began a small shift in the patterns of residential settlement in La Feria. Prior to 1940, with very few exceptions, the area south of the railroad tracks in the city was composed of almost exclusively Anglo residences. A review of property records reveals no clauses in the local property deeds prohibiting Mexican people from purchasing property south of the railroad tracks. Nevertheless, the residential patterns that emerged at the town's inception were such that Anglos exclusively lived south of the railroad tracks, and Mexicans lived in the residences to the north. In the early 1940s, this pattern of residential settlement began to change. From 1940 to 1944, Mexican people purchased nearly two dozen properties on the south side of the railroad tracks. During the latter half of that decade (1945–1949) the number doubled to just over fifty. That no racially restrictive housing covenants existed, coupled with the increased upward economic mobility of the local Mexican population, especially in the latter half of the 1940s, when bracero business had brought a boon to Mexican-owned stores, likely led to this shift. While these numbers were by no means to change the racial/ethnic character of the south side of the tracks, the change was significant because it marked a small opening for Mexican people to claim actual space in an Anglo-dominated town.

Members of the small Mexican American middle class that emerged in La Feria in the first few decades of the twentieth century were among those able to purchase homes on the south side of the tracks. In his study about the emergent Mexican middle class in Texas during this time, the historian Mario Garcia states that people whose families had previously been merchants or those who migrated with enough capital to open a store created a small, viable merchant class that was able to make a living primarily catering to Mexican communities. These merchants "experienced mobility within a Mexican American context" (1989, 27). Garcia notes that a few of these businesses expanded to serve their local Anglo communities. This was the case in La Feria, as well. Juan Hinojosa, a lifelong resident of La Feria whose family traces their ancestry to the first Spanish settlers in the region, recounts that his parents owned a business and home in the Mexican neighborhood in the 1920s and 1930s. As a child in the 1940s, he recalls that because of increased business from braceros, his family was able to establish a second business on the Anglo side of town in 1953. In between that time, in the late 1940s, the Hinojosa family moved the structure of their home to a lot on the south side of the tracks. Additionally, there were a few land-grant families who remained in the area and had managed to maintain enough of their land holdings to have some social and economic capital. The surnames of some of these land-grant families were among those purchasing property on the south side of the tracks. Finally, there were several Mexican American veterans of World War II who returned to La Feria in the mid-1940s. With the money that these returning GIs had saved from their service, they, too, had increased economic flexibility to purchase property on either side of the tracks. The south side of town was desirable for residents because of the spaciousness of its residential areas, its better infrastructure, and its proximity to the financial and political center of town. Moreover, for Mexican-origin people, there was likely an element of social status that came with living on the Anglo side of town.

While the few Mexican families who moved to the *pueblo americano* might have enjoyed higher status among their fellow Mexican residents, it is important to highlight that they were not fully integrated into the neighborhood. Hinojosa recalls that while his mother exchanged pleasantries with her neighbors, no Anglo neighbor ever invited her inside for tea, nor did she invite them. As with the separate Mexican graduation party, social boundaries often remained firmly in place between Anglos and Mexicans, even when the latter were upwardly economically mobile.

Not all Mexican people who had accumulated capital chose to purchase property on the south side of the tracks. Certainly the aesthetics and the infrastructure of the residential areas on the south side of the tracks were more appealing than those on the north side, and some families who were able did purchase homes in this part of town. Nevertheless, other families continued to choose to buy residences on the north side. Still others used their capital to establish businesses such as grocery stores, dry goods stores, and beauty shops on either side of the tracks. On the north side, they would obviously cater to a Mexican clientele, whereas on the south side of the tracks, they might enjoy increased business from both Mexicans and Anglos.

In the 1940s, businesses along South Main Street were generally open to both Anglos and Mexicans. Though some longtime residents recounted a strong sense of discomfort on the south side of town, for others it seemed very normal to shop along this thriving small downtown. The Anglo business community employed and served Mexicans, indicating that they held their profits in higher regard than racial borders. Indeed, Delia Martinez, a native of La Feria and a teenager during the 1940s, worked as the counter girl at a soda shop one summer during high school, serving both Anglo and Mexican town residents. One of her frequent customers, a Mexican American veteran recently returned from service in World War II, eventually became her husband. Romantic notions aside, her story demonstrates that in the business sector of downtown La Feria, Anglo merchants were willing to serve (and even employ) Mexican-origin people as well as the Anglos who lived on that side of town. There was an increased number of Mexican businessmen who held professional relationships with Anglo businessmen in La Feria. One such man was Francisco "Frank" Rodriguez.

Rodriguez was a well-known businessman in both the Anglo and Mexican communities in La Feria in the 1950s. Though Anglo-Mexican relations were often strained, both Anglos and Mexicans recall that Rodriguez "walked both sides of the street." Rodriguez grew up in *el pueblo mexicano*, where his father had owned a small store. High school counselors never encouraged him to pursue college, so after he graduated from high school in 1947, Rodriguez joined a crew that was going to pick cotton in Arizona. When he returned to

La Feria after that summer's work, he remembers that his hands were black. His father asked him if that was what he wanted to do for the rest of his life, and he answered no. Rodriguez could not afford university tuition, but his father and sister worked to put him through a local business college, which he finished in eleven months. Rodriguez met his wife at the college, and when he returned to La Feria with her, Rodriguez worked in different business sectors, including real estate. In 1951, the couple purchased a home on the south side of the tracks.

In the late 1950s, Rodriguez's son was approaching the moment for his first haircut. At the time, Rodriguez had a good friend and business mentor—an Anglo man named Mr. Smith—who had previously been a barber. Acknowledging the special occasion, Smith offered to cut Rodriguez's son's hair in the barbershop where he worked on Main Street. However, when Smith's partner in the barbershop—another Anglo man—found out about these plans, he forbade it. The shop did not cut Mexican hair. Smith returned to Rodriguez apologetically and noted regretfully that there was nothing he could do.

Indeed, the barbershop on Main Street in La Feria was notoriously segregated, and it represented a racial border that Rodriguez, as a Mexican American, could not cross despite his entrée into other Anglo realms (e.g., the business community, the neighborhood south of the railroad tracks). I would like to suggest two reasons for the way that this particular racial boundary was policed. First, it was common for Anglos to hire Mexican people to work in close proximity with them in jobs such as housekeepers, laundresses, and, as previously mentioned, food servers. However, these service positions were not often reciprocated; Anglos did not typically serve Mexicans. Barbers, employees in a service industry, would only serve fellow Anglos, not Mexicans, whom they felt were racially "below" them. This aspect of racist logic could explain why Anglo barbers in town refused service to Mexicans, even if certain Mexicans were to cross racial boundaries in other circumstances.

A second, powerful reason that the barbershop was a space where stringent racial borders were maintained was because of prevailing racist attitudes about Mexican bodies as unclean. George I. Sanchez, a former president of LULAC, offers the following relevant discussion of segregated cemeteries in an article about Mexican discrimination in the U.S. Southwest: "The bodies of 'Mexicans' are denied the right of burial. . . . In those cemeteries where such bodies are received they are assigned a separate plot of land, far enough from the plot destined for the so-called 'whites' so as to be sure that the bodies of the 'whites' will not be contaminated by the presence of the bodies of the Mexicans" (quoted in McWilliams 1948). If even in death Mexican bodies had the potential to "contaminate" white bodies, this would be even more true in a space like a barbershop, where barbers would regularly be in close proximity to the hair and skin of their clients. If Anglo barbers were to offer their services to Mexicans, it would have placed them too close to bodies that were considered unclean and even potentially contaminating. These racist beliefs undergirded the continuing ethos and social structures of segregation.

As Rodriguez's case illustrates, even though Mexican-origin people began to cross certain racial borders in the late 1940s, the logic and culture of segregation remained intact. These could be seen perhaps most vividly in the school district. Sam Houston Elementary School was the town's segregated Mexican school that served students through the third grade. In the so-called integrated junior high and high schools, Mexican students experienced intraschool segregation through the racialized tracking system that privileged Anglo students. During the postwar period, there were exceptions to this school segregation, and there were select Mexican students who were placed in the A (Anglo) tracks in junior high and high schools. Even as Mexican school attrition was a glaring problem in the school system, there were some Mexican students who made their way through the educational pipeline. These students, similarly to Rodriguez, experienced both acceptance and rejection in Anglo-dominant social spheres, largely predicated on the inferiority of Mexican bodies, though in the realm of school, racism was largely coded in terms of intelligence and culture (e.g., language ability).[13]

There were, however, a handful of Mexican-origin students who made their way through the educational pipeline in the La Feria schools during the 1940s. Several women that I talked to recall attending classes alongside Anglo students in high school as well as participating on sports teams with them. Delia Martinez was born and raised on the outskirts of La Feria, and she attended La Feria schools for her K–12 education. She fondly remembers her participation on the high school volleyball team.

> Para las mujeres, hasta que yo llegué a freshman, ninth grade, es cuando me metí a los activities de volleyball y baseball y todo esto. [For girls, it wasn't until I got to high school that I was able to join volleyball and baseball]. I played those, and I loved them. I loved those games. We had our uniforms and everything.
>
> We won some games. We went to the different towns, you know, to Weslaco, Mercedes, Harlingen, para jugar con las otras que iban con el volleyball también [to play with other volleyball teams]. We competed. They came to our school. I'm talking about high school. They came to our school and played with us, competed with us.

Martinez begins her narrative by stating how much she enjoyed participating in team sports. Wearing a team uniform and traveling to neighboring towns to play volleyball was an obvious source of pride for her. She talks about winning some games, but perhaps more powerful is her statement, "We competed." She clearly saw herself and her teammates as competitive athletes engaged with each other in the sport. Martinez's narrative also suggests that she believed herself to be an equal member of a team with both Anglo and Mexican girls.

Belonging to a high school sports team is one way that students claim space for themselves at school. It shows their membership not just to the team, but also to the school. Martinez and her teammates traveled to different towns to compete as representatives of their school. Both Mexican and Anglo girls played for the La Feria High School volleyball team during this time. Martinez does not state what the ratio of Mexican to Anglo girls on the team was, but from the overall school demographics, we can assume that Mexican girls were likely a minority on the team. Nevertheless, as these girls traveled together from town to town, they represented La Feria High School as an "integrated" school.

When questioned about the social relationships within the team, Martinez made it clear that Mexican and Anglo girls, though teammates, were not friends. She remembers, "*No, pues se creían muy superior a nosotros. A nosotros acá . . . 'oh, she's a Mexican.' Y [nosotros] acá abajo, y ellas acá arriba.*" [The Anglo girls thought they were superior. They would say, "Oh, she's a Mexican," as if we were down here and they were above us.] Martinez's narrative reveals that despite the facade of a racially integrated team, there continued to be borders present between them and, as the next portion of her narrative reveals, racial lines that could not be crossed.

During Martinez's senior year, as a treat to the class of 1947, the school arranged a trip to a local park and pool in the neighboring town of Harlingen. She vividly recalls one of the moments in her young life that crystallized the experience of racial discrimination beyond what she sensed from her Anglo teammates.

In my twelfth grade . . . I was real real real angry con las americanas porque, you know Lon C. Hill Park in Harlingen? Las americanas querían ir allí swimming for a treat a los seniors. So they got that pool in the	In my twelfth grade, I was real, real, real angry with the Anglo girls because, you know Lon C. Hill Park in Harlingen? The Anglo girls wanted to go swimming there as a treat for the seniors. So they got that pool in the

park rented in Harlingen, pero no nos dejaron entrar al swimming pool. Tuvimos que estar allí en el deck del pool. . . . Y allí en el deck estábamos viendo nosotros que las americanas acá estaban swimming and having fun and yelling and everything. Y nosotros allá arriba. Just watching them. No nos dejaron entrar con ellas al swimming pool. Porque éramos mexicanas. Imagine that. I was so angry. I'm still angry.

park rented in Harlingen, but they wouldn't let us go into the swimming pool. We had to stay on the pool's deck. . . . And from the deck we were watching that the Anglos were there swimming and having fun and yelling and everything. And we were up there. Just watching them. They didn't let us get into the swimming pool with them. Because we were Mexicans. Imagine that. I was so angry. I'm still angry.

What begins for Martinez as a feeling that her Anglo teammates considered themselves "superior" to their Mexican counterparts is manifested in this senior excursion to a local park and pool. As far as Mexican-origin people in town were concerned, Martinez seemed to be fairly well positioned. Her father owned and farmed his own land. As a teenager, she held a summer job working at the soda counter on the Anglo side of town. Unlike many of her Mexican student counterparts who perhaps had to drop out of school to work to contribute to their family incomes, Martinez successfully navigated the school system through high school, and, in school, she actively participated in sports. Despite her experiences of inclusion, however, Martinez knew that her Anglo contemporaries thought themselves *better* than she was. This feeling came to fruition as she and her Mexican peers were denied entrance to the public pool during a senior trip and were instead made to stand on the deck at the beginning of a South Texas summer and watch as the Anglo students enjoyed what we can only imagine would be refreshing water in the summer heat.

Martinez's experience at the pool in Harlingen, which was echoed in at least one of my other oral history interviews, was not simply a snub that perhaps Martinez had caught from her Anglo peers. It was an overtly humiliating experience for her and her classmates, and it signaled to them that though they enjoyed certain rights—access to public school, the ability to participate in extracurricular activities—these rights were limited by racial discrimination. It is unclear from her narrative whether the park had enacted the pool restriction or the school officials who had orchestrated the excursion did not permit the Mexican girls to swim. Either way, that moment acutely illustrated Martinez's understanding of her Anglo teammates' attitudes of "superiority" to their Mexican counterparts. She knew that they were not allowed in the pool simply because they were Mexican; at that moment, she knew that, to these Anglo people, "being Mexican" meant being dirty.

Martinez emphasizes the feeling of anger, both at the beginning and at the end of her narrative. It is interesting to note that Martinez's anger was directed not at the school officials or at the park facility but at the Anglo girls. However, the pool incident was more than the affirmation of racist attitudes: it was also the result of systemic racist policies toward Mexican people. Forbidding Mexicans from using pool facilities was a common policy of parks throughout Texas (Garcia 1989; Gutierrez 1995; McWilliams 1948). In some cases, Mexicans were allowed to use public pools only on the day before they were to be drained. The implication of this policy, of course, was that Mexican bodies would somehow contaminate the pool. On the other hand, the policy relegated Mexican people only to pool water at its dirtiest. Though these policies were a systemic part of segregation in South Texas, because Martinez had experienced segregation so inconsistently throughout her young life, she directed her anger not at a segregated social system, but rather at the individual Anglo girls on her volleyball team who had treated her with indignity. Ultimately, though the Good Neighbor Policy and the civil rights activism of Mexican Americans pushed for legal changes to stymie practices of segregation, the attitudes and actions of local Anglo people came to define the accommodated form of segregation that Mexican people experienced on a day-to-day basis. While certain Mexican-origin people were accepted into select Anglo-dominated spheres, local Anglo people continued to police the boundaries of integration.

The accommodated form of segregation that emerged in La Feria in the 1940s continued to be characterized by racial boundaries. Though some of these boundaries were more apparent than others, Anglo people continued to control the institutions of power during this time. They determined which Mexicans were permitted into which realms and where racial boundaries would ultimately be drawn. Though people like Frank Rodriguez and Delia Martinez were granted limited incorporation into Anglo-dominant spheres, they still grappled with the racial stigma of being "Mexican" in an era of Anglo dominance. The limits they experienced in the era of segregation had to do with the racialized Mexican body and were evident in nonnegotiable segregated spaces, such as the barbershop and the public pool. Despite Mexicans' increased economic and cultural capital, Anglo people continued to view them as racially inferior. The experiences of these Mexican people were part of the pattern of racial exclusions that defined Mexican segregation in the Lower Rio Grande Valley in the 1940s and the 1950s.

Through the 1930s, Mexican segregation was most often seen as a system of racial exclusion. By the 1940s, however, the culture of segregation had changed, and there were some Mexicans who enjoyed limited rights within the context of an Anglo-dominated society. The previous section has explored some of these new, often contradictory, patterns of racial segregation. Nevertheless, it has shown the ways that Anglo society continued to police certain racial borders against Mexican people. Ironically, it was also during this time that La Feria had its first Mexican American mayor.

A MEXICAN AMERICAN MAYOR IN THE ERA OF SEGREGATION

Originally from Brownsville, Joe Gavito Jr. graduated from Harlingen High School in 1931.[14] He took a job as a janitor at a local business college and worked his way through that same school, graduating in 1934. His first job after business college was for a company that held contracts with tomato canneries. He began work for one of La Feria's prominent businessmen, J. C. Dunn, in 1935. Gavito held several jobs within the cannery, eventually becoming the general manager and president of the tomato cannery in La Feria.

When Joe Gavito and his wife, Bertha (Renaud) Gavito,[15] purchased property in La Feria in 1940, news of the couple building a house was featured in the local newspaper. Other than Gavito assuming a prominent role at the tomato cannery as its general manager and president, it is unclear why this particular Mexican American couple merited news coverage. Whatever the reason, the publication of that article clearly indicated and perhaps introduced the Gavitos as members of "society." The fact that they built their home on the south side of the railroad tracks signified that they would be members of Anglo society.

The couple was extremely involved in the civic life of La Feria from the time they moved to town. Mrs. Gavito was well known in the community for her involvement in the local Catholic church, where she was a member of the Ladies' Altar Society, which was almost exclusively composed of Anglo women. In addition, many people remember that she would travel to the outskirts of town to teach catechism in Spanish to Mexican children. Through the church and other civic organizations, she performed acts of charity for the local Mexican community, including providing food, clothes, shoes, and blankets for those who needed them. Mrs. Gavito's works of charity and involvement in local civic organizations earned her the title of "Woman of the Year" in 1959 by the Zeta Rho Chapter of Beta Sigma Phi, which was an honor because she was selected from among a group that was Valley-wide. Because many civic organizations focused on helping the Mexican community as part of their works of charity, it follows that Mrs. Gavito would be recognized for her efforts in this area.

Mr. Gavito was, likewise, a visible and active member of the community. Several people remember him for his position at the cannery because it employed many Mexican men and woman in the area. In the civic realm, Gavito was involved in various clubs and organizations that were composed of mostly Anglo men. Perhaps most notably he was involved in the La Feria Rotary Club. Celia Garcia, whose husband was also a member of the Rotary Club during this time, recalls that her husband had to fight for admittance, but that once he was accepted, the Anglo Rotary members treated him well. She recalls that her husband would say, "I'm a Mexican. My parents are from Mexico. I'm a pure Mexican." The Anglos in the club would, in turn, pat him on the back and say, "You're a different kind of Mexican, Octavio." Garcia interpreted these exchanges between the Anglo Rotary members and her husband to mean that Mexican Americans like her husband and Joe Gavito were seen as exceptional and thus accepted into the club. However, the prevailing attitudes and beliefs of Anglos were those that continued the view of the Mexican community as racially inferior. Perhaps because he was both economically well positioned and light skinned, these attitudes did not seem to hinder Joe Gavito. He eventually served as president of the La Feria Rotary Club and later went on to found a chapter of the club in the neighboring town of Elsa.

Gavito also served on the La Feria Utilities Board and the Board of Directors for the First National Bank in La Feria. In addition to these city-based organizations, Mr. Gavito was active on committees for Cameron County, such as the Cameron County school board and the Cameron County Housing Authority. Valley-wide, he was president of the Texas Canners Association, director of the Rio Grande Valley Chamber of Commerce, director of the Rio Grande Boy Scouts Council, a member of the Texas Citrus Advisory Council, and vice president of the Good Government League, and he served as chairman of financial drives for organizations such as the Red Cross, the Boy Scouts, and the American Cancer Society (*Valley Morning Star*).

Mr. Gavito's civic involvement also translated to the sphere of local politics. Just five years after moving to La Feria, Joe Gavito was elected to the City Commission. Of the four candidates who ran for two open positions on the commission in 1945, Gavito earned the most votes. He was the only Mexican American candidate and, when elected, he was the only Mexican American on the commission. In 1948, during his term as commissioner, Gavito was named to the committee for the Civic and Education Club of Cameron County. One month later he became president of the Rotary Club. In 1949, the sitting mayor of La Feria stepped down, and Gavito's fellow commissioners appointed him to assume the position of mayor, making him the first Mexican American mayor of La Feria.

During Gavito's two-year tenure as mayor, conditions for Mexican Americans in town largely remained the same. His work as mayor focused on community issues as a whole, such as monitoring city maintenance, issuing permits, and authorizing minor improvements to the town. No policies under his term were specifically geared toward improving the living conditions of Mexicans in the town. It could have been that Gavito saw the latter as something best addressed by the civic organizations and charities with which his wife was so involved. Mexican people's opinions and attitudes about Gavito as a figure of authority were mixed. Whereas some viewed him as a man compassionate to Mexicans, others saw him as more concerned with establishing a place for himself in Anglo society. Either way, that his tenure as mayor had a limited impact on La Feria's Mexican community indicates that his appointment to the post did not reflect a major shift in the patterns of racial inequality and segregation in La Feria in the late 1940s and early 1950s. Certainly, that there would not be another Mexican American mayor for another four decades indicates that Gavito was an exceptional person because of his class status, his white racial aspect, and his cultural ability to navigate both Anglo and Mexican worlds (fig. 4.2).

In April 1951 an entirely new group of people were elected to the commission,[16] and an Anglo man replaced Gavito as mayor. According to records, Gavito expressed his regrets at leaving the commission after six years of service. He would continue to be a prominent citizen through his involvement in the aforementioned organizations, clubs, and advisory boards both in town and Valley-wide. However, after an unsuccessful bid for mayor in 1959, Gavito never returned to politics.

The Gavitos were also well known for their service to the local Catholic parish. In the fifty years that they attended St. Francis Xavier in La Feria, they both served as Eucharistic ministers and lectors for the church. As previously mentioned, Mrs. Gavito was one of the only Mexican American members of the Ladies' Altar Society. At the Valley-wide level, Mr. Gavito served on a council to help local churches follow the new guidelines set forth by Vatican II. In La Feria, he was the first president of the St. Francis Xavier Parish Council. All of the Gavitos' service occurred during an era when the parish was internally segregated. Contemporaries of the Gavitos have conflicting memories about where the couple sat on Sunday mornings. Some recall that they sat with Anglos; others insist that they sat on the Mexican side. These contradictory memories are likely fueled by the people's under-

FIGURE 4.2. Joe Gavito. Photo courtesy of Elsie Ireland

standings of where the Gavitos situated themselves in a racially segregated community. In later years, some community members proposed the construction of a new Catholic church on the north (Mexican) side of town. Gavito's daughter recalls that her father was firmly against such an idea. He believed that all Catholics in the town (regardless of race) should worship together. This is an interesting stance because, on one hand, it indicates his belief that Mexicans and Anglos should be integrated, and on the other hand, his position ignored the fact that Mexicans and Anglos were already separate within one church building.

The Gavitos were an exceptional case in the history of La Feria. There certainly were other Mexican families who were well established, landowning, and educated. The Gavitos, however, were the only family who seemed so fully accepted by and incorporated into Anglo society. They entered the town on the Anglo side of the tracks. They were both part of social clubs that were almost exclusively composed of Anglos. Mr. Gavito was elected to the city commission and appointed mayor by his Anglo peers. There are a number of possible reasons for the Gavitos' exceptional acceptance into Anglo society. As a light-skinned Mexican who was educated and economically stable, Mr. Gavito was already in a privileged position compared to other Mexican-origin people in town. When he and his wife moved to La Feria, he had already been managing the tomato cannery for one of the town's most prominent Anglo citizens, J. C. Dunn. Furthermore, the couple had enough capital to purchase their first home on the south side of the railroad tracks, on Main Street just beyond the business sector. Most likely, it was the convergence of all of these factors as well as delicate race maneuvering that enabled the Gavitos to be so fully integrated into the Anglo sector of town. Both spoke Spanish and regularly interacted with the Mexican community through Mr. Gavito's work at the cannery and Mrs. Gavito's charitable work. A number of their Mexican-origin contemporaries remember them as good people who helped other Mexican people in their times of need. However, another cross section of their Mexican contemporaries remember the Gavitos as an Anglo-identified couple who distanced themselves from the Mexican community, including its groups and organizations. No other Mexican-origin people who crossed racial boundaries in La Feria generated as much discussion or as many opinions in my interviews as did the Gavitos. They certainly seemed to occupy a borderlands social space between Anglos and Mexicans in town.

Mexican people experienced segregation in different and at times contradictory ways in the South Texas town of La Feria beginning in the middle and late 1940s. I argue that this period marked the emergence of an accommodated form of segregation whereby shifts in national and international policy and the increased economic stability of a cross section of Mexican-origin people enabled the blurring of certain racial boundaries. The Texas Good Neighbor Policy placed pressure on the state to lessen discrimination against Mexicans. In turn, Mexican civil rights organizations such as LULAC and the GI Forum used this diplomatic turn as an opportunity to push for increased civil rights for Mexican Americans in the state. While these efforts did not produce widespread systemic change, they did open the path for Mexicans in Texas to claim greater rights. Perhaps even more significant was the economic boom brought by World War II and the bracero program (when it arrived in Texas in 1947). Returning Mexican American veterans and Mexican merchants who benefited from bracero commerce became a small but visible middle class who were increasingly able to cross racial boundaries by purchasing homes on the south side of the tracks and establishing or expanding businesses, and their children were more likely to complete their K–12 education. However, even those Mexican people who were accepted/excepted experienced race-based discrimination, especially around racist attitudes about the Mexican body. Anglo people continued to maintain economic and political control of the city, and they only selectively incorporated Mexican people into their social and political spheres.

This chapter has focused on the experiences of those Mexican-origin people who had more rights than the overall Mexican community, those who were able to cross certain racial boundaries that had been established by de facto practices of segregation. The phenomenon of racial exceptionality that began in the late 1940s occurred in neighborhoods, in businesses, in the schools, and, to a limited degree, in politics. Most of the people who crossed racial boundaries were economically stable, were adept at navigating Anglo social spheres (e.g., they spoke English and were generally more educated), and/or had a white racial aspect. But as we have seen, even those exceptional cases were subject to racial discrimination. In this chapter, we have seen Frank Rodriguez's son refused a haircut at the Anglo-owned barbershop and Delia Martinez and her fellow Mexican American seniors at La Feria High School denied entrance into the local pool in Harlingen. Though Rodriguez and Martinez were allowed into certain Anglo circles, they were never absolved of their race. This becomes painfully clear when it comes to issues pertaining to the Mexican body—a haircut, a chance to swim in a pool alongside Anglo classmates. Both Rodriguez and Martinez know that the reason that they were denied access in these spheres was because they are Mexican and that there was something about the Mexican body that some Anglos found unacceptable. Despite their cultural capital, their racialized bodies limited their civil rights, such as access to public spaces and their human rights, such as dignity and respect.

The accommodated form of segregation that emerged during this time actually prolonged the period of Anglo dominance in La Feria, pushing the process of racial integration well into the 1980s. Because Anglos could point to Mexican "exceptions" to the rule of segregation, it was difficult to file legal actions that would mandate desegregation. In this way, the accommodated form of segregation served to maintain segregation well beyond landmark desegregation legislation. It would not be until Mexican-origin individuals and groups began to challenge prevailing racist ideologies and claim cultural citizenship rights that sustained and long-lasting racial integration would occur.

PART 2

PROCESSES OF RACIAL INTEGRATION

CHAPTER FIVE

TROUBLING THE CULTURE OF SCHOOL SEGREGATION: MEXICAN AMERICAN TEACHERS AND THE PATH TO DESEGREGATION

I think that all the superintendents [in the La Feria School District] were very nice. To us, they were nice. Maybe because we didn't cause any trouble. MARIA PAREDES

Maria Paredes was one of the first Mexican American teacher's aides employed by the La Feria School District in the 1960s. In the above excerpt from her oral history interview, she intimates that Anglo administrators treated her and other Mexican American women who worked as teachers and teacher's aides well during their time working at Sam Houston Elementary School. She reasons that the administration supported them because they were not "troublemakers." Paredes and her Mexican American coworkers were generally among a group of Mexican-origin people whose families attained higher levels of economic and cultural capital beginning in the late 1940s and 1950s. While this increased capital enabled them to cross certain racial boundaries in La Feria, Anglos continued to constrict their access to rights. In this chapter, I argue that Anglos in positions of power in the school district tried to capitalize on the accommodated structure of segregation to maintain their political and social dominance by making targeted hires of Mexican-origin people whom they believed to be conservative. However, the first Mexican American women who worked at Sam Houston as teachers and teacher's aides proved to be more than token hires. This chapter demonstrates that they did indeed trouble the culture of segregation by challenging its dominant ideologies, encouraging students to achieve beyond what was expected of them, establishing caring relationships, and facilitating culturally relevant curricula within the walls of a segregated Mexican school. These educators were an integral part of a larger political movement to dismantle educational discrimination and to challenge the culture of segregation in La Feria.

The 1960s marked the beginning of what I argue was the third and final stage of segregation in La Feria—racial integration. Between 1960 and 1970, the population of the town actually decreased from 3,010 to 2,642 people, most likely due to the settlement of migrant farmworkers outside of the region.[1] Nevertheless, I argue that a convergence of policy, grassroots direct political action, and the everyday actions of individual teachers led to the desegregation of Sam Houston Elementary School. The civil rights movement facilitated several federal and state programs aimed at increasing the quality of education for students of Mexican origin.[2] Most notably, Title I and Title III of the Elementary and Secondary Education Act of 1965 were instrumental in promoting educational equity, providing funds for low-income school districts, and establishing programs for economically disadvantaged students. One year later, Title I allowed for the employment of teacher's aides in the schools, as well as providing funds to hire more instructors and renovate libraries throughout the La Feria school system.[3] In 1967, Sam Houston Elementary School implemented Head Start, which is a federal program intended to provide educational, health, and social services to help communities meet the needs of low-income preschool children.[4] At its inception in La Feria, Head Start enrolled one hundred local Mexican children. Other legislative measures, such as the Economic Opportunity Act (1964), provided money for low-income students to attend college.[5] These pieces of legislation provided federally funded support for low-income Mexican-origin students in the public school system, giving them access to greater resources beginning in elementary school. Resources such as these would be vital to increasing students' access to education beyond their K–12 schooling. Furthermore, for the district to access the funding provided by these programs, it would have to reevaluate its discriminatory practices as well as segregation.

In addition to the implementation of federal and state policies promoting educational equity, the Chicano/a movement was gaining momentum throughout Texas, including in the Lower Rio Grande Valley. During the middle and latter part of the 1960s, a Mexican American third political party called La Raza Unida (LRU) emerged in Texas and elsewhere in the southwestern states (Acuña 1988; García 1990; Navarro 2000). LRU's statewide prominence manifested itself most visibly in Ramsey Muñiz's bid for governor of Texas in 1967, but the party also gained political visibility and strength in South Texas, taking control of prominent political offices in Crystal City and the Rio Grande Valley town of San Juan (García 1990; Navarro 2000). Also in the Valley, the Chicano activist group MAYO (Mexican American Youth Organization) had been successful in organizing a walkout at Edcouch-Elsa High School in 1968 to protest the no-Spanish rule (Barrera 2004; Richardson 1999). Perhaps even more significant was MAYO's establishment of El Colegio Jacinto Treviño in Mercedes, Texas, in 1970. The stated mission of El Colegio Jacinto Treviño was to "develop a Chicano with conscience and skills, [to give] the barrios a global view, [and] to provide positive answers to racism, exploitation, and oppression" (Montemayor n.d.). These political movements demonstrated that radical Chicano/a ideologies and activism were challenging and changing racism and discriminatory practices against Mexican-origin people in different parts of the Valley.

The political manifestations of La Raza Unida and MAYO all occurred within a twenty-five-mile radius of La Feria (the Colegio Jacinto Treviño was only six miles away), but no comparable political activities occurred within its school system. At the end of the 1960s, La Feria youth formed a local version of MAYO that they called the La Feria Youth Organization, and they recruited local students to participate in some of the protests occurring in other towns. These included garnering support for a farmworkers union as well as protests against the Vietnam War.[6] However, in the La Feria school system as a whole, practices of segregation proceeded as they had been for decades. The school district continued to manage its Mexican students by placing them in a segregated elementary school—Sam Houston Elementary School—for kindergarten through third grade and then moving them to Anglo schools on the south side of town, where they were tracked into segregated classrooms. At the high school, Mexican-origin students were severely underrepresented in student organizations and activities throughout the 1960s, indicating their continued social and academic marginalization at school.[7] Nevertheless, the culture of school segregation began to unravel when the district hired its first Mexican American teachers.

If we understand the public school system as an institution of citizen making (Orozco 2009; Tyack and Hansot 1981), the classroom can be a place of empowerment or disempowerment vis-à-vis the nation-state. It is often in the classroom where students learn American history—and their position in it—as well as what teachers expect them to achieve both in and outside of school. For this reason, I highlight the role of the first *mexicana* educators at Sam Houston Elementary School in challenging and changing the culture of segregation through their everyday pedagogical and caring practices in the classroom. I argue that these teachers and teacher's aides drew upon their cultural competency (e.g., behavioral and linguistic acumen) to establish new kinds of teacher-student relationships, including setting higher academic expectations for Mexican-origin students. In this way, Mexican teachers and teacher's aides practiced cultural citizenship, rejecting the notion that children had to assimilate to an Anglo norm to claim rights and envisioning "a more secure cultural and economic future for individuals, their families and their neighbors" (Coll 2010, 169). Their everyday actions opened a space for young Mexican students to imagine racial equality and integration—rights that were previously difficult to conceptualize within the entrenched ideology of segregation.

The project of school desegregation in La Feria required myriad efforts from various cross sections of the community. Scholars of this era tend to focus on the radical politics of the Chicano/a movement and their impact on structural discrimination. While the movement was significant in spurring policy changes and community practices through its often confrontational strategies, I argue that the Chicano/a movement alone did not facilitate a change in the culture of segregation. Indeed, in his monograph *Brown, Not White*, the historian Guadalupe San Miguel (2001) argues that in the Houston public school district, Mexican people had to reconcile generational differences as well as various political positionalities in order to facilitate a large-scale movement for desegregation. In the much smaller context of La Feria, desegregation occurred in similar fashion. Activists both inside and outside of La Feria introduced radical politics at the school and demanded desegregation, filing a lawsuit and a complaint to the U.S. Department of Health, Education, and Welfare (HEW).[8] Also during this time, two politically moderate Mexican American men ran and won positions on the local school board with the goal of enacting school policy that would better reflect the needs of Mexican-origin students.[9] While these political actions converged to facilitate increased racial equity in the La Feria School District, I argue that the first Mexican-origin teachers at Sam Houston Elementary School were particularly important because of the way they dismantled racist ideologies in their everyday practices of teaching. While the civil rights movement engendered policy changes, these women took upon themselves the everyday work of transforming the culture of segregation into claims for cultural citizenship.

INTRODUCING MEXICAN AMERICAN TEACHERS TO THE LA FERIA SCHOOL DISTRICT

In light of the grassroots Chicano/a movement that was growing in the Rio Grande Valley and national civil rights policy changes, it was clear that the Anglo administration of the La Feria School District would have to make changes to redistribute resources to the Mexican-origin community. I argue that the school administration strategically shifted its hiring practices to incorporate more Mexican American teachers, teacher's aides, and counselors in an attempt to maintain an accommodated form of segregation. It is clear that the district, specifically the superintendent of La Feria schools and the principal of Sam Houston Elementary School, facilitated targeted hires of

Mexican Americans whom they considered to be socially or politically conservative. Often these were children of the Mexican American middle class that emerged in the 1940s and 1950s in La Feria. Members of this small group of Mexican Americans were able to cross racial boundaries in business and education. They were English speaking and bicultural, and many had attended or were attending college. Generally, these Mexican Americans did not espouse the same kind of radical politics as Chicanos and Chicanas in other parts of the Rio Grande Valley during this time, and so for this reason Anglos viewed them as desirable candidates for integrating the teaching staff, especially at Sam Houston Elementary School.

In my interviews with the first Mexican American teachers, teacher's aides, and counselors in the district, many intimated that they did not apply for jobs in the La Feria School District; rather, the superintendent of schools personally recruited them for their positions. One candidate was approached at his family's place of business, two others received phone calls, and another was recruited at her university. The following testimony by Maria Paredes recounts how she came to work at Sam Houston Elementary School as a teacher's aide:

> In 1966 I started working as an aide for the school. They just called me. The reason they called me was because my two sisters were already teachers there. I was the only one, the only Hispanic they called. There were four of us—three Anglos and one Hispanic. I guess I was the first aide *mexicana*. That's when they started having aides. They had started earlier, but then they called me. And that principal was the one who told me, "You need to go to college." He was the one. He said, "You go to college and I'll give you a job."

Paredes was among the targeted hires at Sam Houston Elementary School. Her family owned two small businesses in the Mexican neighborhood, and two of her sisters were already employed at that school as teachers. Though she had not yet fulfilled the educational requirements for this position, Sterling Prince,[10] the principal of Sam Houston at that time, went so far as to encourage her to go to college so that he could hire her. Perhaps already being familiar with her sisters, Prince identified Paredes as a desirable employee for the school. Later in her narrative, Paredes recounts that the then superintendent, C. E. Vail, approached her to tell her, "I would like to try to give you a job as a teacher." Although at that time she had completed some college course work, she had still not completed the classes required to become a certified teacher. Nevertheless, the superintendent hired her to teach with an emergency credential.

Through Paredes's experience we can see the Anglo principal of Sam

Houston and the Anglo superintendent of La Feria School District making special efforts to recruit her, a Mexican American woman from a known middle-class family, for positions at Sam Houston Elementary School, first as a teacher's aide and then as a teacher. Upon reflection of this treatment, Paredes stated, "I think that all the superintendents were very nice. To us, they were nice. Maybe because we didn't cause any trouble." Implicitly aware of all of the political "trouble" that was brewing in and around the Valley, in this statement, Paredes positions herself (and her sisters) outside of the political fray. She accepts that Anglo administrators viewed her as someone who was politically conservative, but, as I will discuss later in this chapter, expectations did not prevent her from being critical of the kinds of interactions that she saw between Anglo teachers and Mexican students. Furthermore, Paredes understood herself to be someone who more fully understood and could respond to the cultural cues of her Mexican students, and this knowledge would become integral in her role as a bilingual education teacher.

The logic behind targeted hires of Mexican Americans extended beyond Sam Houston Elementary School. Frank Fernandez, who returned to La Feria after having earned his college degree out of the region, recalls how he vied for a job at La Feria High School: "After I got my master's, I went to a Mexican teacher I knew to ask if he knew of any openings in the system. He told me to cut my hair and put on a tie and go see Mr. Green[11] because he was looking for a conservative Mexican to fill the high school counselor position. I did just that, and Mr. Green gave me the job." A Mexican teacher impressed upon Fernandez that the district was looking for a "conservative Mexican" to hire for the high school counselor position and that he should dress accordingly. After doing so, Fernandez got the job. This account, coupled with Paredes's narrative, gives us insight into the prevailing hiring practices in the La Feria School District during the mid- to late 1960s. The civil rights movement and, perhaps more acutely, the activities of La Raza Unida in Texas and in the Valley were causing dramatic changes in the old social, economic, and political order. The Anglo-dominant school administration in La Feria hoped to circumvent any radical political upheaval by conducting targeted and strategic hires of Mexican Americans whom they viewed as conservative. They seemed to define conservatism by middle-class socioeconomic position in town and modes of dress and appearance. Though the first professional and paraprofessional Mexican American employees in the district did not perform radical Chicano/a identities, their everyday practices of teaching ultimately amounted to a dramatic shift in the racial ideology of segregation for students.

MEXICAN TEACHERS AT SAM HOUSTON ELEMENTARY SCHOOL

Because the first Mexican American teachers and teacher's aides to work for Sam Houston Elementary School were all women with at least some college education and had come from relatively middle-class families, they were generally more privileged than the greater local Mexican-origin community. They all spoke English fluently and were bicultural, having learned how to navigate Anglo and Mexican social spheres as part of their formal and informal education in the town. This type of positionality facilitated their entrance into the Anglo-dominant teaching force in La Feria; it also affected the ways that they experienced their first few years as teachers. This section will examine the experiences of Mexican American teachers and how they affected the culture of segregation within Sam Houston Elementary School. They came to understand the school culture through their relationships with Anglo teachers and administrators and by witnessing the relationships between Anglo teachers and Mexican students. They affected the school culture through their relationships with Mexican students, which often built upon their cultural knowledge and intimate understanding of the local Mexican community.

Accounts vary as to how Mexican American teachers were incorporated into the professional environment of Sam Houston Elementary School. Whereas some teachers recall smooth social relationships between Anglo and Mexican teachers, others recall racial tension. Emilia Treviño, a light-skinned Mexican American woman, came from a family of educators. Her mother and three of her sisters were all teachers. Treviño graduated from the University of Texas–Pan American (UTPA), a university located about thirty miles west of La Feria, and began teaching first grade at Sam Houston in 1967. She recalls:

> As far as I remember, I was the only Hispanic there. I had never had a Hispanic teacher in my whole life, so I didn't feel like it was strange to be around a bunch of Anglo teachers. I don't remember feeling like I was special. I sort of tuned myself to the way they talked and to the way they treated me. They were all very nice. They treated me real good. Of course, I was going around with Mr. Treviño at the time, and he was already a teacher at the high school. . . .
>
> I had Anglo aides, too. I had at least two or three—three Anglo aides. I started with one Anglo lady aide who had been there for a long time. She was very nice. . . . But like I tell you, I never remember having any problems because I was a Hispanic. They treated me just like the other teachers. And my principal, too. He was an Anglo man—Sterling Prince.

Treviño, who felt that she was attuned to the racial climate of the school, has generally positive memories about being one of the first Mexican American teachers at the segregated Mexican school in La Feria. She knew that teaching had historically been an Anglo-dominant profession and generally felt at ease around a majority of Anglo teachers. Furthermore, she remembers that these teachers and her principal, Sterling Prince, treated her well. She felt that they treated her "just like the other teachers."

Treviño's narrative stands in stark contrast to Mine Morales's recollections about being among the first Mexican American teachers at Sam Houston. Although Morales was also a daughter from an economically stable Mexican American family (her parents owned a small business), she followed a more circuitous route to becoming a teacher, attending a technical college, marrying, and then attending UT–Pan Am to earn her degree. Morales recalls that she initially applied for a job as a teacher's aide at Sam Houston, but that upon realizing she had already completed ninety college credits at Pan Am, both Principal Prince and Superintendent Vail encouraged her to apply for a job as a teacher. She did, and she was given the position. Despite her initial positive experience with the principal of the school, she was disappointed with her actual teaching assignment. Morales remembers:

Me dieron una class de retainees. Can you imagine? A full class! (laughs) And me, a first-time teacher. Poor kids! Comoquiera nos dieron los slowest ones. A las americanas les dieron los best kids y a nosotros nos dieron los slowest ones.

En ese entonces, en Sam Houston era puros mexicanos. Cuando empecé yo a trabajar éramos yo y las Quintana . . . como cuatro o cinco mexicanas. Y de allí, fueron entrando más. Pero como te digo, a nosotros nos dieron los slowest kids.

They gave me a class of retainees. Can you imagine? A full class! (laughs) And me, a first-time teacher. Poor kids! They always gave us the slowest ones. They gave the best kids to the Anglo teachers, and they gave us the slowest ones.

At that time Sam Houston was all Mexican students. When I started to work it was me and the Quintana sisters . . . maybe four or five Mexican women. And from there, more came in. But like I tell you, they gave us the slowest kids.

The support that Morales felt after the principal and superintendent encouraged her to apply for a position as a teacher at Sam Houston quickly waned when she received a teaching assignment that she felt ill equipped to handle. Not yet having received her degree or teaching certification, she felt bad for the class of children that she was assigned to teach. Morales quickly noticed, however, the school's de facto policy of assigning the "slowest kids," arguably the most challenging teaching assignments, to the Mexican American teachers at the school.

If Morales understood that there was an implicit kind of discrimination against Mexican teachers based on teaching assignments, her sense of the social relationships between Anglo and Mexican teachers was that they were likewise strained. She states as follows:

Yo me sentí humillada por las maestras americanas. Bueno quizás porque siempre he sido muy tímida. Pero te hacían menos porque eras mexicano.

En el lounge, we always used to be separate, pero eventually ya nos revolvíamos. Eso fue ya cuando no eran tantas [americanas]. Se tenía uno que revolver.

I was made to feel humiliated and inferior by the Anglo teachers. Maybe it's because I've always been shy. But they made you feel like you were "less" because you were Mexican.

We always used to be separate in the teachers' lounge, but eventually we started to hang out together. This was when there weren't as many Anglos. Then they had to hang out with us.

The tension that Morales, a darker-skinned Mexican American woman, sensed between Mexican and Anglo teachers is reminiscent of the tension that Mexicans had been experiencing in so-called integrated spaces in La Feria since the 1940s. This intangible feeling was a major aspect of the culture of segregation, especially as certain Mexican people began to cross racial boundaries. Many Mexican-origin people in La Feria did not experience racial discrimination until they crossed into an Anglo-dominated social sphere. Morales saw racial tension manifested in the way that Anglo and Mexican teachers would self-segregate in the lounge. She states that it was not until much later, when Mexicans outnumbered Anglos, that the latter "had to" mix with Mexican teachers.

Morales's narrative represents a dramatically different experience from that of Treviño. Unlike Treviño, Morales felt that the Anglo teachers treated her differently because she was Mexican. While Treviño remarked that the Anglo teachers were kind to her and that they treated her well, Morales felt that these same women would make her feel as if she were less than they were, causing her to feel "*humillada*." The fact that both women were fully bilingual and raised in economically stable Mexican families indicates that they entered Sam Houston with a similar amount of social and cultural capital. One possible explanation for the differential treatment of the two women could be that Treviño entered Sam Houston having already completed her college degree, whereas Morales began to work at the school when she had not quite finished hers. Furthermore, Treviño had an entire family of educators to serve as a support system for her, while the teaching profession was a completely new occupation for Morales and her family. I would also like to suggest that their differential treatment by the Anglo teachers at Sam Houston might have been the result of racialization. Treviño was light skinned and could pass for white; Morales had a darker complexion. Certainly skin color historically accounted for the way that Mexican-origin people experienced segregation in La Feria; it is likely that in this context of teacher integration, skin color and the spectrum along which Anglos racialized Mexicans continued to be a factor in these historically segregated contexts.

As a teacher's aide, Maria Paredes gained a strong sense of race relations between teachers and students at Sam Houston Elementary School because she worked with various teachers in their classrooms. She remembers:

> There was a lot of discrimination in those days se me hace a mí.[12] The teachers . . . not all of them . . . but I could tell that they did not like the *mexicanos*. See, at that time, they had all the *mexicanos* at Sam Houston school and all the *americanos* were at Lee.
>
> The teachers were nice; they were friendly, but you could tell . . . I don't know . . . with the kids. They never mistreated me; they were nice to me, but with the kids you could tell.

In terms of her professional relationships with the predominantly Anglo teaching staff, Paredes's experience is similar to Treviño's in that she did not feel discrimination directed toward her. However, she viewed the persistence of racial discrimination in two major ways. First, she is critical of the existence of two elementary schools—one for Anglo children and one for Mexicans—aware that this was in and of itself discriminatory. Second, and perhaps most acutely, she viewed discrimination in the way that Anglo teachers interacted with Mexican students. When Paredes observed that some Anglo teachers were less patient and more easily frustrated with Mexican children, she interpreted this behavior to mean that "they did not like the *mexicanos*."

Paredes's observations were reinforced through her conversations with students, who openly told her that they preferred the Mexican American teachers at Sam Houston. She recalls:

When I was an aide, the kids would be very open with me, especially the twelve- and thirteen-year-olds. They would say,

When I was an aide, the kids would be very open with me, especially the twelve- and thirteen-

> "No me gustan Mrs. X and Mrs. Y [Anglo teachers]; son bien malas con nosotros."
> I never saw it, but that's what they would tell me. And then they would say,
> "A Mrs. Alvarez sí la quiero."

> year-olds. They would say,
> "I don't like the Anglo teachers because they're mean to us" . . .
> And then they would say,
> "I love Mrs. Alvarez."

Not all of the Anglo teachers at Sam Houston treated students in a discriminatory fashion; indeed some Mexican American adults recall Anglo teachers who made a positive impact on them during their formative years. Nevertheless, there were enough negative interactions such that Paredes and the students with whom she interacted felt racial tension. Beyond the everyday actions of Anglo teachers, whatever they might have been, the fact that Sam Houston remained a segregated Mexican school provided a racialized context that perhaps engendered such feelings of discrimination and racial tension. The other significant aspect of this narrative is that Mexican students would then contrast their relationships with Anglo teachers to those with their Mexican teachers, stating, "I love Mrs. Alvarez." This affection is indicative of different kinds of teacher-student relationships between Mexican students and their Mexican American teachers. I will return to the subject of teacher-student relationships later in this chapter.

Paredes and Treviño understood that some of the tension between Anglo teachers and Mexican students was a lack of cultural understanding. Both women recounted the scenario in which Anglo teachers would become frustrated with the way that Mexican children responded to discipline. Paredes states:

> I remember cuando los regañaban, agachaban la mirada. De respeto, de vergüenza, agachaban la mirada.[13] But the Anglo teachers didn't understand that. They would grab the kids by the chin and say, "Look at me while I'm talking to you! Look at me!" They didn't understand that the kids were well mannered. No como ahora, when they'll look up at you and say, "What?! Whatever!" Those kids had respect.

Both women recount Anglo teachers' misinterpretation of the simple act of children casting their gaze downward as one of defiance and perhaps unwillingness to face up to their misdeeds. However, both *mexicana* teachers realized that, on the contrary, by looking downward while being scolded, Mexican children were expressing not only respect for their teacher but also shame at what they had done wrong. As cultural insiders, Mexican American teachers understood these children's reactions differently than their Anglo counterparts did. Education scholars have written about this type of cultural "mismatch," which Gándara and Contreras describe as a "lack of understanding of students' social and educational circumstances and inability to communicate with students and parents who do not have a good command of English" (2009, 107). In this case, the misunderstanding was cultural rather than linguistic. Mexican students' body language reflected remorse in a way that Anglo teachers did not understand; in effect, this body language made teachers even more upset. Garcia concludes that the difference between students' school and home culture "leads to an educationally harmful dissonance" (1996, 803). The cultural divide between Anglo teachers and Mexican students was a long-standing characteristic of the culture of school segregation.

Indeed, teacher-student relationships were a key factor in shaping the culture of school segregation in La Feria. In Paredes's narrative, she recounts how Mexican students would talk about Mexican teachers with affection, a marked contrast from how they would talk about certain Anglo teachers. The first Mexican American teachers at Sam Houston occupied a unique positionality and had different kinds of relationships with their students. Emilia Treviño recalls:

> Since I was teaching the little six-year-olds, I think they felt like they were at home with their mothers. It was their first year away from home, and so it was their first teacher who was a Hispanic. . . .
>
> If you're a little Hispanic child and you've never had any contact with an Anglo and then you see your teacher who's young—I was only twenty-three years old at the time—and also Hispanic and female, I think you feel like—[she exhales, as if sighing relief]. "My teacher is someone I can relate to." If I were a little Hispanic girl going to school for the first time and saw that my teacher was a Hispanic, I think that I would feel relieved. I think that's what a lot of Hispanic kids relate to—someone like their mother. And I hope that I made a difference.

Treviño recognizes the context of segregation as impacting the way that children related to their Anglo teachers. Because of residential segregation, children had very limited contact with Anglo people. She recognized that, as a young Mexican American woman, her presence might allay the anxieties of children who were entering school for the first time. In their study about effective African American teachers, Hudson and Holmes (1994) find that these teachers play many roles in the lives of African American students, including surrogate parent and role model. The fact that Treviño compares herself to "someone like their mother" indicates that she also saw her position as a teacher to be not only a purveyor of knowledge but also someone who would care for the students.

Caring teacher-student relationships were instrumental in changing the educational experience of Mexican children at Sam Houston Elementary School. While cultural familiarity was an important aspect of these relationships, so were the extra efforts that Mexican teachers expended for their students. Mine Morales remembers:

> We went out of our way to help the kids. Las americanas no. They just did what they had to do.
>
> Los mexicanos a veces pidieron que pusieran sus kids con las maestras americanas. I know some mexicanos who did that. But maybe they just wanted que their kids hablaran inglés bien. Pero ya después, no. Habían personas que nos pidieron a nosotros porque they would see that we went out of our way [to help Mexican children].

> We went out of our way to help the kids. The Anglo teachers didn't. They just did what they had to do.
>
> Sometimes Mexican parents would ask for their kids to be placed with the Anglo teachers . . . but maybe they just wanted for their kids to speak English well. But after a while they didn't request Anglo teachers anymore. There were people who would ask for us because they knew that we went out of our way [to help Mexican children].

Morales remembers that she and her fellow Mexican American teachers would go above and beyond to help their Mexican students. In her ethnography about a predominantly Latino high school in Houston, Texas, Valenzuela (1999) argues that students respond more positively to those teachers who develop authentically caring relationships with them. These types of relationships often extend beyond the classroom and involve coming to understand the student as well as his or her family and community background. Morales recalls that when she and her Mexican American colleagues first began to work at Sam Houston, some Mexican parents would request that their children be placed with Anglo teachers. However, upon realizing that Mexican teachers were putting in extra effort with the children, that they *cared*, these same parents began to request Mexican teachers. It was most likely empathy that led Mexican teachers to put in extra effort with their students at Sam Houston.[14] As I stated earlier, most of these teachers were privileged compared to the majority of the Mexican-origin population in La Feria in that they were more economically stable and had enough formal education to secure white-collar jobs. Furthermore, Anglo administrators and teachers (at least nominally) accepted them as professional coworkers. Nevertheless, because these women had been raised in segregated Mexican neighborhoods and had social and familial connections with the larger Mexican-origin community, they had a more intimate understanding of Mexican children's struggles with language, poverty, and discrimination.

I do not mean to suggest here that there were no caring Anglo teachers. My oral histories recall incidents when compassionate and kind Anglo teachers provided rich educational experiences for Mexican children. Nor do I mean to suggest that all Mexican teachers engendered caring relationships with their students. Garcia and Guerra (2004) caution that cultural disconnects, especially as informed by class status, occur with teachers of color, as well. The argument here is that, overall, Mexican teachers brought unique cultural resources to their work at Sam Houston. These resources often led to more positive relationships between Mexican students and teachers and also more positive schooling experiences. Among these more positive schooling experiences was a shift in teacher expectations for their Mexican students.

It has been well documented that teachers throughout the Southwest held low expectations for Mexican students during the first half of the twentieth century. Generally speaking, Anglo educators did not believe that Mexican children were capable of academic excellence, especially compared to Anglo children. The social distance between Anglo educators and Mexican students likely contributed to low expectations for Mexican students (Gándara & Contreras 2009, 104). Even among the progressive principal of Sam Houston Elementary School in the 1930s, the solution to the "Mexican problem" in education was the implementation of more vocational training programs (Armour 1932). This attitude demonstrates that even educators who were compassionate held low academic expectations of Mexican students (Garcia and Guerra 2004). Indeed several scholars have argued that the goal of Mexican education during the first half of the twentieth century was to reproduce a racialized labor market in which Mexicans were relegated to the lowest occupational sectors (Garcia 1989; González 1990).

One of the most important changes that the first *mexicana* educators brought to Sam Houston was holding higher expectations for their young Mexican students. Emilia Treviño recounts the way that she would teach and encourage her young students:

> I loved the children. I loved going to work in the morning. Not all children learn the same way. Sometimes you have to explain things in different ways for them to understand. To see their faces when they would say, "Oh! Now I know what they're talking about!" That was tremendous to me.
>
> I remember so clearly, I would tell them, you can grow up to be anything

> you want to as long as you put your mind and soul to it. You can be president! Even though they're only six! I would ask them, "Do you want to grow up like your parents, out in the fields, in the sun?" They're doing the best with what they have so you can do better. My mother always said, if you want a better life, education is the way to do it.

Treviño's narrative reveals not low expectations for her Mexican students, but a hope for their educational achievement. She recognizes the need to employ different strategies in the classroom because "not all children learn the same way." I would suggest here that Treviño's pedagogical approach was informed by her cultural understanding. In her article about African American teachers and students, Mitchell asserts that minority teachers "are particularly adept at motivating and engaging minority students because they often bring knowledge about students' backgrounds to the classroom that enhances students' educational experience" (1998, 104–105). Treviño's commitment to her students' education was fueled by her belief that they could grow up to achieve parity with anyone else in society; they could even become president. In this portion of the narrative, Treviño borders on becoming self-conscious about suggesting such possibilities for her students when they were just six years old. However, Gándara and Contreras cite a study that found that teachers' low assessments and expectations of first graders resulted in lower academic achievement in later years (2009, 104). In fact, several studies indicate that teacher expectations directly affect student performance (Gándara and Contreras 2009; Garcia 1996; Garcia and Guerra 2004). Treviño recognized her students' working-class backgrounds and valorized the hard work that their parents performed, telling her students that their parents' labor could be a stepping-stone for them to achieve even more. She believed that education was the means to achieve their dreams.

The way that Mexican American teachers experienced and affected the school culture of Sam Houston Elementary School was predicated upon their relationships at the school. After having been targeted as good hires for positions as teachers and teacher's aides by Anglo administrators, the women had mixed experiences with their colleagues. While some felt completely accepted, others sensed racial tension in their interactions with Anglo teachers. Racial tensions were more obvious when observing the ways that Anglo teachers interacted with Mexican students. While some of this tension was obviously the result of discriminatory attitudes cultivated in the context of racial segregation, it was also the result of the Anglo teachers' lack of cultural understanding. I have argued that Mexican teachers during this time were able to affect the school culture by building on their cultural assets of bilingualism and biculturalism, establishing caring relationships with Mexican students, and holding higher expectations of students. These everyday pedagogical actions reflect a sensibility of cultural citizenship in which teachers created a culturally accepting environment for students and envisioned for them a future as citizens who would be able to claim increased rights. Even though these actions occurred within the context of a segregated school, I argue that they were the foundation for a shift in the prevailing culture and ideology of segregation. The structure of school segregation would erode more fully in the early 1970s with the introduction of a federal lawsuit, the election of the first Mexican American school board members, and a complaint filed with the U.S. Department of Health, Education, and Welfare.

SCHOOL POLITICS AND THE DESEGREGATION OF SAM HOUSTON ELEMENTARY SCHOOL

In the middle of November in 1969, La Feria High School senior Lucinda Escalante[15] attended a regularly scheduled meeting of the La Feria Youth Organization. This group, composed mostly of Mexican American high school students from La Feria, was modeled after MAYO, which, as indicated earlier in this chapter, had organized a major student walkout at Edcouch-Elsa High School and was in the process of establishing an alternative, Chicano-centered high school in Mercedes, Texas. Among the items on the agenda for the La Feria Youth Organization's meeting that day were the plans for a Moratorium Day to protest U.S. involvement in the Vietnam War the following weekend in nearby McAllen.

Escalante arrived at school early the next morning and began to distribute flyers for the protest to her classmates. These flyers announced the date, time, and reason for the protest in Spanish on one side, and on the other included statistics of the disproportionately high numbers of Mexican Americans enlisted or drafted to serve in the war. A teacher approached Escalante and sent her to Principal Green's office. Green told Escalante that it was against school rules to distribute such flyers at school. When Escalante asked Principal Green what the school policy was, he informed her that it was *his* policy that flyers not be distributed. As a result of her actions, Escalante was suspended from school for three days, as were two other members of the La Feria Youth Organization who had also been passing out event flyers.[16]

With the support of her mother, Bertha, Escalante filed a lawsuit against the La Feria School District to protest her suspension. Filemon Vela, local counsel for the newly formed Mexican American Legal Defense and Education Fund (MALDEF), was her lawyer.[17] *Escalante v. La Feria Independent*

School District was ultimately decided in the Southern District Court of Texas by Reynaldo Garza, a native of Brownsville in the Rio Grande Valley and the country's first Mexican American federal district judge. Judge Garza ruled in August of 1970 that Escalante's suspension was unconstitutional, writing that "expression cannot be prohibited because of disagreement with or dislike for its contents."[18] He furthermore ordered that Escalante's record of the unconstitutional suspension be expunged. The ruling took La Feria school board members by surprise. At the school board meeting following the rendering of the court's decision, board members did not discuss the decision on the record, citing the need for time to read the court decision and "digest" its meaning.[19] This court decision demonstrated that the political empowerment of Mexican Americans in other parts of Texas was now beginning to have an impact in La Feria. Escalante had enlisted the help of an organization that was founded to litigate against Mexican American discrimination, and their case was heard by the first Mexican American federal judge. The shock that La Feria school board members experienced and their need to "digest" the meaning of this decision reflected their newfound realization that their carefully constructed racialized political structure was about to crumble.

The following spring, Tony Guevara[20] decided to run for a position on the La Feria school board. Born in La Feria, Guevara grew up on Villareal Street in *el pueblo mexicano*. He played football for La Feria High School, graduated in 1954, and joined the navy. After completing his military service in 1958, Guevara and his wife returned to La Feria, where he was involved in the local business community. Then, in 1971, he made a bid to secure a seat for himself on the local school board. Unlike Escalante and the high school members of the La Feria Youth Organization, Guevara was not involved in the Chicano/a movement. He viewed himself as a political moderate, someone who was "well accepted" by both Mexicans and Anglos in town. Guevara recalls that his decision to run for school board was motivated by his receiving anonymous letters that were allegedly written by Anglo members of the community:

> I got some anonymous letters, which were always on a positive side. These letters from Anglos telling me that it was about time that somebody did something. I don't know. I never found out who these people were, but I imagine they were feeling remorse for things that they had done. They felt bad about it. I did not get any letters condemning me or telling me not to run. I only got two letters and they were both positive.

Though Guevara's story runs parallel, in some ways, to the stories that the first Mexican American teachers and teacher's aides recount about being recruited to apply for their positions, he interprets the letters he received from Anglo community members as an appeal for change in the district precisely because of the history of discrimination against Mexicans. Indeed, given that some people recall instances of charitable and sympathetic Anglos in their school experiences, it is likely that some Anglos did not agree with the ideology and structure of segregation in La Feria. While these people may not have been willing to speak out publicly, they might have been amenable to offering their support anonymously through letters and with their votes. Guevara was indeed motivated to run for school board, and he won the open position, garnering more votes than either of the two Anglo candidates on the ballot and thus becoming the first Mexican American school board member in the history of La Feria.

Just two months after Guevara's election, two major events set in motion perhaps the final blow to segregation at Sam Houston Elementary School, both of which were discussed at length at the June 1971 school board meeting. That evening, Antonio Pérez and Pedro Guzmán,[21] representatives from the activist group Colonias del Valle, presented a list of grievances to the La Feria school board. Among other things, they were calling for the end of segregation at Sam Houston Elementary School. The discussion was cut short because of time constraints, so Pérez and Guzmán requested a special session where they could more fully engage with the board members about their complaints. The school board denied the group's request for a special meeting, stating that they would meet and discuss the issues again during their regularly scheduled time at the beginning of the following month.[22]

With those grievances tabled, the board proceeded to briefly discuss and approve the appointment of a citizen's advisory committee per federal policy. La Feria Independent School District had applied for state and federal aid under Title I, including the Migrant Education Program (MEP), because it served a large number of children from low-income families as well as children from migrant farmworker families. The district also applied for aid under Titles II and III, the latter of which provided aid to schools whose student body included English-language learners. One of the requirements to receive aid was to establish an advisory committee composed of parents of children who would benefit from the programs. The board appointed and approved an eight-member committee, all of whom were Mexican American women.[23] National civil rights legislation had a far-reaching impact. In the case of La Feria, the district applied for increased federal funding to support its population of low-income Mexican students. In order to comply with policy requirement, the administration had to include more Mexican-origin people in its decision-making processes.

The following month, when the school board convened again at their regularly scheduled meeting, there were over two hundred community members present. At this meeting, held in the high school auditorium, school board members attempted to address the grievances that had been brought to them the month before. Among the various issues discussed at this meeting were the lack of a PTA at Sam Houston, the failure to get students the benefits for which they were eligible through Title I, the retention of a particular student, and the fact that another student had not received a letter jacket in athletics. Though none of these complaints was an overt accusation of racial discrimination, racial tension was evident at the meeting. In the school board president's opening remarks, he emphasized, "We are all Americans, no matter the ancestry." At one point during the meeting, some members of the audience cheered when a Mr. J. A. Hawkins praised the work of the school board. The local newspaper reported that Hawkins "advocated putting a stop to 'this type of harassment,' or no good men would want to serve on the School Board" (*La Feria News*, July 8, 1971). The school board president's comments about all the people being "American" regardless of ancestry likely rang hollow in the ears of Mexican people who had experienced the structures and culture of segregation for so long. In characterizing the grievances as "harassment" that, if left unchecked, would dissuade "good men" from serving on the school board, Hawkins reflected the racist logic of segregation, rendering legitimate complaints made by Mexican people as illegitimate acts of aggression. Furthermore, his use of the phrase "good men" only thinly veiled his preference for Anglo men on the school board. Finally, a Mexican American community member that evening implored in Spanish, through a translator, that "all the people work together so all could see each other as brothers." Ultimately, the board presented justifications for the grievances presented and stated that it was working on solutions to some ongoing problems (ibid.).

Not satisfied with the outcome of that meeting, Guzmán told the local newspaper that he planned to register an official complaint against the La Feria School District with HEW (ibid.). In the spring of 1972, members of the La Feria school board were indeed grappling with how to respond to the HEW. By that time, another Mexican American, Sam Martinez, had been elected to the school board. Minutes from that time reveal meetings of the school board's policy committee to address issues presented by HEW representatives as well as a lawsuit filed against the school district. Martinez recalls that the board was hesitant to integrate Sam Houston, but realized that it would be necessary if they wanted to continue to receive federal funding.

Beginning in the 1972–1973 school year, eighteen years after *Brown v. Board of Education* ruled racially segregated schools unconstitutional, the La Feria

Independent School District changed its enrollment policy to desegregate its Mexican school. All La Feria children who were to be enrolled in kindergarten through second grade would enroll at Sam Houston, all third- and fourth-grade children would report to Lee School, fifth graders would be divided between Lee and Roosevelt Schools, and all sixth graders would meet at Roosevelt. Enrollment for the junior high and high schools was to remain the same (*La Feria News*, August 10, 1972).

An early Mexican American educator offers his memories of that time:

> Locally, I don't remember the ins and outs. There were charges brought against the school district of perpetuating educational guidelines that were detrimental to Hispanic children. There was tracking that always placed Anglos in the top two classes and then Sam Houston School for Mexican children. . . . In the early 1970s, most of that came to a screeching halt. I'm not sure if it was a lawsuit or if it was a threat of withholding federal funds. But the concept that all first graders had to go to Sam Houston, that was like—gasp—you mean my child has to go to school in the Mexican town?!?!

Norma Sánchez, who attended Sam Houston Elementary School herself in the late 1940s, remembers that her son was to begin his education as a kindergartener at Sam Houston in the fall of 1972. Aware of the new school policy, she arrived at the school curious to see how others in town would respond to the change. She recalls that Sam Houston was still primarily Mexican that year and for a few more years after that; rather than send their children to Sam Houston, many Anglo parents opted to send them to private elementary schools in nearby Harlingen. Over the years, however, more Anglo children began to enter kindergarten at Sam Houston and to proceed through a more racially integrated K–12 pipeline.

It is important to consider the way that federal and state policies influenced local educational policy. The Escalante federal lawsuit was a strong indication that the Anglo administration could no longer easily quash radical political viewpoints that differed from its own. Furthermore, the school administration in La Feria realized that if it wanted to continue to receive federal and state funding, it had to demonstrate that it was in compliance with nondiscrimination policies. These large-scale government policies led the school district to finally desegregate Sam Houston Elementary School, which had been the "Mexican School" for almost half of a century.

INTRODUCING BILINGUAL EDUCATION

The official policy mandate for desegregation was a decisive victory for the Mexican-origin community in La Feria. Changing the culture of segregation, however, involved the committed and sustained actions of groups and individuals; facilitating a culture of racial integration involved working to transform the way that people understood race and engaged in race relations in their everyday lives. Mexican American teachers and teacher's aides at Sam Houston Elementary School had already been enacting such a project with Mexican children. Within the context of segregation, they had facilitated positive teacher-student relationships, which were often based on linguistic and cultural understanding. Perhaps more important, they held higher expectations for their Mexican students, helping them to imagine themselves in positions that had previously only been held by Anglos. After the policy mandate for desegregation, *mexicana* teachers at Sam Houston were able to further such pedagogical endeavors through the introduction of bilingual education.

At the beginning of 1968, President Lyndon B. Johnson signed the Bilingual Education Act, Title VII of the Elementary and Secondary Education Act of 1968, into law. This legislation offered funding to those schools that wanted to develop bilingual education programs (Blanton 2004; San Miguel 1984). Bilingual education had been one of the major demands of Chicano and Chicana student activists across the Southwest. Generations of Mexican students had been subjected to English-only policies at their schools. While these policies were decidedly curricular in original intent, they were found to often extend outside the classroom, and students who were caught speaking Spanish faced punishment. At the heart of cries for bilingual education, however, was the desire for a new kind of education. Because school curricula had for so long enabled discrimination and the reproduction of a racially stratified class structure, bilingual and bicultural education programs were seen as a way by which racial integration might occur (Blanton 2004, 148). Indeed the education historian Carlos Blanton asserts that proponents of the Bilingual Education Act "conceived it not just as a linguistic tool in the education of non-English speakers but also as a mechanism of empowerment and integration for language minorities[,] mostly Hispanic, into the mainstream of American life" (2004, 124).

Bilingual education was implemented at Sam Houston Elementary School during the academic year beginning in 1974. Irma Dublin, a Valley native and *mexicana* teacher, was director of the district's bilingual education program for nearly thirty years. Her recollections of those first years of the program indicate her commitment to education, for both teachers and students. When she assumed the position as director, Dublin recalls that there were already about four Mexican American bilingual teachers. She reinforced to them that they needed to establish caring relationships with their students. In terms of her relationship with teachers at the time, she remembers: "I always give the teachers the benefit of the doubt. But I tell them, you're going to treat these kids as if they're your own. You want them to learn all that they can before they move to the next grade. If they were your kids, you'd want them to learn as much as they could. I was all about empowerment." In this part of her interview, Dublin's teaching philosophy echoes that of Isabel Treviño when she recalled that her students most likely saw her as a mother figure. Dublin encouraged her bilingual education teachers to embrace those roles and relationships and to use them to further their learning goals.

Dublin was a firm believer in bilingual education, in part because she knew that the program would have a positive impact on students. Though initially the Spanish language was used between teachers and students to foster positive relationships and cultural understanding, the bilingual education program had a very specific pedagogical imperative. Dublin knew that bilingual education would immediately impact student performance. She recalls:

> I told [the teachers], don't get disillusioned, because your kids are going to start doing better on the tests after we started the bilingual program. And they did. Because they understood! When they took the test, that TAAS test or the other one—I can't remember what it's called—they did better and better. . . . I tell you, I remember that first batch of kids that I had in bilingual when they graduated from high school. Every single kid that was in that program graduated from high school. And that speaks for itself.

A strong proponent of bilingual education from its early period, Dublin knew that the Mexican children would learn better in a setting where their native language was not just utilized but also built upon. She was proud of her students' improved test scores on the annual Texas state tests as well as the increased graduation rate of students who had participated in her bilingual education program. The outcome of the first generation of students who participated in the program in La Feria reflects the results of a 1966 Texas study that found that after intensive Spanish instruction, Mexican American children's attitudes toward themselves and toward school improved dramatically (Blanton 2004, 125–126). Bilingual education was effectively changing educational outcomes for Mexican-origin children in La Feria.

So strongly did Dublin believe in the effectiveness of bilingual education, she extended her everyday activism within the schools to the larger political realm, testifying before politicians in Austin and Washington, D.C.

> I had Title VII—for bilingual education—for twenty years. We had it from 1975 to 1995. I never asked for a lot of money. I never asked for more than $100,000. I went to Washington to testify for bilingual education. I also went to Austin because they wanted to do away with bilingual education. And really, ¿qué se hace que sepan en español o en inglés? [Who cares if they learn in Spanish or English?] The important thing is that they learn. . . . I was for the kids. If you're not for the kids, then you don't belong [in] teaching.

Dublin's testimony in favor of bilingual education programs was necessary because opponents of such programs continued to push for their elimination (Blanton 2004). Dublin's antiracist attitude is clearly noted when she states, "*¿Qué se hace que sepan en español o en inglés?* The important thing is that they learn." Defying attitudes that favored English above all else in the education of Mexican children, Dublin firmly refutes that sentiment, emphasizing that the truly important thing is that the children learn. An educator by training, she assumed the role of activist when confronted with the possibility that a program that so benefited her students might be cut—an occurrence more common among caring teachers of color than others(Galindo et al. 1996; Hudson and Holmes 1994). When Dublin finally resigned from teaching, it was because of changes the legislature wanted to enact, namely, either limiting the use of Spanish in bilingual classrooms or eliminating the classes altogether.

In 1974, nearly a decade after the school district began to hire Mexican American women to serve as teachers and teacher's aides at Sam Houston Elementary School, the cultural tide began to turn in the schools. As Dublin stated in her narrative, there was a critical mass of bilingual and bicultural teachers at the newly integrated Sam Houston. In addition to these teachers, according to a survey of high school yearbooks, La Feria High School employed a record six Mexican-origin teachers during the 1973–1974 school year, a dramatic increase from the one to two Mexican teachers that had been on staff over the previous decade. This demographic shift among teachers in the La Feria school system also coincided with nearby Texas A&I's implementation of the first master's degree program in bilingual and bicultural education in 1974 (*La Feria News*, May 2, 1974).

The demographic composition of the teaching staff was not the only change seen in the schools. At La Feria High School, Mexican students were more visible in the school's honor society and as student council members than they had been in previous decades. During the 1973–1974 school year, Mexican girls held three of the five positions as school cheerleaders for the first time in the history of La Feria High School, positions that throughout the school's history had been occupied almost exclusively by Anglo girls. Also in that same school year, a group of students formed the Pan American Student Forum, a club that celebrated and promoted Mexican culture. The most visible activity of this club was Mexican folkloric dancing, for which the students were recognized with various competitive awards. The graduation rate of Mexican students at the high school increased around this time, and the increased Mexican social and cultural presence at the high school not only reflected an increased enrollment of students but also represented their broader political and cultural empowerment during that era.

During the latter half of the 1960s, the culture of segregation in the La Feria School District began to unravel. Civil legislation rights intended to provide services for economically disadvantaged students enabled the district to hire its first Mexican-origin teachers and teacher's aides. While the Anglo district officials made a concerted effort to hire "conservative" Mexican Americans to fill these positions, these *mexicana* educators challenged racist ideologies of segregation in their everyday practices of teaching. Drawing on their cultural capital, these women cultivated caring relationships, challenged low expectations of Mexican students, and ultimately fought for and enacted linguistically relevant curricula. Through their everyday pedagogies, the first Mexican and Mexican American teachers opened a space for Mexican children to understand that their culture was not a liability that would preclude them from becoming fully enfranchised members of the community. These acts of cultural citizenship were instrumental in challenging and dismantling the culture of segregation in the La Feria School District.

The process of school desegregation in La Feria required the efforts of a cross section of the community, many members of which held different ideas about the best way to enact change. Civil rights legislation and the growing momentum of a Valley-wide Chicano-Chicana movement opened channels through which segregation could occur at the local level. Local and regional activists filed legal actions against the district for its restrictions on freedom of political speech and because of the continued racial segregation of Sam Houston Elementary School. Meanwhile, politically moderate Mexican Americans assumed positions on the school board, working to change policy by negotiating with Anglo school officials internally. While these were significant policy changes, I have argued that the everyday pedagogical work of

Mexican and Mexican American teachers was vital to dismantling the culture of segregation. Before Sam Houston Elementary School was desegregated, these educators had already laid an ideological foundation for racial integration. Their belief in and commitment to racial equality was critical to enacting racial integration in the La Feria School District.

CHAPTER SIX

SURGIENDO DE LA BASE: COMMUNITY MOVEMENT AND THE DESEGREGATION OF THE CATHOLIC CHURCH

Una de las primeras veces que yo fui a misa aquí a St. Francis . . . entramos yo y Javier y Alma y Noe. . . . Fuimos y nos sentamos en una banca. Y fue el Señor Harper . . . y le tocheó a Javier y quién sabe que le dijo; yo estaba allá (sentada en el otro lado). Y volteaba Javier y no más dijo que no.

Y le dije a Javier, "¿Qué te dijo?"

Dijo Javier, "Que no podemos sentarnos aquí . . . que tenemos que estar en el otro lado."

"Y después ¿qué? ¿Te dijo por qué?"

Y dijo "Que este lugar está apartado."

"Oh," le dijo, "¿Está reservado o qué?"

"No, no más es aparte."

"No, pues no," dijo Jaime, "No vamos a mover."

Y no nos movimos.[1] VICTORIA SANTOS

The preceding vignette represents a typical experience for Mexican Catholics in La Feria during the period of segregation throughout the first half of the twentieth century. In discussing incidents of racial separation within the context of the local Catholic church, several Mexican-origin community members recounted similar stories to me. Though Anglo and Mexican parishioners worshiped in the same sanctuary, Mexicans were relegated to a separate side of the church. Many Mexican people remember that an Anglo usher would make them feel "uncomfortable" if they were to sit on the "wrong" side of the church. After years of coerced separation, Mexican families came to accept the internal segregation of their church as common sense. For the Santos family, however, the separation did not make sense. After Mr. Santos completed his college degree at a university in the Midwest, he and his family returned to South Texas. Though Mr. and Mrs. Santos were originally from other Valley towns, upon returning to the region, they chose to make their home in La Feria because they thought it would be a good place to raise their young family. The year was 1979, and the town was again experiencing an increase in its population, from 2,642 people in 1970 to 3,495 people in 1980. At that historical moment, though Anglo ushers attempted to police the racial boundaries of the Catholic church, the Santos family, newcomers to La Feria, refused to move aside.

Despite the strides that had been made toward racial integration in the La Feria school system, St. Francis Xavier, the sole Catholic church in La Feria, remained entrenched in the culture and ideology of segregation in the late 1970s. Because it was not a governmental agency, the church remained outside of the purview of the government, which had taken the lead in pressuring federally funded institutions to desegregate. Consequently, the church in La Feria maintained a culture of segregation well beyond the time that public institutions had grown increasingly integrated. Anglo ushers continued to usher Mexican parishioners to a separate side of the church, and many Mexicans felt culturally marginalized within the parish. While actions such as those taken by the Santos family were significant in challenging racial segregation, in this chapter I argue that people of Mexican origin had to organize and engage in new practices in order to claim increased rights for themselves at St. Francis Xavier. For this reason, I focus on the creation of *comunidades de base*, small faith-based communities, and their revival of Mexican popular religion; the actions of these faith-based communities were instrumental to the racial integration of the church. By enacting *religión popular*, Mexicans created a culturally relevant religious space for themselves, and from the position of religious cultural empowerment, they began to challenge the Anglo hegemony that dominated their local Catholic church.

At the same time that the civil rights movement in the United States was gaining momentum and radically changing the political fabric of American society, the Catholic Church underwent a radical institutional shift that had a ripple effect in parishes worldwide. The meetings of the Roman Catholic Church's Second Vatican Council (1962–1965) marked dramatic changes in its policies, many of which were intended to more effectively meet the cultural and material needs of Catholics, in addition to fostering their spiritual development (Medina 2004). Shortly after Vatican II, in 1968, the Latin American Conference of Bishops met and developed the concept of liberation theology, which identified institutional oppression as "structural sin" and encouraged the poor to engage in social struggle for their own liberation from such sin (Medina 2004). Building on these changes and social movements internally and outside of the church, Chicano priests and Chicana nuns in Texas served communities by engaging in political activism as well as by building a church that was more culturally relevant to Mexican-origin parishioners (Martinez 2005; Medina 2004). These shifts in doctrine, theology, and service challenged the discrimination that Mexicans continued to face in Texas.

The process of dismantling the culture of segregation in the local Catholic church occurred mostly in the 1980s, long after what is typically considered the period of segregation. That practices of segregation endured so long reflects not only the deep entrenchment of the culture of segregation but also the effectiveness of the "accommodated" form of segregation that allowed for the selective incorporation of Mexican people into Anglo spheres of influence. This selective incorporation, which began in the late 1940s, served to maintain Anglo racial hegemony well beyond the 1960s and 1970s and required people to utilize a range of tactics to facilitate racial integration and cultural inclusion. In this chapter, I will demonstrate that in the case of the Catholic church in La Feria, priests, Spanish-speaking nuns, and Mexican laity worked in different ways to create a church that was fundamentally racially and culturally integrated. In this discussion, I highlight the activities of *comunidades de base*, which forged a sense of community for Mexican Catholics and revived popular religious practices. Through their regular meetings and their cultural performances, members of the *comunidades de base* served to expand notions of belonging in La Feria's Catholic Church.

Previously, much of the struggle for racial integration for Mexican people in La Feria was centered on the ability to claim civil rights, rights that should have been legally guaranteed. The struggle for full incorporation into the local Catholic church, however, was a struggle of cultural citizenship. If, as scholars of cultural citizenship suggest, citizenship entails a discussion and struggle over who truly belongs to a community and how they belong, the actions of the *comunidades de base* in La Feria fell within the purview of broadening the scope of citizenship to include working-class Mexican-origin people. With the establishment of *comunidades de base*, Mexican Catholics began to revive the popular religious practices that Anglo Catholics had forbidden in the parish during the first stage of segregation. As anthropologist Richard Flores has argued, "Collective forms of cultural practice assert social rights, and . . . social rights can lead to an expanded view of communal action in the civil sphere" (Flores 1997, 150). The actions of *comunidades de base* and the revival of popular religious practices, which began in individuals' homes in Mexican neighborhoods, empowered Mexican people to claim space for themselves within their local parish. Buttressed by institutional change and grassroots social movements, Mexican and Mexican American Catholics in La Feria propelled a dramatic shift toward racial integration and meaningful inclusion in St. Francis Xavier.

SOCIAL JUSTICE MINISTRIES IN THE SOUTHWEST, 1960S AND 1970S

The latter part of the 1960s and the 1970s were a critical time period for Mexican Americans in the United States. The Chicano/a movement was gaining momentum throughout the Southwest, fueling many political projects, from school reform to farmworker rights (Medina 2004; Treviño 2006). It was becoming apparent that Chicanos/as were increasingly emboldened to challenge their subjugated positions in society. At the same time, the Catholic Church was undergoing dramatic changes. The meetings of the Second Vatican Council transformed the way that Catholic churches around the world operated on a daily basis. Perhaps one of the most significant changes was the Council's recognition that "God speaks through cultures" (Medina 2004, 19). This new institutional stance opened space for Chicano/a activists to work from within the Catholic Church to facilitate social change. The intersection of Chicano/a activism and the meetings of the Second Vatican Council led to the establishment of PADRES and Las Hermanas in Texas, organizations of Chicano/a priests and nuns, respectively, that used their faith as a basis by which to conceptualize and promote social justice for Mexican Americans.

As early as the 1940s, the Catholic Church began to institutionalize its charity work with Mexican and Mexican American communities in the Southwest. In 1945 the Bishops' Committee for the Spanish Speaking was organized with progressive archbishop Robert E. Lucey at the helm. Under Archbishop Lucey's leadership, the committee constructed medical clinics, settlement houses, and catechetical centers in Los Angeles, Santa Fe, Denver, and San Antonio (Medina 2004, 17). Furthermore, the committee was responsible for establishing child-care centers, promoting youth work and public housing, and working with cities to bring services to Mexican neighborhoods (Treviño 2006, 172). The historian Roberto Treviño (2006) credits the archbishop with ushering in the first era of Catholic social action, including involvement in farmworker advocacy. In general, the position of the Catholic Church by the 1960s was that parish societies, political gatherings, and civic organizations—the laity—should take it upon themselves to address social issues (Treviño 2006). Beyond its charitable actions, the institution of the Church in the United States did not actively engage in political issues, such as the civil rights movement. There were, however, individual priests and nuns who became politically involved in the Mexican American community to enact radical structural change. Their activist stance marked a departure from the service and charity approach that the Church had historically taken (Martinez 2005; Medina 2004; Treviño 2006).

In 1966, one such activist priest from Houston, Father Antonio Gonzales, along with the Reverend James Novarro and the labor organizer Eugene Nelson, led a march of farmworkers from the Rio Grande Valley to Austin. Initially intended as a march from Starr County to the San Juan shrine in the Rio Grande Valley to bring attention to the plight of striking farmworkers, the march gained momentum and significance, drawing attention to the abysmal working conditions of Mexican laborers and demanding a minimum-wage law in Texas. The marchers were met with hundreds of supporters along the path from the Valley to Austin in the middle of a brutal South Texas summer. The protesters finally reached the Texas State Capitol on Labor Day, where ten thousand supporters joined them. A former farmworker himself, Gonzales was a key organizer of the successful march and protest. Though the demands of the protesters were not immediately met, the march served to raise political and ethnic consciousness among Mexican American Catholics in Texas (Treviño 2006).

Over the next few years, activist priests and nuns established organizations that solidified and provided a conduit for their social justice missions. In October of 1969, a group of about fifty priests converged in San Antonio and formed Padres Asociados para Derechos Religiosos, Educativos y Sociales (PADRES), a national activist priests' organization. These priests came together because of their common desire for social justice and also at the behest of the Mexican American Catholic laity. Treviño states, "These Chicano clerics vowed to take 'the cry of our people' to the hierarchy of the church, and to involve the institution in *el movimiento*" (2006, 182). From its inception, PADRES made a clear investment in mobilizing the institution of the Catholic Church to work for social justice in the Mexican community.[2] The following year, Gloria Gallardo and Gregoria Ortega, both activist nuns, founded Las Hermanas. Through this organization, Gallardo and Ortega "reinterpret[ed] the traditional role of a nun" (Treviño 2006, 193). Like the priests active in PADRES, Las Hermanas was invested in mobilizing the Mexican American community to enact social change. Las Hermanas dedicated themselves to raising awareness of community needs, promoting social change, and increasing Latino/a leadership, while lobbying the Church to support its organizational goals (Flores n.d.; Medina 2004; Treviño 2006).

PADRES and Las Hermanas exerted considerable influence in their roles as Catholic activist groups. Together, these two organizations founded the

Mexican American Cultural Center (MACC) in San Antonio in 1971 (Cadena 1987; Medina 2004). MACC had two main goals. The first was to train religious leaders to work in Mexican American communities. To this end, it played an important role in developing religious materials for U.S. Latinos while simultaneously helping non-Latinos to better serve local Spanish-speaking populations (Cadena 1987). The center's second goal was to empower the poor so that they could "control and direct their own destinies" (Medina 2004, 70). MACC was directly influenced by the guiding principles of Latin American liberation theology, with its emphasis on activism, justice, and liberation. Inspired by the Latin American Conference of Bishops in 1968, liberation theology reflected a religious ideology that "moved beyond a concern for personal sin and identified the reality of structural sin or institutionalized systems of oppression" (Medina 2004, 26–27). Liberation from such structural sin would originate from the poor themselves "acting as agents of social transformation or subjects of their own history" (ibid.). Under this theology, Chicano/a religious interpreted social struggle as a kind of Christian discipleship. Recognizing that these principles would benefit the Mexican poor in Texas, Cadena argues that activist clerics in Texas were attempting to forge a U.S. version of liberation theology (1987).[3] Indeed, MACC connected the religious in Texas to Latin American liberation theologians who would teach courses and attend meetings at the center (ibid.).

SURGIENDO DE LA BASE

In May 1978 Father Francisco Aguirre, the first Hispanic priest at St. Francis Xavier, wrote a letter to Sister Maria Elena Ortiz, the mother superior of the Congregation of Franciscan Eucharistic Missionaries. Father Aguirre's letter requested that two nuns be sent to La Feria to help with the religious education of La Feria's Mexican Catholic community. During this time, in the whole of the United States there was only one house of Mexican-origin sisters, and this house was, perhaps not coincidentally, located in San Antonio, Texas. Because the sisters had been considering extending their ministry, they decided to visit La Feria to familiarize themselves with the town, its people, and the work they could perform there. A written narrative of the nuns' experiences in La Feria explains their decision to send two sisters to minister in La Feria:

Conociendo la realidad y la urgente necesidad de evangelizar en especial a los inmigrantes de habla	[They] saw the reality and the urgent need to evangelize, especially to Spanish-speaking immigrants, of whom there are

> española que son mayoría [*sic*], se encontraron familias que no hablan el inglés, otras que lo hablan poco, cosa común aquí en el Valle. (Pineda 1991)

> many. They found families who did not speak English and others who spoke only a limited amount [of English], a common characteristic of the [population] in the [Rio Grande] Valley. (Pineda 1991)

After their brief sojourn in La Feria, the nuns returned to San Antonio to make arrangements to establish residence in town. In August of that same year, Sister Margarita Vargas and Sister Maria de los Angeles Enriquez[4] arrived in La Feria, occupying a house designated for them near the parish. It was decided that Sister Margarita would assume the responsibility of organizing and directing CCD (Catholic Christian Doctrine) classes, and Sister Angeles would dedicate herself to *la pastoral*.

Vocation dedicated to *la pastoral* meant becoming acquainted with the needs of the Mexican-origin community. Sister Angeles walked through the Mexican neighborhoods in town, knocking on doors and familiarizing herself with the people and their concerns. Sister Rosa Romero, a nun who worked alongside Sister Angeles in La Feria, narrated to me the work the latter performed in the late 1970s and the early 1980s:

> [La Hna. Angeles] se encargaba de visitar casas en los barrios para ver lo que necesitaba la gente. Y la gente expresaba que quería conocer su fe. Compartían sus vidas con ella—todo lo social y religioso. Tenían muchas preguntas. Después del Segundo Congreso del Vaticano, sucedieron muchos cambios en la iglesia. La gente no entendía los cambios.

> Sister Angeles was in charge of visiting houses in [Mexican] neighborhoods to see what people needed. And people expressed to her that they wanted to learn more about their faith. They shared their lives with her—both social and religious aspects. They had a lot of questions. After Vatican II, there were a lot of changes in the Church. People didn't understand those changes.

Sister Angeles arrived in La Feria at an opportune moment to answer the questions that the Spanish-speaking members of the community had about their faith. Because the Second Vatican Council had enacted several changes that affected local parishes, parishioners wanted to more deeply understand what these changes meant. Though Sister Angeles's narrative focuses on questions of faith, one can imagine that as Mexican people shared "their lives" with Sister Angeles, including "*todo lo social*," issues of poverty and discrimination would also be a major part of their stories. Sister Angeles's service to the Mexican-origin community had to address both the spiritual and social needs of the people.

Individual meetings with Sister Angeles soon converted into small home groups, where people could learn more about the practice of their faith and build a stronger community that provided mutual aid to each of its members. Sister Rosa explains:

> Les dieron la idea—¿por qué no formamos pequeños grupos de reflexión bíblica? ¿Cómo estoy viviendo el evangélico que me pide a mí las lecturas de domingo? Entonces invitaban a sus vecinos, amistades de sus vecindades para esos grupos.

> They got the idea—why don't we form small groups for biblical reflection? How am I living the teachings that the scriptures ask of me on Sundays? So they invited their neighbors and friends of their neighbors for these groups.

These small home groups were organized in Mexican neighborhoods and usually hosted about ten people once a week. Each week, a different family would take their turn to host the group. In these neighborhoods, people would organize days and times to meet, according to their schedules.

In the spring of 1984, Sister Ana Maria de la Torre[5] arrived in La Feria from San Antonio, where she had received training at MACC with Father Marins (Pineda 1991). She reorganized the existing groups and formed new ones, introducing the themes and techniques of *comunidades de base*. *Comunidades de base* originally emerged in parts of Latin America where there was a scarcity of priests. Led by the laity, these small groups "became the seeds of the base community movement that fostered a radical Christian faith critical of systems of oppression" (Medina 2004, 27). This lay movement emerged in the U.S. Catholic Church in the 1970s. Gilbert R. Cadena (1987) describes *comunidades de base* as "basic Christian communities" and as groups that "study the Bible and link the words of scripture to the conditions in which the participants live. The *comunidades de base* bring together fellowship and engage in consciousness-raising and community action" (8). In an interview, Sister Clara Garcia, another nun who ministered to La Feria's Spanish-speaking population in the 1980s, maintains that, unlike the *comunidades de base* prevalent in Latin America, U.S. *comunidades de base* were related to charismatic rather than liberation theology movements within the Catholic Church. Though its emphasis might have been on creating a charismatic Mexican Catholic community, self-determination and social justice did appear as these groups came together to study various *temas*, or "themes."

Members of La Feria's *comunidades de base* recognize that perhaps the most characteristic difference between a *comunidad de base* and a bible study was the *tema*. Antonio Tenorio, an immigrant to La Feria and a longtime member of the *comunidades*, recounts, "*El tema ya los transportaba a hacer comunidades de base y no grupo de biblia. Aunque usaba la biblia, ¿verdad? Pero había que llamarle la comunidad que sea de base*."[6] *Comunidades de base* focused on *temas* that would relate the scripture to their lives. According to Tenorio, *temas* would include issues of alcoholism, spousal abuse, and discrimination. The theme would guide members to discuss how to address social problems in their own lives rather than to accept such problems as a cross to bear. In terms of political activism, Tenorio recalls *temas* discussing farmworker activist César Chávez, as well as those that encouraged members of the *comunidades de base* to participate in local, state, and national elections. These *temas* reveal that the *comunidades de base* sought to improve social relations within families and communities. By addressing issues of discrimination and recognizing the work of César Chávez, they also promoted a level of political involvement and social justice.[7]

As the *comunidades de base* began to grow in La Feria, so did a particular community identity among Mexican people. In his article about a Mexican Catholic performance community, Richard Flores argues that such performances are about the "formation of a community through a religious idiom, not about religious formation" (1997, 148). Within the context of La Feria's *comunidades de base*, I would argue that community formation and religious formation developed hand in hand. Mr. and Mrs. Zamarripa, longtime parishioners at St. Francis Xavier and active members of the *comunidades de base*, recount to me how weekly meetings of the *comunidades de base* created a strong sense of unity among members of the group.

Mr. Z: Lo mejor que tuvo todo [fue que] . . . tuvimos una comunidad de base aquí en esta casa, la siguiente semana en otra casa, la siguiente en otra casa, y en otra casa. Entonces nos unimos todos. En Arroyo Heights. En Rancho Solis. Comunidades de base en muchas partes.

Mrs. Z: Y de allí nos uníamos y hacíamos una comida para convivir todos. No era para otra cosa. Si nada más era para convivir.

Mr. Z: The best thing of all was that we would have a *comunidad de base* meeting here in this house, the next week in another house, and in another house. Then we became closer. In Arroyo Heights. In Rancho Solis. There were *comunidades de base* all over.

Mrs. Z: And from there we became close and we would have meals so that we could come together. Just so that we could be together.

Mr. Z: Allí sí había mucha unidad.	Mr. Z: We were very united.
Mrs. Z: Entonces nos fuimos uniendo más y más. La comunidad de base tuvo que ver con ésta.	Mrs. Z: Then we became more and more united. The *comunidades de base* had to do with that.
Mr. Z: Y compartíamos y de allí a otros y a otros . . .	Mr. Z: We would share with other people.
Mrs. Z: Y así fue como fuimos creciendo.	Mrs. Z: And that was how we began to grow.

Mr. Zamarripa's narrative asserts that the best thing that the *comunidades de base* had to offer was that members would meet in different people's houses every week, in Mexican neighborhoods in town and in outlying rural communities. For Mr. and Mrs. Zamarripa, the intimacy of people's homes, where they would share food and music, was instrumental in getting to know the members of the group more deeply and in becoming involved in each other's lives. As their enthusiasm for the *comunidades de base* grew, so did their desire to expand and include more members. The increased development of the *comunidades* was directly related to their providing a space of belonging for Mexican-origin Catholics in La Feria and its surrounding rural neighborhoods.

Providing a space of cultural and spiritual belonging for Mexican-origin Catholics was a catalyst for the development of economic and social mutual aid. Flores asserts the importance of cultural performances, that is, "those enactments and practices that forge a sense of community and belonging, lead to renewed experiences of identity, and provide a social space for the formation of collective practice and its concomitant forms of power" (1997, 125). In the case of La Feria's *comunidades de base*, collective practice included the redistribution of economic, social, and spiritual resources. According to Tenorio, members of the *comunidades de base* studied the bible through certain *temas*, but were also able to learn about the particular social and economic circumstances of their fellow community members. They pooled resources to help members of the group who needed them. If people who attended meetings were struggling with their spouses or their children, the group would support them in whatever way they could. If others did not have money to pay utility bills, the group would take a small collection. If someone were to pass away, the group would pay for flowers and take food to the grieving family. They would pray for each other's needs and provide as much social and material support as possible. This informal system of mutual support paralleled the activities of Mexican mutual-aid societies in the 1930s (Orozco 2009; Zamora 1993). Mutual aid continued to be necessary because of the ongoing economic and political disenfranchisement of the Mexican community.

La Feria's *comunidades de base* were the conduit for both religious formation and community formation. While the formal content of their meetings fortified members' understandings of the role of faith in their everyday lives, the practice of the meetings and the development of relationships in those spaces led to a strong sense of community identity. As Mr. Zamarripa stated, "*Nos fuimos uniendo más y más*." We became more and more united. Community building and identity, in this case, were achieved through the development of a social network of mutual support and concern. As Flores indicates, community identity holds the potential for its members to engage in collective action (1997, 150). Members of the *comunidades de base* began such action with the redistribution of resources to meet the economic, social, and spiritual needs of its members. As they began to grow, the *comunidades de base* identified cultural and racial inclusion as another need that had yet to be met.

After a long period of segregation and discrimination, one of the most obvious needs of the Mexican-origin people in La Feria was to become more fully integrated into the church. Since the first decades of the twentieth century, local Mexican Catholics had been marginalized within St. Francis Xavier, unable to practice their culturally specific religious customs, and literally relegated to a separate side of the church. Sister Angeles's pastoral ministry in the late 1970s marked the beginning of the Church reaching out to the Mexican Catholic community in La Feria. Mexican Catholics who were involved in the *comunidades de base* saw their actions in the group as furthering the church's mission in the community. Mr. Zamarripa recalls: "*No no más hacíamos en la pura iglesia, sino en las casas. Salía la gente. Hazte cuenta que la iglesia se le hacía para afuera. A las casas.*" [We weren't just doing this in the church, but in people's homes. People would come out. Imagine the church going outside. To people's homes.] It is clear from his statement that Mr. Zamarripa believed himself and other members of the *comunidades de base* to be "the church." They were the church, and they were serving the needs of the Mexican people. In this way, the *comunidades de base* created space where the institution of the Church and the people of the church were reconciled with each other. Establishing a strong Mexican Catholic community identity and attaining a sense of belonging to the Church led to a deeper cultural engagement with the St. Francis Xavier parish community. The *comunidades de base* decided to reinvigorate Mexican popular religious practices.

In the 1930s and 1940s, Anglo Catholics in La Feria shamed Mexican Catholics in La Feria out of their culturally specific religious practices at St. Francis Xavier. Treviño refers to this way of practicing one's faith as "ethno-Catholicism" (2006, 4). While the institution of the Church did not always accept Mexican popular religious practices, for the Mexican faithful, these practices defined what it meant to be Catholic (Espinosa 2008; Treviño 2006). Treviño continues, "Mexicans in the United States have had an interactive relationship with the institutional church, one that at different historical moments has been characterized by varying degrees of resistance and accommodation" (2006, 5). Mexican Catholicism, as with many ethnic Catholicisms, engaged in religious cultural practices that were not always sanctioned by the Church. In the case of La Feria, however, it was Anglo Catholic parishioners who defined the cultural position of the Church, and that position had rejected Mexican people's popular religious practices.

Although the Mexican Catholics in La Feria were able to practice their faith by attending Mass at St. Francis Xavier on Sundays, people missed the Mexican Catholic celebrations they had practiced in Mexico and in Texas before Anglo settlement. Sister Rosa explains:

Éso se llama religiosidad popular. La cultura mexicana es muy rica. Los miembros de las comunidades de base son inmigrantes e hijos de inmigrantes. Cuando empezamos ya no celebraban la virgen de Guadalupe, las posadas. La gente decía, nuestros hijos no saben de nuestra cultura. Aquí no tenemos nada. Era el deseo de celebrar lo que ya no se celebraba. Para ellos era su deseo. Les daba tristeza que pasaran [los días festivos] como cualquier día. Querían revivar su cultura.

It's called popular religion. Mexican culture is very rich. The members of the *comunidades de base* are immigrants and children of immigrants. When we began, they no longer celebrated la Virgen de Guadalupe, Las Posadas. . . . People would tell us, our children don't know about our culture. We seem to have nothing here. The desire was to celebrate what was no longer celebrated. It was their desire. It made them sad that their traditional days of festivity would pass like any other day. They wanted to revive their culture.

The sense of loss that Mexican immigrants expressed to the nuns was both cultural and religious in nature; they could still be Catholics, but not in the way that they had once been. Furthermore, within the walls of the church they were unable to pass on their culturally specific faith practices to their children. Mexican-origin people told the nuns that here in the United States they felt they had nothing. "Nothing" most likely referred to economic as well as political and social clout. Perhaps more painful, however, was the sense that they were also losing their culture. In order to help the Mexican Catholics of La Feria regain some of what they felt they had lost, the nuns and the members of the *comunidades de base* began to take charge of reviving some of these Mexican Catholic celebrations. Celebrations for la Virgen de Guadalupe, Las

Posadas, and las vías cruces began to take root in La Feria. One of the largest of these was the annual celebration of Las Posadas.

The celebration of Las Posadas is a reenactment of the biblical journey Joseph and Mary make in Bethlehem looking for shelter the night of Jesus's birth. It recounts how the couple is denied a place to stay at various houses. Finally, they find one person willing to open their doors to them. Mr. Tenorio explains how the Posadas transpire in La Feria:

Tienen dos niños que van a representar a José y a María.

Entonces nosotros ya traemos hechos los cantitos, las lecturas bíblicas y esa noche comenzamos en una casa a pedir posada. . . .

Se junta de cien, ciento y pico de gente esa noche. Bajan según el tiempo a cuarenta o treinta.

Cantamos de casa en casa, vamos cantando o rezando. Y pedimos posada en la primera casa, luego en la segunda y nos responden que no hay posada. Vámonos a la otra. . . .

José y María siguen caminando en frente. . . . Lleva la lamparita prendida que lleva José cargando, la virgen la lleva pescada siempre con él. . . . Toda la gente espera en la última casa porque saben que allí sí les van a abrir y saben que allí ya dan la entrada a los peregrinos.

Hay muchos niños. Ése es lo que el padre le gusta mucho ver. Muchos niños. Porque . . . cuando ya terminamos en la última casa, la monjita que está con nosotros les da muchas explicaciones a los niños . . . y contesta sus preguntas también. . . .

Es parte de la celebración. Cuando viene la piñata y viene todo el convivio allí. . . .

There are two children who represent Joseph and Mary.

At that point, we have our songs and our Bible passages ready. And that night we begin at one house to ask for posada (a place to stay).

A hundred or more people will gather that night. The number of people will go down according to the day to forty or thirty.

We sing going from house to house. We sing and pray. And we ask for posada (a place to stay) at the first house, then the second and they respond that they will not give us posada. Then we go to another house.

Joseph and Mary continue to walk in front. Joseph carries a small lamp, the Virgin always by his side. Everyone waits at the last house because they know that there they will open the doors to us. They know that they will let the pilgrims enter.

There are a lot of children. That's what the priest likes to see. A lot of children. Because when we arrive at the last house, the nun who is with us will explain everything to the children. She answers their questions.

It's all part of the celebration. Then there is a piñata and time to enjoy each other's company.

Siempre [hay] comida tradicional mexicana. Tamales. . . . Chocolate cuando da el friazo. Nosotros no cancelamos posada. Si está helando o no está helando.

Las ocho posadas están en comunidades de base. La novena la hacemos allí en la iglesia. En el salón. Allí reunimos a todas las comunidades y más gente aparte todavía. . . . Allí ya damos regalos para los niños, jueguetitos.

[Todos llevan algo]. La gente toda coopera para celebrar.

There is always traditional Mexican food. Tamales. Mexican hot chocolate when it gets very cold. We never cancel the Posadas. Even if it's freezing.

The first eight days of posadas are in the *comunidades de base*. The ninth is at the church hall. We all get together there—the *comunidades de base* and people from outside of the *comunidades de base*. There we give gifts to children, little toys.

Everyone takes something. Everyone gives something to celebrate.

The celebration of Las Posadas is significant because it represents the revival of a popular religious practice that Mexican-origin people felt that they had lost. I would like to suggest, however, that more than a simple cultural revival, the celebration of Las Posadas also reflects how Mexican people forge a system of mutual self-reliance and community building. As a cultural practice, the Posadas celebration is decidedly Mexican in nature. The songs and prayers of the procession occur in Spanish. At the end of the procession, the community enjoys traditional Mexican food, and the children celebrate with a piñata. In addition to the positive cultural and religious aspects of the celebration, Las Posadas demonstrates how members of the *comunidades de base* facilitate community building in the Mexican community. They coordinate which houses the procession will visit and who will host the parties; people must practice the songs and prayers to lead the procession; and they cooperate to make food and bring toys for the children. All of these elements of the celebration demonstrate the effective way by which an economically disenfranchised community pools its resources to promote the celebration. Furthermore, the inclusion of children in the procession and the subsequent celebrations ensure that the next generation is educated about Mexican Catholic culture so that these practices will continue. In this way, *las comunidades de base* not only reinforce the bonds and support of the local Mexican-origin community but also revive a popular religious practice.

Enacting Las Posadas and the other popular religious practices revived by the *comunidades de base* was both a struggle for cultural survival and a political struggle. In an essay about Latino popular religious practices, the theologian Roberto Goizueta states that "precisely because these practices emerge on the margins of society and the official Church, they are nurtured by the spiritual and intellectual demands of the struggle for survival, by the everyday resistance to vanquishment" (1997, xvii). While the marginalization Mexicans experienced (being ushered to one side of the church) at St. Francis Xavier was painful, many of the members of the *comunidades de base* also lamented the loss of their culturally specific practices within the Catholic Church. It upset them that they were not able to pass these practices—part of their culture—on to their children. The theologian Orlando Espín asserts that "popular Catholicism stands out as one of the very few social (public and private) spaces that have been able to preserve some high degree of protagonism for Latinos" (1997, 102). In reviving their popular religious practices, Mexican-origin Catholics asserted their right to place their culture at the center of their Catholicism, thus resisting the Anglo religious hegemony. The activities of the *comunidades de base* and the enactment of their popular religious practices were thus political in nature, part of the struggle for cultural visibility and racial integration within the local Catholic church.

Racial integration occurred not only through creating cultural space within the parish in La Feria, but also through literally occupying space in the sanctuary. The community building that occurred outside of the church facilitated Spanish-speaking parishioners' increased attendance inside the church. Prior to the ministry of Spanish-speaking nuns from San Antonio, many Mexican-origin Catholics did not attend St. Francis except for special occasions (e.g., baptisms, weddings, Christmas, Easter). This could have been because many lived in the rural outlying areas of La Feria or because of racial discomfort and a sense that they did not belong at the church. One of my oral history interviewees explicitly recounted to me that her father did not permit his daughters to attend church because of the segregation Mexicans experienced in the church's sanctuary. For many Mexican people, the nuns' ministry and the activities of *las comunidades de base* inspired a renewed interest in and connection to the local parish. Several interviewees reveal that the number of Spanish-speaking Catholics who attended St. Francis began to grow. By building community outside of the church, Mexican-origin people began to feel empowered to integrate themselves by attending church in larger numbers, making literal space for themselves inside the sanctuary.

ADDITIONAL MOVEMENTS TOWARD DESEGREGATION

In addition to the activities of *las comunidades de base*, other church groups as well as individual priests contributed to the involvement of Mexican-origin people in the Church and the shifting attitudes of parishioners about race relations. There were several groups, or movements, at St. Francis Xavier in the 1970s and 1980s; while some specifically targeted the Mexican population, others had a more broad demographic focus. According to a parish history, a Guadalupana Society was organized in 1980. Many members of the parish also participated in the Cursillo, Charismatic, and Marriage Encounter movements, some of which had implications for social change (St. Francis Xavier 1930–1980; Treviño 2006). Longtime parishioner Mr. Zamarripa also recalls the *movimiento familiar cristiano* (Christian Family Movement) and *grupos de oración* (prayer groups) as significant movements whereby people would come together to actively participate in their faith.

New parish priests also facilitated a shift in people's attitudes about the politics of racial inclusion and exclusion in the Church. Mr. and Mrs. Zamarripa recall Father Buckholt and Father Gomez[8] as two priests who began to change the way parishioners thought about each other. Mrs. Zamarripa recounts that it was in their homilies that these priests facilitated change:

En sermones decía . . . Comenzó él a trabajar sobre éso y a decirnos, a inculcarnos que todos éramos hermanos. Todos éramos hijos de Dios. A Dios no dividía ni color ni raza. Entonces hay ésto en los sermones, ésos fuertes que él ponía.	In his sermons he [the priest] would say . . . He started to work on this and tell us, to ingrain in us that we were all brothers and sisters. We were all children of God. God did not divide by color or by race. He would put those [themes] in his sermons, those strong [sermons] he would give.

The priests at St. Francis Xavier were well positioned to influence people's moral positions and attitudes every Sunday at the pulpit. They gave powerful sermons about how parishioners were all children of a God who did not divide them by race. The Zamarripas believe that these sermons effected change within the church. Mr. Zamarripa asserts that the efforts of the priests, along with the movements, helped to "*componer*" (repair) broken relationships in the Church. It is interesting to note his choice of words. Discrimination against Mexican Catholics and the segregation they experienced within the church had, in a way, broken the Catholic community. While the work of the nuns, the *comunidades de base*, and other local church groups and ministries began to repair this fragmentation, new priests used their influence to push forward the project of racial reconciliation.

Finally, I would like to argue that many of the vestiges of discrimination and segregation that Mexican-origin people experienced within the local Catholic church were both unearthed and put to rest by the construction of the new church. At the groundbreaking ceremony for the new church on December 3, 1992, Norma Sánchez, a Mexican American woman who has been involved in the church for several years, narrates how she came to an understanding of race relations then and now within the church.

> One of the things that I always remember is when the priest, which was Father ——, [who] . . . was here the whole time. . . . On December the third . . . we dedicated the new church . . . and they announced how long he had been here. And it was a long time. But I'm sitting there, already as an adult, already married. . . . And they said how long he had been here and I'm thinking, why didn't I ever have a personal conversation with him? You know, like I do now with [the current priest].
>
> And it hit me.
>
> And I remember so vividly that we would walk out of church and he would walk. You know how they greet the people? It was in the *capilla* [the old church], so he would go like halfway . . . and everybody was around him, talking with him. And I always wondered, "Why can't we [the Mexican people] do that?" But I don't think we were ever told not to do that. I just remember seeing all the Anglos. . . .
>
> It kind of made me sad because I thought . . . he was such a good priest and I loved him and everything. And he was the one who married me. That I remember. When we got married, we had one conversation with him. And you know, what he told us was good, but that was the only time I remember just talking to him personally.

While Mr. and Mrs. Zamarripa hold very early memories of the discrimination they experienced within the Catholic church in La Feria, Sánchez comes to the realization only as parish members closed the doors to the old church and opened those of the new church. Unlike Mr. and Mrs. Zamarripa, who are in their late seventies and early eighties, Sánchez is in her early sixties, having grown up in the church when the racial order had already been established. At that point, Anglo members of the congregation had already effectively suppressed Mexican Catholic customs. Mrs. Sánchez grew up in the church not necessarily questioning why her family sat on a particular side of the church. When asked why she sat there, she stated, "That's where we sit as a family. . . . I thought it was normal." This normalized set of racial rules was disrupted only by the construction of the new church.

The first Catholic church in La Feria was built by Anglo residents, with the land and financial support coming from one of La Feria's first land speculators, a resident who was originally from the Midwest, S. J. "Duke" Schnorenberg

(McNail 1975). His support, along with that of other Anglo Catholics, set a precedent for Anglos to feel a sense of ownership of the church. Sánchez recalls how this kind of religious empowerment shifted to the larger community of La Feria with the construction of the new church in 1992:

> When we moved into the new church, all the confirmation students and everybody was working together. Not just the students but the adults. I could see vividly. . . . On the last day . . . I remember Father Tom making the comment that this is everybody's church. This church doesn't belong to just this people; it belongs to everyone. . . . And I was like, wow. And I think it's true. I think in the other church we felt like it was their church.

Sánchez recognizes that moment as a turning point in the church's history. She sees all the confirmation students as well as the adults—both Mexican and Anglo—working together. She understands Father Tom's implication when he says that this is *everybody's church*. This church will not divide Mexicans from Anglos by an aisle. It will not belong to one group. It will belong to everyone. Unlike the original church, whose pews were organized in two long columns facing the altar, the new church is constructed such that there is a semicircle of pews facing the front. This new architecture positions the parishioners face-to-face as they celebrate the Mass together.

SACRED AND SECULAR STRUGGLES

> *Here, in the everyday, common struggle for our survival as a people with a dignity bestowed on us by God, the political and the personal, the economic and the spiritual, the intellectual and the emotional, the sacred and the secular are united.*
> ROBERTO GOIZUETA

While Mexican racial segregation was affected by the law and manifested in public institutions and spaces, it also had a deep personal, even spiritual, impact on Mexican-origin people in La Feria. The theologian Roberto Goizueta beautifully expresses how the personal, the spiritual, and indeed the political are united in people's quests for dignity, which he argues is a divine right. For Mexican Catholics in La Feria, the struggle for dignity in the place where they worshipped was long and required the efforts of many individuals and groups—both clergy and laypeople. In this chapter, I have highlighted the actions of members of the *comunidades de base* as instrumental to racial integration. Their actions of social, economic, and spiritual reciprocity within the context of home group Bible studies created a strong sense of identity and community for Mexican Catholics in La Feria. This translated into increased visibility, participation, and belonging within the actual church. Particularly through their reinvigoration of Mexican popular religious practices, members of the *comunidades de base* claimed rights of cultural citizenship, creating a culturally viable space for themselves at St. Francis Xavier. This was a key element of racial integration in the church.

While civil rights legislation and radical elements of the Chicano/a movement in the Valley were effective in dismantling practices of segregation in public institutions, such as the schools, de facto practices of racial segregation in the church were more difficult to legislate. The Second Vatican Council's changes with regard to cultural evangelization laid some of the foundation for Mexican-origin Catholics to feel a greater sense of inclusion, while liberation theology in Latin America provided a radical theology by which working-class Catholics could combat the "structural sin" of economic oppression (Medina 2004). In Texas, the establishment of groups such as PADRES and Las Hermanas as well as the Mexican American Cultural Center in San Antonio helped in the struggle for Mexican American rights—both inside and outside of the church (Martinez 2004; Medina 2004). While all of these were important shifts in theology and practice, at the end of the 1970s Mexican Catholics in La Feria continued to experience marginalization and discrimination within their local parish.

Within the community of La Feria, we can see how the struggle for racial integration was dependent upon grassroots social action. Inspired by the pastoral work of a Spanish-speaking nun, Sister Angeles, Mexicans were able to organize to create a kind of homegrown Catholicism that ultimately led them to feel a stronger sense of belonging within the local church. They achieved this through the creation of a strong social network of mutual aid and through the revival of popular religious practices that had been suppressed within the historically Anglo-dominant church. In this way, Mexican Catholics engaged the institution, and as Edward Said has remarked, engagement with a dominant power has the potential to "dispute its hierarchy and methods, to elucidate what it has hidden, to pronounce what it has silenced or rendered unpronounceable" (quoted in Goizueta 1997, xi). Members of the *comunidades de base* established strong Mexican Catholic identities outside of the community, but were able to translate that into an increased presence within and engagement with the local institution of the church. Their revival of Mexican popular religion was a way by which Mexican Catholics claimed cultural citizenship, the right to be culturally different and yet to belong fully to the local church.

I have argued that the social actions of La Feria's *comunidades de base* reflect grassroots critique and resistance. These home group communities not only created cultural space for Mexican-origin people within the local Catholic church but also challenged national racial attitudes and set the stage for broader racial integration and community transformation.

EPILOGUE

I APPROACH THE brightly lit stadium nervously that fall Friday night. Because I have arrived late, I have had to park on the frontage road along the expressway instead of at the high school. There are throngs of people in maroon on the La Feria side, blue and gold on the opposing side, representing the Brownsville-Lopez Lobos. I climb the stadium steps feeling lost in the crowd; everyone has already taken their seats and is engrossed in the game. I finally spot the roped-off section along the fifty-yard line that marks the beginning of the reserved section. Through new friendships I have made in town, I have been able to procure a ticket for a seat in this section. I show my ticket to the woman at the entrance, and she lets me pass. I quickly find my friends and their family and am pleased to see that I am sitting between them and another couple I know. The couple, an old family friend of my mother and his wife, do not have children in high school. Their youngest graduated from La Feria High School perhaps a decade prior. I am happy to be surrounded by more familiar faces, though I am surprised by their attendance.

Settling into my seat, I am slightly overwhelmed by the scene around me. The stadium lights gleam against the black sky. The baritone of the football announcer resonates, drowning out the traffic along the expressway. The band, loud and rambunctious, beats out rhythms to energize the fans. The cheerleaders, skinny and peppy and silly, yell to the crowd to arouse team spirit. I cannot help but notice as they dance and bounce around the sidelines that all but two of them are Mexican American, a demographic shift that would have been unthinkable when my mother attended La Feria High School in the 1960s. Likewise, the jerseys of the football players are adorned with Spanish surnames—Zambrano, Molina, Rodriguez. Their protective gear seems too heavy for their teenage frames as they plow toward first downs or sacrifice their bodies to prevent them.

Though the sun has set long ago, the air is still heavy and warm. The stadium is full. All but a handful of people around me are Mexican American. I watch school board members, city commissioners, the mayor, and local clerics and business owners smiling, shaking hands, and speaking amicably with people in the crowd. There are people of all ages, from silver-haired elderly women in wheelchairs to dark-haired toddlers in La Feria Lions cheerleader uniforms. Most are riveted by the game, yelling in exasperation at the coaches, the players, the referees. A seemingly demure woman behind me suddenly yells, "Kill him!" in reference to a player from the opposing team running toward the goal. A man seated to the side of me yells to the Catholic priest several rows down to "pray harder" for the Lions to win.

We are uncomfortable in our backless bleacher seats; we are exasperated that our team is not performing better; we are hoarse from yelling. We are hot and thirsty—the warm sodas from the concession stand never quench our thirst. We are being mercilessly bitten by mosquitoes hovering around the bleachers, even though in at least every other row, someone is spraying Off!

It is a perfect night.

JUST A FEW YEARS EARLIER, I was at a family function when my eldest aunt found out that I was going to be attending graduate school in Texas. She pulled me aside and warned me to "be careful" because Texas was different from California. Texas did not treat Mexicans well. My family left La Feria in 1965, just before the process of desegregation had begun in earnest. The Texas of their memories has remained in that historical moment, the period of "accommodated segregation" for middle-class Mexican people, which was nearly an absolute segregation for my working-class immigrant family. When my mother and my aunts attended schools in La Feria, they began at Sam Houston Elementary and continued through the school system on the B track alongside other Mexican children. Ironically, the aunt who issued me the warning about Texas was an exception. Fiercely competitive and intelligent, she was placed on the A track alongside Anglo students. It was perhaps in those "integrated" classrooms in the 1950s and early 1960s that she most acutely felt the weight of Anglo discrimination against Mexicans. Though most of my years in Texas were spent in Austin, I decided to make La Feria the site where I would conduct fieldwork for my dissertation. It was apparent to me early in my stay there that it was no longer the town of my aunt's memories.

The autumn that I lived in La Feria I became addicted to football games. I bought season tickets—in the reserved section—for the remaining games and became a permanent fixture at these games, both at home and away. I found myself swept up in the exuberance of high school football in a small Texas town. The games provided a space for the entire community to come together; they gave everyone a common cause. I was taken by the fact that it was a Mexican American space precisely because I knew this town's history of racial segregation. Forty years ago, it would have been unimaginable for Mexican-origin people in La Feria to hold so many positions of economic and political power and social prestige. My first La Feria Lions football game signaled to me the dramatic shift that had occurred in this town and suggested to me that racial equality had taken root.

DURING A VISIT with a family friend, I meet Maria, an immigrant from Mexico. My friend introduces us, telling Maria that I am writing a history of La Feria. They point out to me some important historical sites in town. They mention the Henry Tichenor Mansion in La Feria, which sits squarely on the south side of town, west of Main Street. The mansion encompasses an entire block and strongly resembles a southern plantation home—gleaming white and with pillars adorning its facade. Palm trees and bright flowers flank its periphery. Maria, who has lived in La Feria for the past twenty years, remarks that she has heard a "Mexicano" now owns the property, a hint of pride in her voice.[1]

I enjoy my conversation with my mother's friend and this woman. Maria is personable and funny. We get along well, talking and laughing into the evening. Eventually she reveals to me that her son plays football for the La Feria Lions.

I feel my face light up. I tell her how I love high school football in the Valley. How much more exciting it is than in California. That I go to every game. It occurs to me suddenly that I have never seen her at any of them.

"*¿Va usted a los games?*" I ask her.

She tells me that she goes to every one.

I am puzzled for a few seconds before I feel a pang of guilt. One of my friends, a school board member, has helped me to buy season tickets in the reserved section, away from the general public.

A FEW WEEKS LATER, my friends and I make plans for the upcoming away game.

One of them remarks, "I don't think that they have reserved seating there."

I catch knowing looks but don't exactly understand what I am supposed to know.

They tell me that it is not a big deal. It is just annoying sometimes because people sound these loud, handheld horns and throw confetti that often lands in your drink. Just louder. Messier.

I HAVE LIVED IN La Feria for a few months now, and I have come to know several people. I attend school board and city council meetings; I teach catechism and attend Mass on Sundays; I frequent local establishments and attend every football game. It is a small town, after all, and people are very open and welcoming to me. Nonetheless, at the away game, where there is no reserved seating, I am surprised to find myself in a sea of unfamiliar faces, people who are also La Ferians. They are also Lions fans, dressed in maroon and gold and unabashedly cheering for the team. There is as much, if not more, team spirit among this *un*reserved crowd of fans. My friends are right. It is louder in this section. People do throw confetti into our drinks.

The teenagers I had become accustomed to in the reserved section had "preppy" aesthetics. They were often wearing name brands—Abercrombie and Fitch and American Eagle ensembles. Young Mexican American girls often used only light makeup and adorned their ponytails with bows. In the general section, there are alternative types of teenagers. While some wear name brand clothes, many do not. Hair and makeup styles are varied, ranging from preppy to Goth to more rebellious aesthetics. While English was the dominant language in the reserved section, here it is a mix of Spanish and English. I am surprised to see a couple of pregnant teenage girls, La Feria Lions T-shirts stretched taut across their bellies, carefully navigating their paths through the bleachers. I have heard that teenage pregnancy is a problem in La Feria, as it is in many Valley towns. I recall a conversation with a town advocate for these teenage mothers. She told me that one of the biggest obstacles she faces is convincing people that teenage pregnancy is a problem at all. Many community members deny its existence.

I wonder if these people are sitting in the reserved section at the football games.

Investigating the issue, I find out that school board members have priority for the purchase of their seats and that those residents interested in reserved seats must buy tickets for the season in advance. While many people can spend four dollars a week on a football game, not as many can pay for season tickets all at once.

I start to think about the reserved section of the football stadium and wonder if such a thing existed forty years ago. If so, I am positive that it would have been filled with Anglo residents. Now it is filled with high-profile residents, business owners and politicians, most of whom are Mexican American.

I wonder about the economic class and immigrant status of the people who are not sitting in the reserved section.

MEXICAN REFLECTIONS/INFLECTIONS

This book serves as a historical ethnography about the culture of segregation in the South Texas community of La Feria, Texas. It serves also as an examination of the various stages of segregation in La Feria, from its early establishment in the first part of the twentieth century to its accommodated form beginning in the late 1940s to its gradual unraveling after the civil rights and Chicano movements. In this book, I highlight how the ambiguous racial positionalities of Mexican people affected the way that they experienced segregation during those epochs. By including in my analysis Mexican-origin people who could cross certain racial boundaries, sometimes enjoying rights and at other times being denied them, I illustrate how many people of Mexican origin had a borderlands experience of race in this community. Instead of reading these contradictions within the structure of segregation as indicative of the permeability of racial borders, I argue that the practices of segregation persisted well beyond landmark national legal mandates of desegregation precisely through these processes of selective and limited incorporation. The durability of de facto segregation meant that grassroots efforts in conjunction with broader civil rights movements were integral to facilitating long-lasting, meaningful Mexican racial integration. During this process, I highlight how Mexican people worked for both political and cultural citizenship rights.

At the heart of this study has been a processual analysis of culture. During the era of segregation—at its beginning and in its accommodated stage—the Mexican-origin people in La Feria constituted a primarily working-class and immigrant community. While there were a handful of families who traced their ancestry to Spanish colonialism and a small Mexican merchant class, intracommunity differences were often obscured by Anglo practices of racial segregation. Though during the accommodated era of segregation Anglos accepted some Mexicans into their spheres of influence, there were always racial borders that these exceptional Mexican people could not cross. For this reason, common experiences of discrimination and segregation often engendered a kind of unity among La Feria's Mexican community.

Now, several decades into a period of racial integration, divisions within the Mexican-origin community along lines of class and immigrant status have come into sharper relief. David Gutierrez (1995) characterizes the history of the complex relationships between Mexican Americans and Mexican immigrants as "walls and mirrors." In a contemporary context, the sociologist Gilda Ochoa (2004) illustrates that in the California city of La Puente, relationships between Mexican immigrants and Mexican Americans reflect "a continuum of conflict and solidarity that includes antagonism, a shared connection, and political mobilization," and she notes that people's attitudes are neither "mutually exclusive [n]or static" (2004, 15). Ochoa's findings reflect what can be seen occurring in contemporary La Feria between Mexican immigrants and Mexican Americans, but I would build upon her and Gutierrez's analyses to include socioeconomic class divisions between the growing middle class and the working class in the Mexican-origin community.[2] At times, such differences engender conflict, whereas at other times common historical and cultural genealogies or contemporary experiences draw Mexican-origin people in La Feria together.

Intra-race relations in La Feria have unique characteristics because of the town's history of segregation and its close proximity to the U.S.-Mexico border. Today the city's population is nearly double what it was during the period of my study. There are now 7,302 residents, 85 percent of whom identify as Mexican origin,[3] and these people inhabit previously segregated spaces in different ways. The old Catholic church, where for decades Mexican parishioners were ushered to one side, has been repurposed as a small chapel, with adjoining rooms that function as office space and religious-education classrooms. For many years, Sam Houston Elementary School was the early elementary school for all children in town, but it has recently been vacated in favor of a newly constructed school on the south side of the tracks. The city's current high school and junior high school are both located on the north side of the railroad tracks. These new school locations indicate that—for the schools—the railroad tracks no longer function as a racial boundary. The neighborhood north of the railroad tracks known as the *pueblo mexicano* continues to be characterized by narrow streets and small wood-framed homes nestled closely together. Though the town is only 18 percent foreign born, immigrants are twice as likely to live on the north side of the tracks than on the south side.[4] The neighborhood is also home to working-class Mexican Americans as well as those who are economically stable but have chosen not to leave their longtime homes. The south side of the railroad tracks is now populated by a majority of Mexican-origin people, and the city has actively sought to build affordable housing units on that side of the town as well.

During my fieldwork, I found that sometimes class divisions between Mexican Americans assumed a "racial" tone, which seemed to be a residual aspect of the culture of segregation. One evening during a catechism class I was teaching, I divided the students into small groups to answer questions. The class of high school students was predominantly of Mexican origin; there were only two Anglo kids out of about fifteen enrolled. One Mexican American boy protested aloud when he realized that he would be in a group with an Anglo boy and a preppy Mexican American girl. "Why do I have to be in the group with the white kids?!" I was caught off guard by his comment, but the Mexican American girl in the group immediately and indignantly responded, "I'm not white!" The Anglo boy, normally a kind of jokester in the class, remained quiet. They settled down and were able to work together for the short activity, but the minor outburst left me thinking about contemporary assignations of race among these young people. The boy who made the initial statement racialized the girl in the group as "white" based on his perception of her cultural performance. This could have been because of the way she dressed, the way she talked, her friends, or any number of social or economic factors. In his articulation of the difference he perceived between them, he fell back onto old racially divisive categorizations. She, on the other hand, was quick to claim her nonwhite identity, pushing him to recognize that she, too, was Mexican. In doing so, she was not only challenging his notions of "whiteness" but also his ideas about who was culturally "Mexican." In this case, both Mexican American teenagers quickly claimed nonwhite Mexican identities. However, in border communities such as La Feria, being "Mexican," particularly a Mexican immigrant, can mean being subject to symbolic as well as physical violence.

When I lived in La Feria in 2002 and 2003, white and green Border Patrol SUVs were a regular part of the landscape of the Valley. While for me these "police" vehicles seemed ominous, most Mexican Americans I knew in the region did not seem fazed by them. Though their casual attitudes might have been the result of regional acclimation, the past two decades have actually been marked by rapid border militarization in Texas. Operation Hold the Line in El Paso in 1994 and Operation Rio Grande in McAllen in 1997 reflected a new kind of "concentrated border enforcement" that included increased numbers of Border Patrol agents, increased fencing and lighting, and a myriad of old and new technologies (Cornelius 2001). Border militarization, especially in California and Texas, has led to spatial reorganization (e.g., more migrants moving through Arizona) and increased acts of violence. These include migrant deaths in the unforgiving Arizona desert, violent confrontations with Border Patrol agents, and the everyday harassment of migrants by Mexicans and Americans on both sides of the border (Cornelius 2001; Rosas 2012). Jonathan Inda (2006) refers to this policing as a kind of "anti-citizenship technology"—attempts to ensure that migrants are not meaningfully integrated into the nation-state.

Migration, race, and racialization, prominent characteristics of the contemporary U.S.-Mexico border, necessitate complex negotiations of border identities for Mexican-origin people. The anthropologist Gilberto Rosas argues that "surging militarized policing practices and its own racial politics of migration" are characteristics of what he calls "the new frontier" (2012, 15). Certainly, the new racial politics includes the regularity with which one sees Mexican American Border Patrol agents manning checkpoints both at border crossings into Mexico and at the interior checkpoints in Sarita and Falfurrias. These men (I have seen few women) essentially profile the people who are crossing to determine who might be traveling without papers or who might be smuggling drugs. Anecdotally, people tell stories about Mexican American Border Patrol agents as "the worst ones" because they have something to prove. Other stories include those of family members who are Border Patrol agents who turn a blind eye to that particular member of the extended family everyone knows is undocumented. These intra-racial negotiations of power represent the new ways Mexican Americans negotiate racialized identities in the Lower Rio Grande Valley border region.

In La Feria the relationships between Mexican Americans and Mexican immigrants range from vehement disassociation to political alliance. There is, for example, the Mexican American woman who, in helping to plan for the city's annual Fiesta de La Feria, suggests the need to bring "Mexican" musical performers in addition to the regular Tejano groups. Noting an increase in Mexican people in town, she wants these residents to feel as if they belong to the community. On the other hand, there is the high school boy who breaks up with his girlfriend when he realizes that she is undocumented, hurling at her the word "wetback."[5] Then, there is my friend Celeste De Luna, who has spent the past several years creating art that critically engages with subjects such as border violence, family separation, and the border wall, just to name a few. She has exhibited her work in the Valley and throughout Texas and California and participated in shows that focus on human rights as well as on art in protest of the border wall. Though she is a Mexican American, De Luna takes a markedly proimmigrant stance in her work, writing "but for the grace of God me and my family have supposedly been lucky enough to end up on the 'right side' of Anzaldua's razor's edge.[6] I'm proimmigrant because I see myself in other immigrants."[7] On the border, where there are native people, descendants of colonists, migrants, immigrants, Mexican Americans of many generations, and those whose relationships to the U.S. nation-state defy easy categorization, the potential for slippage to the wrong side, as De Luna implies, is real and potentially menacing. For those of us whose histories are tied to immigration, some of us are painfully aware that today's undocumented immigrants could easily have been us if immigration legislation had not come down in our favor at a particular historical moment. Whereas some Mexican Americans see boundaries—cultural and/or political—between themselves and Mexican immigrants, others continue to see their experiences—real and imagined—mirrored in each other's.

For their part, Mexican immigrants in La Feria continue to create culturally relevant space for themselves, which is often shared by Mexican Americans. If you were to enter St. Francis Xavier parish just after 8:00 a.m. on a Sunday morning, you would be among the people walking briskly through the parking lot toward the church because you are all a few minutes late to the Spanish-language Mass.[8] Entering from the back, you would see that people are already standing shoulder to shoulder and singing the entrance song. As you take tentative steps in either direction of the sanctuary's semicircle of pews to find a seat, your gaze takes in a cross section of the community. There are elderly people with canes, young families with antsy children hanging off the pews, and gangly teenagers in jeans and T-shirts. Some men are dressed in their Western finest, with Wranglers, pointy boots, and Mexican-embroidered leather belts. Others are in Dockers with loose-fitting button-down dress shirts and loafers. If you know some people in town, you would notice that there are a good number of Mexican Americans who attend this Mass, some of whom serve as lectors, Eucharistic ministers, and religious education teachers. As you squeeze into a pew behind a familiar couple, you see some members of the *comunidades de base* in the choir. You join in singing, grateful that the lyrics are projected onto the walls in front of the sanctuary. The heavy strumming of the guitar and people's strained voices echo and fade as the priest welcomes the congregation.

El Señor esté con ustedes.

MY MOM FIRST INTRODUCED me to La Feria thirty-five years after she and her family had made their final migration to California. We arrived to town on a warm summer afternoon in August after a five-hour drive from Austin. Exiting the expressway, my mom navigated us through the narrow streets of the *pueblo mexicano*—the side of town she had known best in her youth. She pointed out houses where people she knew had once lived—buildings that certain neighborhood stores had occupied. Some of these had been reincarnated as other kinds of stores; others looked to be abandoned. The cotton gin had been torn down and a tract of housing erected in its place. A few houses with windows and doors boarded up signaled to her that the family inside had gone to pick crops elsewhere for the summer, as she and her family used to do. When I think about my first tour of La Feria, I think about the histories and current realities of Mexican-origin people that are mapped on to that place.

The literary critic Mary Pat Brady writes, "[S]pace is processual, it changes, goes extinct" (2002, 5). Experiences of segregation continue to haunt many Mexican people of my mom's generation and older. This project has given me the opportunity to investigate and dig more deeply into the historical record about Mexican segregation as well as into the archives of people's memories. Memories are what keep places alive; and histories, at their best, enable us to move forward, reconciled and creating a more just future.

NOTES

INTRODUCTION

1. In this book, I use the term "Anglo" to designate non-Hispanic whites. Though whites in the region may or may not have been of Anglo-Saxon descent, this is the term most commonly used in the region.

2. Suzanne Oboler (1997) describes how throughout the Southwest, Mexican people experienced racial segregation based on custom rather than law.

3. Romano's arguments in this essay can be seen as part of a larger critique against the so-called culture of poverty, first theorized by Oscar Lewis in his ethnographic work in Mexico (1975). Lewis argued that it was the values and behaviors of a working-class community that led them to remain in poverty. Subsequent scholars refuted Lewis's claims by shifting the analysis of poverty to structural inequities.

4. See Montejano 1987 and Zamora 2008 for a more in-depth discussion about the political economy of South Texas and the Lower Rio Grande Valley.

5. I use pseudonyms for my interviewees except where I indicate otherwise.

6. Blackwell (2011) and Delgado Bernal (1998), for example, provide excellent examples of the ways that Chicana feminist scholars have theorized and utilized oral history narratives.

7. Ranajit Guha, quoted in "Introduction: Historical Anthropology and Its Vicissitudes," in *From the Margins: Historical Anthropology and Its Futures*, ed. Brian Keith Axel (Durham, NC: Duke University Press, 2002).

8. Nugent (1993) and Alonso (1997) offer similar methodologies in their work on the Namiquipans of Chihuahua, Mexico.

CHAPTER 1: THE BORDERLANDS OF RACE AND RIGHTS

1. In the early stages of the war for Mexican independence, the Spanish government passed the Law of Cádiz (1812), which abolished the racial caste system in colonial Mexico. However, this political move proved to be insufficient to quell the discontent of Spain's colonial subjects (Menchaca 2001).

2. Vélez-Ibáñez (1996) notes a parallel phenomenon among Anglo and Mexican elites in Arizona.

3. See also Ken Gonzales-Day's book *Lynching in the West: 1850–1935* (2006) for an analysis of lynching practices in California that disproportionately affected Native Americans, Chinese, Mexican Americans, and other groups of Latin American descent.

4. See Sanchez 1995 and Garcia 1989, respectively, for in-depth histories of those two cities.

5. For a more in-depth discussion about the ways that land-grant families steadily lost land after the Mexican-American War, see Alonzo 1998 and Chavana 2002.

CHAPTER 2: ESTABLISHING A CULTURE OF SEGREGATION

1. City records also refer to the area north of the railroad tracks as "Mexicata" and "Mexiquito."

2. Darla Jones, La Feria city commissioner, in discussion with the author, September 11, 2002.

3. Protestant newcomers to the area worshipped in various town spaces, including in a local pool hall and beer parlor and then, later, in the one-room school building (McNail 1975). In 1914, Union Church was constructed as a place of worship for the town's Protestants. A Methodist church was built later that same year; Baptist and Presbyterian churches appeared soon thereafter (McNail 1975).

4. The original Catholic church burned down in 1930 and was reconstructed that same year.

5. Similarly, one of my oral history interviews revealed that the Mexican Baptist Church, which began to advertise its services in the local newspaper in September 1947 (*La Feria News*), began as a mission of the La Feria Baptist Church.

6. A parallel phenomenon that Orsi (1985) notes in his study on Italian Catholics in Harlem was that they were made to sit in the basement of the church.

7. Not a pseudonym.

8. Not a pseudonym.

9. Not a pseudonym.

10. Not a pseudonym.

11. La Feria, Texas, City Commissioner Minutes. November 6, 1922; January 12, 1923; February 13, 1923. City of La Feria.

12. Not a pseudonym.

13. The 1920 United States census.

14. Johnson (2003) argues that the intense racial violence engendered by the Plan de San Diego uprising was actually an impetus for Anglos to enact strict policies of racial segregation in South Texas.

15. Cameron County Clerk, Property Records, 1913–1915, 1919, 1924–1931.

16. Beatris Villareal Delgado, affidavit, Cameron County Clerk, June 23, 1945.

CHAPTER 3: FORMAL AND INFORMAL MEXICAN EDUCATION WITHIN THE CONTEXT OF SEGREGATION

1. "If in the American schools our children attend they are taught Washington's biography and not Hidalgo's, and instead of teaching the glorious deeds of Juárez, they refer to Lincoln's accomplishments, though these might be noble and just, these children will not know the glories of their homeland, they will not love it and they will even view their parents' compatriots with indifference" (cited in Limón 1974, 90; translation mine).

2. This ruling was only a partial victory for the Mexican community because it did not challenge the segregation of "nonwhite" Mexicans (Menchaca 2001).

3. "That's where I went, to Sam Houston School for primary. It was in Mexiquita (Little Mexico). They called that part of town, on the other side of the tracks, Mexiquita because the Mexican people lived there, on the other side of the tracks, and that school was the Mexican school for Mexicans. Anglo people used to be very discriminatory in those days."

4. It is not insignificant that Anglos decided to name the school after Sam Houston. Houston led the troops that defeated General Santa Anna at the Battle of San Jacinto, the battle that marked the victory of the Texas War for Independence. Subsequently, Houston became the first president of the Republic of Texas (Acuña 1988).

5. The degree of segregation also depended on the amount of opposition presented by the local Mexican-origin community (San Miguel 1987).

6. First conceptualized by C. M. Pierce (1970), racial microaggressions are defined by Solórzano et al. as "subtle insults (verbal, nonverbal, and/or visual) directed toward people of color, often automatically or unconsciously" (2001, 60).

7. See Ngai 2004 for an incisive account of how the 1920s were a critical epoch in the making of "illegal" Mexican subjects.

8. Not a pseudonym.

9. Not a pseudonym.

10. "Somebody had a cannon. I don't know where they got it, but they would sound it at five in the morning."

11. "We would go see the floats. They would decorate them with multi-colored ribbons—green, white, and red, you know. And they would dress us [the children] in 'china poblana' dresses [traditional Mexican dresses]."

12. "There were people who would recite the histories from that era."

13. "They would choose girls to be queen, and these girls had to get votes. The queens had beautiful crowns and capes made out of velvet."

14. Christmas season was well celebrated in La Feria.

15. See Vargas 2012 for an incisive analysis about the way that Silva's renderings of the bolero disrupted normative understandings of Chicana gender and sexuality.

16. "In '39 there was a big package program. Somebody came and excited us with the prospect that the Mexican government was going to be giving away land on March 18th. At that time, my dad was one of the people who wanted to go, and I told him, 'No, sir, if you think it's bad here, it's probably worse over there.' It was in '39 when everyone was excited. Several families were going, but we didn't."

17. Not a pseudonym.

CHAPTER 4: AN ACCOMMODATED FORM OF SEGREGATION

1. The 1940 United States census.

2. There are several key texts that discuss various aspects of the bracero program as it was manifested in different parts of the United States. Galarza 1964 remains a cornerstone text in outlining the terms of the program, the many contract violations that occurred, and its impact on domestic labor. Gamboa (2000) highlights the significance of World War II as an economic impetus for the program and similarly notes depressed working conditions in the Pacific Northwest. More recently, Kim (2004) and Ngai (2004) both offer an excellent discussion of the program's legal foundations and the way that it was intertwined with larger immigration policy. Finally, Cohen (2011) offers an insightful discussion about the transnational impact of the program, focusing on the desires of the Mexican government to use the program as a segue into socioeconomic modernity.

3. In her historical ethnography about Santa Paula, California, Menchaca (1995) writes about a parallel phenomenon in which famers organized in an attempt to stymie labor organizing. One of their goals was to lobby for a Mexican guest-worker program to hinder farmworkers from striking. Interestingly, Gamboa (2000) notes that the braceros in the Pacific Northwest successfully organized labor strikes of their own.

4. A dramatic example from Santa Paula, California, was that the major agricultural

union was disbanded in 1942, and no new union was organized for the next thirty years (Menchaca 1995, 92).

5. "My grandmother had a restaurant, and there were a lot of braceros, men who came [from Mexico]."

6. "We worked hard at my father's store, too. It was a lot of work because it was the time of the braceros, and we had a lot, a lot of work. We wouldn't close the store until one in the morning."

7. See Ramos 1998 for a comprehensive history of the GI Forum.

8. Orozco argues that in addition to being a euphemism for the word "Mexican," the term "Latin American" "tied them to their *hispanidad* and Spanishness. Most México Texanos were Spanish-dominant and read Spanish language newspapers" (2009, 223; emphasis hers). She continues by saying that members of LULAC never tried to deny their Mexican identity.

9. This phenomenon runs parallel to what George Sanchez (1995) writes about in his history of Mexican Americans in Los Angeles. Repatriations in that city left behind Mexican-origin people who were less invested in maintaining ties to Mexico and who had developed a unique Mexican American cultural and political sensibility.

10. "They would rope off the street [in the Mexican neighborhood], and there would be a dance. People would dance in the street. It was really nice back then."

11. "There were societies. Columbus and who knows what else. There were many societies of this and that. They would sponsor those dances in the street."

12. See Manuel Peña 1999 and José Limón 1994 for an in-depth analysis of the function of Tejano music and dance in working-class Mexican communities of South Texas.

13. See Gonzalez 1991 and Valencia 2008.

14. Not a pseudonym.

15. Not a pseudonym.

16. Among the newly elected was R. G. Pena Jr., a Mexican American whose well-established family owned a business on the north side of town. Pena served only one two-year term on the commission; an Anglo man replaced him in 1953.

CHAPTER 5: TROUBLING THE CULTURE OF SCHOOL SEGREGATION

1. Saenz (1989) writes that from 1960 to 1970, Texas experienced the most dramatic decline in its share of the Mexican-origin population. He cites data that indicate that in the 1960s, about 60 percent of migrants with Spanish surnames settled in California, whereas only 17 percent moved to Texas.

2. As early as 1960, a Texas state program made funds available for the establishment of "preschools" for non-English-speaking children in Texas. The purpose of the program was to teach children enough English-language skills that they would be able to communicate with their teachers when they began elementary school (Blanton 2004, 141–142). That year, increased enrollment in the Mexican elementary school in La Feria led to a record high overall student enrollment for the school district. This prompted the district to initiate a summer language program for Spanish-speaking children to prepare them for entrance to Sam Houston Elementary.

3. *La Feria News*, January 6, 1966.

4. *La Feria News*, June 22, 1967.

5. *La Feria News*, December 17, 1964.

6. MALDEF archives (SA/69/238 *Escalante v. La Feria Independent School District*).

7. La Feria (Texas) High School. *Leonidas* yearbooks, 1960–1969.

8. *La Feria News*, July 8, 1971.

9. La Feria school board minutes, April 5, 1971, and April 11, 1972.

10. Not a pseudonym.

11. Not a pseudonym.

12. "It seemed to me that there was a lot of discrimination in those days."

13. "I remember when the Anglo teachers would scold the Mexican children, the children would look down. Out of respect, out of shame, they would lower their eyes."

14. See Galindo et al. 1996 for an excellent article that engages the narrative life stories of Mexican American teachers and how these life experiences informed their teaching of students with similar socioeconomic and cultural backgrounds.

15. Not a pseudonym.

16. Harmon Wilson 2003; MALDEF archives (SA/69/238 *Escalante v. La Feria Independent School District*).

17. MALDEF was founded in 1969 with the support of a grant from the Ford Foundation, and its initial headquarters was in San Antonio.

18. *Corpus Christi Caller-Times*, August 2, 1970, 16.

19. La Feria school board meeting minutes, August 3, 1970.

20. Not a pseudonym.

21. Not pseudonyms.

22. La Feria school board meeting minutes, June 3, 1971.

23. Ibid.

CHAPTER 6: SURGIENDO DE LA BASE

1. "[One of the first times that] I went to Mass here at St. Francis, Javier, Alma, Noe, and I went in. We went and sat down in a pew. And Mr. Harper went and touched Javier and who knows what he told him; I was over there on the other side of the pew. And Javier turned around and just told him, no.

And I asked Javier, 'What did he tell you?'

Javier said, 'That we can't sit here, not in this spot. That we have to be on the other side.'

'Why? Did he tell you why?'

He said, 'That this space is separate.'

'Oh,' Javier told him, 'Is it reserved?'

'No, it's just separated.'

'No,' Jaime said, 'we're not going to move.'

And we didn't move."

2. In 1970, Father Patricio Flores, a member of PADRES, was appointed as the first Mexican American bishop in 1970 (Cadena 1987; Martinez 2005; Treviño 2006). Bishop Flores took strong political positions, including support of the United Farm Workers Union (UFW) and denouncement of the lack of educational opportunities for Mexican American youth. He actively attempted to focus the Church's attention on such issues (Treviño 2006).

3. In California, the Chicano activist group Católicos Por La Raza were similarly trying to "propose a theology of liberation East L.A. style" (Garcia 2008, 130).

4. I use the real names of these two nuns because their story has been told in both published and unpublished accounts of church history.

5. Not a pseudonym.

6. "The '*tema*' was what distinguished *comunidades de base* from Bible studies. Though we would use the Bible. But they were *comunidades de base*."

7. In the mid-1980s, members of La Feria's *comunidades de base* became involved in helping Central American refugees who were being detained in the Rio Grande Valley. The groups took up small collections and donated clothes and food, performing, as Sister Clara said, "*muchas obras de misericordia*" ("many acts of charity").

8. Not a pseudonym.

EPILOGUE

1. The mansion is still owned by the Tichenor family.

2. See Zavella 2011 for an ethnography that offers an integrative analysis of immigration, class, and assimilation in Santa Cruz County.

3. The 2010 United States census.

4. U.S. Census Bureau, 2007–2011 American Community Survey.

5. This extreme reaction demonstrates the depth of what Leo Chavez (2008) calls the "Latino threat narrative," an ideology that criminalizes and dehumanizes undocumented immigrants that is promulgated by the media. See also Zavella 2011.

6. Reference to Gloria Anzaldúa 1987.

7. Celeste De Luna, electronic message to author, June 2, 2013.

8. The introduction of Spanish-language masses was another change enacted by Vatican II. Previously, masses were celebrated in Latin.

REFERENCES

Acosta, Teresa Palomo, and Ruthe Winegarten. 2003. *Las Tejanas*. Austin: University of Texas Press.

Acuña, Rodolfo. 1988. *Occupied America*. New York: HarperCollins.

Alonso, Ana Maria. 1997. *Thread of Blood: Colonialism, Revolution, and Gender on Mexico's Northern Frontier*. Tucson, AZ: University of Arizona Press.

Alonso, Armando C. 1997. *Tejano Legacy: Rancheros and Settlers in South Texas, 1734–1900*. Albuquerque: University of New Mexico Press.

Anderson, Benedict. 1991. *Imagined Communities*. Rev. ed. New York: Verso.

Anzaldúa, Gloria. 1987. *Borderlands/La Nueva Frontera*. San Francisco: Aunt Lute Books.

Armour, Basil. 1932. "Problems in the Education of the Mexican Child." *The Texas Outlook* 16:29–30.

Axel, Brian Keith, ed. 2002. "Introduction: Historical Anthropology and Its Vicissitudes." In *From the Margins: Historical Anthropology and Its Futures*. Durham, NC: Duke University Press.

Barrera, Aida. 2006. "The 'Little Schools' in Texas, 1897–1965: Educating Mexican American Children." *American Educational History Journal* 33 (2): 35–45.

Barrera, James. 2004. "The 1968 Edcouch-Elsa High School Walkout: Chicano Student Activism in a South Texas Community." *Aztlán* 29 (2): 93–122.

Blackwell, Maylei. 2011. *¡Chicana Power!* Austin: University of Texas Press.

Blanton, Carlos Kevin. 2004. *The Strange Career of Bilingual Education in Texas, 1836–1981*. College Station: Texas A&M University Press.

Cadena, Gilbert R. 1987. "Chicano Clergy and Liberation Theology: A Descriptive Analysis." SCCR Working Paper no. 23. Stanford, CA: Stanford Center for Chicano Research.

Carrigan, William D., and Clive Webb. 2003. "The Lynching of Persons of Mexican Origin or Descent in the United States, 1848 to 1928." *Journal of Social History* 37 (2): 411–438.

Chavana, Herminia Balli. 2002 [1989]. *The History of the Prestigious Balli Family: Story of the First Pioneer Settlers of the Rio Grande Valley*. Sioux Falls, SD: Pine Hill.

Chavez, Leo. 2008. *The Latino Threat: Constructing Immigrants, Citizens, and the Nation*. Stanford, CA: Stanford University Press.

Cohen, Deborah. 2011. *Braceros: Migrant Citizens and Transnational Subjects in the Postwar United States and Mexico*. Chapel Hill: University of North Carolina Press.

Coll, Kathleen M. 2010. *Remaking Citizenship: Latina Immigrants and New American Politics*. Stanford, CA: Stanford University Press.

Cornelius, Wayne A. 2001. "Death at the Border: The Efficacy and 'Unintended' Consequences of U.S. Immigration Control Policy 1993–2000." Working paper. Center for Comparative Immigration Studies, UC–San Diego.

Dávalos, Karen Mary. 1998. "Chicana/o Studies and Anthropology: The Dialogue That Never Was." *Aztlán* 23 (2): 13–45.

De Leon, Arnoldo. 1983. *They Called Them Greasers: Anglo Attitudes toward Mexicans in Texas, 1821–1900*. Austin: University of Texas Press.

Delgado Bernal, Dolores. 1998. "Grassroots Leadership Reconceptualized: Chicana Oral Histories and the 1968 East Los Angeles School Blowouts." *Frontiers* 19 (2): 113–142.

Espín, Orlando. 1997. *The Faith of the People: Theological Reflections of Popular Catholicism*. Maryknoll, NY: Orbis Books.

Espinosa, Gastón. 2008. "Conclusion: Reflections on Mexican American Religions and Culture." In *Mexican American Religions: Spirituality, Activism, and Culture*, edited by Gastón Espinosa and Mario García, 381–386. Durham, NC: Duke University Press.

Flores, María Eva. n.d. "Las Hermanas." *Handbook of Texas Online*. http://www.tsha.utexas.edu/handbook/online/articles/LL/ixl3.html.

Flores, Richard. 1997. "Aesthetic Process and Cultural Citizenship: The Membering of a Social Body in San Antonio." In *Latino Cultural Citizenship*, edited by William V. Flores and Rina Benmayor, 124–151. Boston: Beacon.

———. 2002. *Remembering the Alamo: Memory, Modernity, and the Master Symbol*. Austin: University of Texas Press.

Foley, Douglas. 1988. *From Peones to Políticos*. Austin: University of Texas Press.

Galarza, Ernesto. 1964. *Merchants of Labor*. Charlotte, NC: McNally and Loftin.

Galindo, Rene, Madeline Aragón, and Ruby Underhill. 1996. "The Competence to Act: Chicana Teacher Role Identity in Life and Career Narratives." *Urban Review* 4:279–308.

Gamboa, Erasmo. 2000. *Mexican Labor and World War II: Braceros in the Pacific Northwest, 1942–1947*. Seattle: University of Washington Press.

Gándara, Patricia, and Frances Contreras. 2009. *The Latino Education Crisis*. Cambridge, MA: Harvard University Press.

Garcia, Eugene E. 1996. "Preparing Instructional Professionals for Linguistically and Culturally Diverse Students." In *Handbook of Research on Teacher Education*, edited by J. Sikula, 802–813. New York: Simon and Schuster.

García, Ignacio. 1990. *United We Win: The Rise and Fall of La Raza Unida Party*. Tucson: University of Arizona Mexican American Studies Research Center.

———. 2009. *White but Not Equal: Mexican Americans, Jury Discrimination, and Supreme Court*. Tucson: University of Arizona Press.

Garcia, Mario. 1989. *Desert Immigrants*. New Haven, CT: Yale University Press.

———. 2008. "Religion and the Chicano Movement: Católicos Por La Raza." In *Mexican American Religions: Spirituality, Activism, and Culture*, edited by Gastón Espinosa and Mario García, 125–149. Durham, NC: Duke University Press.

Garcia, S. B., and P. L. Guerra. 2004. "Deconstructing Deficit Thinking: Working with Educators to Promote More Equitable Learning Environments." *Education and Urban Society* 36:150–168.

Goizueta, Roberto. 1997. Foreword. In *The Faith of the People: Theological Reflections on Popular Catholicism*, by Orlando Espín. Maryknoll, NY: Orbis Books.

Goldfarb, Ronald L. 1981. *Migrant Farm Workers: A Caste of Despair*. Ames: Iowa State University Press.

Gómez, Laura E. 2007. *Manifest Destinies: The Making of the Mexican American Race*. New York: New York University Press.

Gonzales Day, Ken. 2006. *Lynching in the West: 1850–1935*. Durham, NC: Duke University Press.

González, Gilbert G. 1990. *Chicano Education in the Era of Segregation*. Philadelphia: Balch Institute Press.

González, John Morán. 2009. *Border Renaissance*. Austin: University of Texas Press.

González, Jovita. 2006. *Life along the Border*. College Station: Texas A&M University Press.

Government Service Agency. 1999. *La Feria, Texas: Comprehensive Development Plan*. Dallas, TX: GSA.

Gutierrez, David. 1995. *Walls and Mirrors: Mexican Americans, Mexican Immigrants, and the Politics of Ethnicity*. Berkeley: University of California Press.

Haney López, Ian. 2006 [1996]. *White by Law*. 10th anniversary ed. New York: New York University Press.

Harmon Wilson, Steven. 2003. *The Rise of Judicial Management in the U.S. District Court, Southern District of Texas, 1955–2000*. Athens: University of Georgia Press.

Hendricks, David, and Amy Patterson. 2002. "Genealogy Notes: The 1930 Census in Perspective." *Prologue* 32 (2). http://www.1930census.com/us_census_history.php.

Houston, Ramona. 2000. "African Americans, Mexican Americans, and Anglo Americans and the Desegregation of Texas, 1946–1957." Ph.D. diss. *University of Texas*. Dissertation Abstracts International (UMI No. 9992818).

Hudson, M. J., and B. J. Holmes. 1994. "Missing Teachers, Impaired Communities: The Unanticipated Consequences of *Brown v. Board of Education* on the African American Teaching Force at the Precollegiate Level." *Journal of Negro Education* 63 (3): 388–393.

Inda, Jonathan Xavier. 2006. *Targeting Immigrants: Government, Technology, and Ethics*. Malden, MA: Blackwell Publishing.

Johnson, Benjamin Heber. 2003. *Revolution in Texas: How a Forgotten Rebellion and Its Bloody Suppression Turned Mexicans into Americans*. New Haven, CT: Yale University Press.

Kibbe, Pauline. 1946. *Latin Americans in Texas*. Albuquerque: University of New Mexico Press.

Kim, Joon. 2004. "The Political Economy of the Mexican Farm Labor Program, 1942–64." *Aztlán* 29 (2): 13–53.

Lassiter, Matthew. 2006. *The Silent Majority: Suburban Politics in the Sunbelt South*. Princeton, NJ: Princeton University Press.

Lewis, Oscar. 1975 [1959.] *Five Families: Mexican Case Studies in the Culture of Poverty*. New York: Basic Books.

Limón, José E. 1974. "El Primer Congreso Mexicanista de 1911: A Precursor to Contemporary Chicanismo." *Aztlán* 5 (1–2): 85–117.

———. 1994. *Dancing with the Devil*. Madison: University of Wisconsin Press.

Madsen, William. 1973 [1962]. *The Mexican Americans of South Texas*. 2d. ed. New York: Holt, Rinehart and Winston.

Martinez, George A. 1997. "The Legal Construction of Race: Mexican Americans and Whiteness." *Harvard Latino Law Review* 321 (2): 321–328.

Martinez, Richard E. 2005. *PADRES: The National Chicano Priest Movement*. Austin: University of Texas Press.

McNail, Eddie. 1975. *The Bicentennial History of La Feria, Texas*. N.p.: n.p.

McWilliams, Carey. 1948. *North from Mexico*. Philadelphia: J. B. Lippincott.

Medina, Lara. 2004. *Las Hermanas: Chicana/Latina Religious-Political Activism in the U.S. Catholic Church*. Philadelphia: Temple University Press.

Menchaca, Martha. 1993. "Chicano Indianism: A History of Racial Repression." *American Ethnologist* 20 (3): 583–603.

———. 1995. *The Mexican Outsiders*. Austin: University of Texas Press.

———. 2001. *Constructing Race, Recovering History*. Austin: University of Texas Press.

Mitchell, Antoinette. 1998. "African American Teachers: Unique Roles and Universal Lessons." *Education and Urban Society* 31: 104–122.

Montejano, David. 1987. *Anglos and Mexicans in the Making of Texas, 1836–1986*. Austin: University of Texas Press.

Montemayor, Aurelio M. n.d. "Colegio Jacinto Treviño." In *Handbook of Texas On-Line*. http:/www.tsha.utexas.edu/handbook/online/articles/CC/Kbc51.html.

Navarro, Armando. 2000. *La Raza Unida Party: A Chicano Challenge to the U.S. Two-Party Dictatorship*. Philadelphia: Temple University Press.

Newcomb, William W. 1961. *The Indians of Texas, from Prehistoric to Modern Times*. Austin: University of Texas Press.

Ngai, Mae. 2004. *Impossible Subjects: Illegal Aliens and the Making of Modern America*. Princeton, NJ: Princeton University Press.

Noriega, Chon, ed. 2001. *The Chicano Studies Reader: An Anthology of Aztlán, 1970–2000*. Vol. 2. Los Angeles: UCLA Chicano Studies Research Center.

Nugent, Daniel. 1993. *Spent Cartridges of Revolution: An Anthropological History of Namiquipa Chihuahua*. Chicago: University of Chicago Press.

Oboler, Suzanne. 1995. *Ethnic Labels, Latino Lives*. Minneapolis: University of Minnesota Press.

Ochoa, Gilda. 2004. *Becoming Neighbors in a Mexican American Community: Power, Conflict, and Solidarity*. Austin: University of Texas Press.

Omi, Michael, and Howard Winant. 1994. *Racial Formation in the United States: From the 1960s to the 1980s*. New York: Routledge.

Orozco, Cynthia. 2009. *No Mexicans, Women, or Dogs Allowed*. Austin: University of Texas Press.

Orsi, Robert. 1985. *The Madonna of 115th Street: Faith and Community in Italian Harlem*. 3rd ed. New Haven, CT: Yale University Press.

Paredes, Américo. 1958. *With His Pistol in His Hand*. Austin: University of Texas Press.

———. 1978. "On Ethnographic Work among Minority Groups." In *New Directions in Chicano Scholarship*, edited by Ricardo Romo and Raymund Paredes, 1–32. La Jolla: University of California Press.

Peña, Manuel. 1999. *Música Tejana: The Cultural Economy of Artistic Transformation*. College Station: Texas A&M University Press.

Perales, Monica. 2010. *Smeltertown: Making and Remembering a Southwest Border Community*. Chapel Hill: University of North Carolina Press.

Pierce, C. 1970. "Offensive Mechanisms." In *The Black Seventies*, edited by F. Barbour, 265–282. New York: Basic Books.

Pineda, Sr. Clara Amelia. 1991. *Crónicas de la Comunidad de La Feria, Texas*. Unpublished report.

Portelli, Alessandro. 1998. "What Makes Oral History Different." In *The Oral History Reader*, edited by Robert Perks and Alistair Thomson. New York: Routledge.

Ramos, Henry A. J. 1998. *The American GI Forum: In Pursuit of the Dream, 1948–1983*. Houston: Arte Público.

Richardson, Chad. 1999. *Batos, Bolillos, Pochos, and Pelados: Class and Culture on the South Texas Border*. Austin: University of Texas Press.

Romano-V, Octavio Ignacio. 1968. "The Anthropology and the Sociology of the Mexican Americans: The Distortion of Mexican American History." *El Grito* 2 (1): 13–26.

Rosaldo, Renato. 1985. "Chicano Studies, 1970–1984." *Annual Review of Anthropology* 14: 405–427.

———. 1993 [1989]. *Culture and Truth*. Boston: Beacon.

Rosas, Gilberto. 2012. *Barrio Libre: Criminalizing States and Delinquent Refusals of the New Frontier*. Durham, NC: Duke University Press.

Rubel, Arthur. 1971. *Across the Tracks: Mexican Americans in a Texas City*. Austin: University of Texas Press.

Ruiz, Vicki. 1998. *From Out of the Shadows: Mexican Women in Twentieth-Century America*. New York: Oxford University Press.

Saenz, Rogelio. 1989. "Mexican-American Interstate Migration Flows among Arizona, California, Colorado, New Mexico, and Texas." *Sociology and Social Research* 73 (3): 153–157.

Saint Francis Xavier Catholic Church, La Feria, Texas, 1930–1980. Waco, TX: United Church Directories.

Salazar-Lozano, Molly. 1995. "School Days: A Recollection of Life at La Feria's Sam Houston Elementary School from September 1934 through May 1937." In *Sketchbook '45*, edited by Emily E. J. Rice, unpaginated.

Saldívar, Ramon. 2006. *The Borderlands of Culture: Américo Paredes and the Transnational Imaginary*. Durham, NC: Duke University Press.

Salinas, Martin. 1990. *Indians of the Rio Grande Delta*. Austin: University of Texas Press.

Sanchez, George. 1995. *Becoming Mexican American*. New York: Oxford University Press.

San Miguel, Guadalupe. 1984. "Conflict and Controversy in the Evolution of Bilingual Education in Texas—An Interpretation." *Social Science Quarterly* 65 (2) (June): 505–518.

———. 1987. *"Let All of Them Take Heed": Mexicans Americans and the Campaign for Educational Equality in Texas, 1910–1981*. Austin: University of Texas Press.

Smith, J. B. 1939. "A Survey of Pupil Failure in the La Feria Schools with Suggested Remedial Measures." Master's thesis, University of Texas at Austin.

Solórzano, Daniel, Miguel Ceja, and Tara Yosso. 2000. "Critical Race Theory, Racial Microaggressions, and Campus Racial Climate: The Experiences of African American College Students." *Journal of Negro Education* 69 (1–2): 60–73.

Spicer, Edward. 1962. *Cycles of Conquest*. Tucson: University of Arizona Press.

Treviño, Roberto R. 2006. *The Church in the Barrio: Mexican American Ethno-Catholicism in Houston*. Chapel Hill: University of North Carolina Press.

———. n.d. "Mexican Americans and Religion." In *Handbook of Texas Online*. http://www.tsha.utexas.edu/handbook/online/articles/MM/pqmcf.html.

Tyack, David, and Elizabeth Hansot. 1981. "Conflict and Consensus in American Education." *Daedalus* (Summer): 1–26.

Valencia, Richard. 2008. *Chicano Students and the Courts: The Mexican American Legal Struggle for Educational Equity*. New York: New York University Press.

Valenzuela, Angela. 1999. *Subtractive Schooling*. Albany: State University of New York Press.

Vargas, Deborah R. 2012. *Dissonant Divas in Chicano Music: The Limits of La Onda*. Minneapolis: University of Minnesota Press.

Vélez-Ibáñez, Carlos G. 1996. *Border Visions: Mexican Cultures of the Southwest United States*. Tucson: University of Arizona Press.

Walsh, Casey. 2008. *Building the Borderlands: A Transnational History of Irrigated Cotton along the Mexico-Texas Border*. College Station: Texas A&M University Press.

Wells, Miriam. 1978. "Emigrants from the Migrant Stream: Environment and Incentives in Relocation." *Aztlán* 7 (2): 267–289.

Zamora, Emilio. 1993. *The World of the Mexican Worker in Texas*. College Station: Texas A&M University Press.

———. 2008. *Claiming Rights and Righting Wrongs in Texas: Mexican Workers and Job Politics during World War II*. College Station: Texas A&M University Press.

Zavella, Patricia. 2011. *I'm Neither Here nor There: Mexicans' Quotidian Struggles with Migration and Poverty*. Durham, NC: Duke University Press.

INDEX